Teaching Poetry

Teaching Poetry is an indispensable source of guidance, confidence and ideas for all those new to the secondary English classroom. Written by experienced teachers who have worked with the many secondary pupils who 'don't get' poetry, this friendly guide will help you support pupils as they access, understand, discuss and enjoy classic and contemporary poetry.

With an emphasis on active approaches and the power of poetry to enrich the lives of both teachers and students, *Teaching Poetry*:

- provides a succinct introduction to the major ideas and theory about teaching poetry
- covers the key genres and periods through tried and tested favourites and a range of less well known new and historical poetry
- illustrates good practice for every approach covered, through case studies of theory and ideas in action in the classroom
- includes activities, ideas and resources to support teaching at Key Stages 3, 4 and 5.

Teaching Poetry tackles head-on one of the aspects of English teaching that new and experienced teachers alike find most difficult. It offers both a comprehensive introduction to teaching poetry and a rich source of inspiration and support to be mined when faced with an unfamiliar text or an unresponsive class.

Amanda Naylor is Lecturer in English Education at Hull University, Lecturer in English at Selby College and Visiting Tutor at York University, UK.

Audrey B. Wood is Head of KS3 English at a mixed comprehensive school in South London, UK. She is also a teacher trainer and school-based tutor for in-service Master's-level accreditation.

Teaching Poetry

Reading and responding to poetry
in the secondary classroom

Amanda Naylor and
Audrey B. Wood

Routledge
Taylor & Francis Group

LONDON AND NEW YORK

KH

First published 2012
by Routledge
2 Park Square, Milton Park, Abingdon, Oxon OX14 4RN

Simultaneously published in the USA and Canada
by Routledge
711 Third Avenue, New York, NY 10017

Routledge is an imprint of the Taylor & Francis Group, an informa business

© 2012 Amanda Naylor and Audrey B. Wood

British Library Cataloguing in Publication Data
A catalogue record for this book is available from the British Library

Library of Congress Cataloging in Publication Data
Naylor, Amanda.
Teaching poetry : reading and responding to poetry in the secondary classroom / by Amanda Naylor and Audrey Wood.
   p. cm.
   Includes bibliographical references and index.
   1. Poetry--Study and teaching (Secondary) 2. Poetry--Authorship I. Wood, Audrey.
   II. Title.
   PN1101.N36 2012   808.1071'2--dc23
   2011028313

ISBN: 978-0-415-58567-5 (hbk)
ISBN: 978-0-415-58568-2 (pbk)
ISBN: 978-0-203-13924-0 (ebk)

Typeset in Times New Roman and Gill Sans
by Bookcraft Ltd, Stroud, Gloucestershire

MIX
Paper from
responsible sources
FSC
www.fsc.org   FSC® C004839

Printed and bound in Great Britain by
TJ International Ltd, Padstow, Cornwall

4/15/13

Contents

Acknowledgements   vi
Preface   viii

1   Why poetry?   1

2   Critical perspectives on teaching poetry   11

3   Aspects of form   23

4   Words and imagery   36

5   Voice in poetry   51

6   Settings as mirrors   65

7   Constructions of character through time   83

8   Narrative in poetry   102

9   The poetry of conflict   117

10 Multi-modality and new technologies   135

    Appendix: The Haward Version of 'To His Coy Mistress'   143

References   144
Index   150

Acknowledgements

Audrey would like to register her appreciation for the help and encouragement received from her parents Daphne and Brian, who enabled her to write by helping with the day-to-day chores that get forgotten when writing. Appreciation also goes to her children April, Laura, Matthew and Rosalind, who allowed her time and space to write, to her life partner Robert Pontefract, for his encouragement and understanding, and to her dear friends Karen Nicholson and Suzanne Long, for their unfailing belief in her ability.

She would also like to thank Heather Swinnerton for being an inspirational teacher and everything you could wish for in a colleague, and her pupils at Coopers Technology College for being so willing to trial new ideas, particularly class 9a/En1, whose interest and enthusiasm have made them a joy to teach.

Amanda would like to thank her husband Ross Wiltcher for his support and encouragement, and her parents Diana and Ron, who listened patiently and made suggestions. Thanks also go to the Hull University ITT English trainees, who developed some of the ideas with her, and also to the York University English in Education students. I must mention Nick McGuinn, my colleague, and both Noreen Nelson and Gillian Heslop. We all have people who have inspired along the path of our professional life, and these three people have been inspirations and wonderful role models.

Finally, thanks from both of us must also go to staff at the Poetry Library, for helping us with referencing, to Emma Davis who chased up permissions for us, and to Helen Pritt at Routledge, for her unfailing confidence, sensible advice and guidance.

The publishers would like to thank the following for permission to reprint their material:

Carcanet Press for permission to reprint 'What lips my lips have kissed, and where, and why', StVincent Millay, E. (ed. Falck 1992) *Selected Poems*, Manchester: Carcanet, Press p.56;

The Millay Society for permission to reprint 'What lips my lips have kissed, and where, and why' © 1923, 1951 by Edna St Vincent Millay and Norma Millay Ellis. Reprinted by permission of Holly Peppe, Literary Executor, The Millay Society;

David Higham Associates Limited for permission to reprint 'The Ballad of Charlotte Dymond', Causley, Charles (1992) *Collected Poems 1951–1997*, London: Macmillan, p.108;

Faber & Faber for permission to reprint 'Roger the Dog', Hughes, Ted (1995) from *What is the Truth?* London: Faber & Faber, pp.97–8, originally published 1984;

HarperCollins for permission to reprint 'Roger the Dog', Hughes, Ted (1995) *What is the Truth? A Farmyard Fable for the Young*, by Ted Hughes, and drawings by R. J. Lloyd, London: Faber & Faber, pp.97–8 © 1984 by Ted Hughes. Reprinted by permission of HarperCollins Publishers;

'Lone Dog', Irene Rutherford McLeod (1916) in McLeod, I. R. *Songs to Save a Soul* Chatto and Windus, p.89;

Faber & Faber for permission to reprint 'Thistles' by Ted Hughes in Hughes, Ted (1972) *Wodwo*, London: Faber & Faber, p. 17, originally published 1967;

Farrar, Straus and Giroux LLC for permission to reprint 'Thistles' from *Selected Poems 1957–1994* by Ted Hughes;

AK Press for permission to reprint 'It's Work', Benjamin Zephaniah in Zephaniah, B. (1997) *School's Out: Poems Not for School*, Edinburgh AK Press, p.45;

The Estate of Wilfred Owen for kind permission to reprint 'Dulce et Decorum est', by Wilfred Owen, in *Wilfred Owen: The War Poems*, ed. Jon Stallworthy, London: Chatto & Windus, 1994;

'Rain' by Edward Thomas in *The Collected Poems of Edward Thomas*; Oxford University Press, 1978, p.259;

Faber & Faber for kind permission to reprint 'The Waste Land' by T. S. Eliot in *The Waste Land: Poems 1909–1925*; Faber, 1922, p.83;

Carcanet Press for permission to reprint 'This is Just to Say' by William Carlos Williams in *Collected Poems Vol 2, 1939–1962*, Paladin Poetry, 1991, p.372;

New Directions Publishing Corporation for permission to reprint 'This is Just to Say' by William Carlos Williams, from *The Collected Poems: Volume I, 1909–1939*, copyright ©1938 by New Directions Publishing Corp., reprinted by permission of New Directions Publishing Corp.;

Faber & Faber for permission to reprint 'The Barn' by Seamus Heaney in *Death of a Naturalist*, Faber, 1966;

Farrar, Straus & Giroux, LLC for permission to reprint 'The Barn' from *Opened Ground: Selected Poems 1966–1996* by Seamus Heaney;

Cambridge University Press for kind permission to reprint 'City Blues' by Mike Hayhoe in *I Look Into My Glass Thomas Hardy*, first 4 lines as edited by Mike Hayhoe in Hayhoe, M., and Parker, S., 1(998) *Words Large as Apples*, Cambridge University Press;

Pan Macmillan for permission to reprint 'Mrs Midas' by Carol Ann Duffy, *The World's Wife*, Picador, 1999, p.11; and 'Medusa' by Carol Ann Duffy in *The World's Wife*, p.40;

Carcanet Press Ltd for permission to reprint 'Miracle on St David's Day' by Gillian Clarke from *Letter from a Far Country,* 1982;

Faber & Faber for permission to reprint 'Vergissmeinnicht' by Keith Douglas in *The Complete Poems of Keith Douglas*, Oxford University Press, 1978, p.111;

The Estate of Wilfred Owen, for kind permission to reprint 'The Sentry', from *Wilfred Owen: The War Poems*, edited by Jon Stallworthy (London: Chatto & Windus, 1994);

'Perhaps' by Vera Brittain in *Poems of the War and After*, Victor Gollancz, 1934, p.42. Vera Brittain's 'Perhaps' is reproduced by permission of Mark Bostridge and T. J. Brittain-Catlin, Literary Executors for the Estate of Vera Brittain 1970;

SSgt Colin N. Clark for kind permission to reprint 'The Last Patrol', by SSgt Colin N. Clark, published in *The Sapper*, June 2010, p.572;

B. Wynick, Literary executor of the estate of Isaac Rosenberg for permission to reprint 'Dead Man's Dump' by Isaac Rosenberg from Stallworthy, J. (ed.) (1984) *The Oxford Book of War Poetry*, Oxford: OUP.

The publishers have made every effort to contact authors and/or copyright holders of works reprinted in *Teaching Poetry*, and to obtain permission to publish extracts. This has not been possible in every case, however, and we would welcome correspondence from those individuals or companies whom we have been unable to trace. Any omissions brought to our attention will be remedied in future editions.

Preface

Both authors are secondary English teachers, with some 30 years of classroom experience between us. We have both been involved with teacher training for many years, Amanda as an English AST and mentor on the Bromley Schools' Collegiate SCITT scheme, where she first met and mentored Audrey as a trainee, and latterly as a lecturer in English Education at the Universities of York and Hull. Audrey has been an English mentor herself for some years on the Bromley Schools' Collegiate SCITT scheme and is currently involved in tutoring on the MTL programme in association with the University of Hull.

This book is the result of our belief in the power of poetry to enrich our lives and those of our pupils and students. The book is a joint effort, resulting from our love of poetry and our passionate belief in the importance of active approaches to teaching poetry in the classroom. We have had many conversations with people who say they hated poetry at school and that it was taught really badly, and with trainee and newly qualified teachers who are insecure about teaching it themselves, because of their own poor experiences at school.

In this book we suggest ways to move away from a model of teaching poetry from the front, where the teacher explains meanings that pupils passively accept, to an active approach where pupils are able to access the ideas behind the poetry, enabling them to make their own meanings and respond to the poetry on a personal level. We have researched many of the major ideas about teaching poetry in an active fashion, and condensed them here for the busy teacher who may not have time to do the research they would like to do themselves.

We offer this book not as a definitive guide, but more as a selection of ideas and approaches to be mined when faced with an unfamiliar text or an unresponsive class. The ideas have been trialled by us in our own teaching, and have been written up for you here with confidence that they are successful methods. Whilst we both have our own voices, we have written as we would speak to you were we your mentors and you our trainees or NQTs, offering what we hope is clear guidance on the sometimes daunting prospect of getting pupils to read and respond to poetry. We hope that you will find it useful.

Chapter 1

Why poetry?

The poet's eye, in fine frenzy rolling,
Doth glance from heaven to earth, from earth to heaven;
And as imagination bodies forth
The forms of things unknown, the poet's pen
Turns them to shapes and gives to airy nothing
A local habitation and a name.
   (*A Midsummer Night's Dream*, Act 5, Scene 1, ll.13–18)

This chapter presents some significant ideas about poetry that have been expressed over the course of the development of English as a subject. It does not present a comprehensive review, but rather examines a few particular moments in the history of poetry on the curriculum and as a social phenomenon. These ideas input into the complex relationship that we as contemporary English teachers have with poetry and the reasons why we believe that teaching it is important.

As English teachers we believe that poetry offers something that other forms of writing do not. We enjoy it and seek to pass on that enjoyment to our pupils. We also believe in the particular power of poetry to express ideas, captured by Thomas Gray in *The Progress of Poesy* as 'Thoughts that breathe, and words that burn' (Quiller-Couch 1927: 526). Poetry is integral to the way that we acquire language, rhyme and rhythm being essential to the ways that we learn. Poetry has been assigned a variety of roles in our society over time. The debate is ongoing about what poetry should be taught and in what quantities. This is not a new debate and one particularly important era for the position of poetry in the curriculum is the nineteenth century, when public education was being developed and the curriculum being established for a wider audience than just those in the grammar and public schools.

Matthew Arnold: poetry and the decline of religion

One significant figure in the debate over the school curriculum and the position of poetry is Matthew Arnold. His ideas have provoked much discussion over the years, and he is regarded with mixed opinions, yet his position as an educationalist and poet enabled him to develop very interesting views on the development of the curriculum with regards to poetry. He held the position of school inspector for 36 years in the mid-nineteenth century and argued vociferously for English literature, and specifically poetry, to have a place in the curriculum for pupils in elementary schools.

Arnold was appointed school inspector in 1851, the same year as the Great Exhibition was held at Crystal Palace, celebrating the commercial and inventive successes of Britain and the Empire. This was an event that in Britain was followed by 'a period of immense commercial prosperity – and immense self-complacency' (Arnold 1932: xvii), as trade, manufacturing and the population boomed over the following twenty years. This was also a time of great scientific advances, as *The Origin of Species* was published in 1859, presenting the theory of evolution, challenging the essential precept of Christianity that God created man and signalling a scientific challenge to faith. Arnold saw these two forces as placing pressures on society and on the individual. Arnold was himself a writer of poetry and Oxford Professor of Poetry for ten years. He was appointed professor of poetry in 1857, and he was the first appointee to give his inaugural lecture in English, rather than Latin, which signals in itself a more democratic approach to the study and criticism of poetry than that held by previous incumbents of the post. Arnold was concerned that poetry should be accessible not only to those from élite, highly educated backgrounds and believed that literature could help guard against the twin assaults of materialism and the loss of faith.

Arnold's most well-known poem, 'Dover Beach', published in 1867 but written much earlier, expresses 'Arnold's negative vision of modernity' (Campbell 2008: 27) and his fears at the impact of the twin pressures of materialism and the loss of religion on the emotional welfare of his contemporaries and particularly the pupils he encountered daily. The poem, written around the time of Arnold's honeymoon, is both a lyrical love song, expressing private emotions, and also an expression of public disquiet where Arnold 'charge(s) science with draining the natural world of spiritual and metaphysical meaning' (Brown 2000: 148). The poem opens:

> The sea is calm to-night.
> The tide is full, the moon lies fair
> Upon the straits; on the French coast the light
> Gleams and is gone; the cliffs of England stand,
> Glimmering and vast, out in the tranquil bay.
> Come to the window, sweet is the night-air!
>
> (Arnold 1965: 254)

The scene seems to be in a room, perhaps the bedroom, and the speaker looks out at the English Channel, about to embark on a journey over the sea, and the mood is tranquil and lyrical. The tone is intimate and joyful, 'sweet is the night-air!':

> Only, from the long line of spray
> Where the sea meets the moon-blanch'd land,
> Listen! you hear the grating roar
> Of pebbles which the waves draw back, and fling,
> At their return, up the high strand,
> Begin, and cease, and then again begin,
> With tremulous cadence slow, and bring
> The eternal note of sadness in.
>
> Sophocles long ago
> Heard it on the Ægæan, and it brought
> Into his mind the turbid ebb and flow

Of human misery; we
Find also in the sound a thought,
Hearing it by this distant northern sea.
The Sea of Faith
Was once, too, at the full, and round earth's shore
Lay like the folds of a bright girdle furl'd.
But now I only hear
Its melancholy, long, withdrawing roar,
Retreating, to the breath
Of the night-wind, down the vast edges drear
And naked shingles of the world.

(Arnold 1965: 256)

The tone has shifted from private to public, where the 'Sea of Faith' has withdrawn, and the 'eternal note of sadness', which was part of the classical world as well as our own, is the only song remaining. Religion, faith, once a protection, 'a bright girdle furl'd', is now retreating, leaving the speaker in the silence, listening to the noise of its retreat. So the only consolation is in love:

Ah, love, let us be true
To one another! for the world, which seems
To lie before us like a land of dreams,
So various, so beautiful, so new,
Hath really neither joy, nor love, nor light,
Nor certitude, nor peace, nor help for pain;
And we are here as on a darkling plain
Swept with confused alarms of struggle and flight,
Where ignorant armies clash by night.

(Arnold 1965: 256)

Arnold characterises the world, modernity, as one without certainty 'nor help for pain', it is a 'darkling plain', where confused armies 'struggle' and 'clash'. Brown argues that 'a readership acquainted with Darwin's researches – as indeed most of its readership is likely to have been' (Brown 2000: 146) would understand the allusion to the struggle and flight, 'as animals prey upon one another in an ongoing "struggle" responding instinctively with "fight or flight"' (Brown 2002: 146), that is, the allusion to the theory of the survival of the fittest. Arnold expresses a vision of a modernity where there is a loss of faith, a sadness, where the only consolation is in other humanity, the love of others, to replace the gap left by the withdrawal of the 'Sea of Faith'.

Arnold held the position of school inspector from 1851 to 1887. His day-to-day work, visiting schools, advising and reporting on the education of pupils across southern and western England brought him into close contact with the reality of education for pupils who were not being educated in élite establishments. At the point in which Arnold was appointed inspector, the education of the poor was provided by religious bodies, with some small grants from the state. Very few children attended, and those that did struggled to attend for an extended period. The system of teaching was through the use of pupil-teachers, who were trained by the teacher and then taught younger pupils by rote, so that teaching consisted of drilling pupils mechanically in spelling and memorising 'elementary knowledge' (Wardle

1970: 86), which conjures up visions of Dickens' Mr Gradgrind. In his report of 1867 Arnold records one pupil-teacher for every 57 pupils. During the period in which Arnold worked, state provision for the working class was being slowly developed and investigated by a number of commissions. Arnold believed that school pupils could be prepared for life, given moral strength and imaginative capabilities, through what they read. In his report of 1878 he writes:

> A power of reading, well trained and well guided, is perhaps the best among the gifts which it is the business of our elementary schools to bestow; … good and sterling poetry learned for recitation … should be made to contribute to the opening of the soul and imagination, for which the central purchase should be found in poetry.
>
> (Arnold 1910: 191–2)

Arnold also allies poetry in his report of 1880 with the formation of the 'soul and character' and with 'high and noble principles' (Arnold 1910: 200–1). Arnold was an admirer of the Romantics, writing essays about Keats, Shelley, Wordsworth, Byron and Coleridge and although 'these writers' Romanticism differs greatly', Campbell notes that 'they share values that centre on the importance of the individual, self-expression, feelings, creativity, imagination and nature' (Campbell 2008: 19). Arnold believed in a 'humanized democracy' (Novak 2002: 595) and that schooling played a pivotal part of this. This 'humanizing' was best brought about by the use of English literature, and in its highest form, poetry. Arnold writes of poetry that:

> No man … can fully draw out the reasons why the human spirit feels itself to attain to a more adequate and satisfying expression in poetry than in any other of its modes of activity. For to draw them out fully we should have to go behind our own nature itself, and that we can none of us do.
>
> (Arnold 2000: 549)

Poetry is compared with religion in *Culture and Anarchy* as a force for moral good, in that it typifies perfection, an ideal to aspire to, 'the idea of beauty and of a human nature perfect on all its sides, which is the dominant idea of poetry, is a true and invaluable idea' (Arnold 1932: 54). During Arnold's time as writer and inspector by 1871 English literature and grammar was a subject on the curriculum, and in 1880 elementary schooling was compulsory up to the age of ten. Arnold's views have caused much debate, not least, as with the ideas of F.R. Leavis, over the question of who is to determine what aspects of culture exemplify 'sweetness and light' (Arnold 1932: 43) and who should determine what should be studied. As Eagleton, a Marxist and brilliant critic put it, Arnold's ideas suggest that culture will have the anaesthetising effect of 'controlling and incorporating the working class' (Eagleton 1996: 21) into the social hierarchy and that will ensure stability, not revolution. If education does not provide culture, the working class may rebel, 'If the masses are not thrown a few novels, they may react by throwing up a few barricades' (Eagleton 1996: 21). Whichever viewpoint one subscribes to, there is no doubt that Arnold was convinced of the power of poetry, and argued for its centrality in the curriculum for English:

> Arnold played the pied piper of poetry for the cause of national education; he convinced education's overseers to create a legal mandate for English literature's place in the lives of the young. Where the Bible served as the reading matter of the poor in Charity

Schools, and the classics served the privileged in Grammar Schools, English poetry had little place at all until it finally gained status as a 'specific subject' in 1871.

(Willinsky 1990: 345)

Material culture: poetry as a social object

Another lively moment in the development of the significance of poetry is the Early Modern period (1450–1700) because, 'from this time the English were aware of their own literary culture' (Palmer 1965: 2). The printing press had been introduced in England in 1476 and throughout this period printing was on the increase, although most texts were still in manuscript form. Literacy levels are difficult to assess, but a study of literacy levels in Norwich between 1580 and 1700, discussed in David Cressy's *Literacy and the Social Order: Reading and Writing in Tudor and Stuart England*, reveals very few of those at the top of the hierarchy, such as the clergy and professional people, were illiterate whilst a very large number of labourers were unable to write their names. There was an improvement in general literacy rates in the Elizabethan period as well as a growth in the founding of grammar schools, such as the one that Shakespeare attended. University attendance reached a high point under James I, 'peaking in Cambridge in the 1620s and in Oxford in the 1630s' (Cressy 1980: 122) with 'some 400 students a year matriculating at Cambridge' (Cressy 1980: 122). The curriculum would have been based on 'learning to speak and write classical Latin' (Palmer 1965: 2) in the grammar schools, along with Greek and Hebrew, and at university studying rhetoric and a 'close scrutiny of the classical texts prescribed' (Palmer 1965: 3). Thus, the élite were highly educated in classical and rhetorical forms, and it is in this context that poetic forms, such as the sonnet, developed in English and held a place in the social interchange. Poetry, in the circles of the court and educated households, had a more significant daily presence in people's lives than, arguably, it does today.

In the Early Modern period, people mostly read in manuscript form, that is, texts that are handwritten. Manuscripts were collected and circulated in miscellanies by many people in various different social environments. They were compiled from a variety of different texts that were circulated within specific groups and included poems, prose and translations of various lyrics. In 1557 *Totell's Miscellany* was printed, one of the first of such collections to be published, which included poetry by courtly writers such as Wyatt and Surrey, whose work had previously only been circulated in manuscript. It contained 'the sorts of verse that someone in contact with the political and social elite might include in a private compilation' (Marotti 1995: 214). It demonstrated that 'within the court circle it [poetry] was used to grace and comment on virtually every happening in life' (Saunders 1951: 151) and that 'the courtiers' immediate experience is often reflected in this poetry' (Marotti 1995: 52). In a system where poems are passed around between members of a group, there is much more interchange and exchange of ideas, motifs and styles than in one where text is stabilised in print. As Marotti comments, the 'social and occasional character of composition' (Marotti 1995: 52) marks poetic discourse 'as continuous with other forms of communication' (Marotti 1995: 52). To the modern reader, this marks a contrast to the use of poetry today, where it tends to be more isolated, used in a celebratory capacity in public and as a mode of self-expression in private.

The Early Modern period used poetry on many more occasions than we do today, as part of everyday life, more akin to the way that song lyrics are integrated into our lives, along with text messages and email.

We can see this use of poetry as 'continuous' with other forms of social communication in *The Adventures of Master F.J.* This is a sort of proto-novel written in 1573 by George Gascoigne. Gascoigne hoped for career advancement at court through his presentation of poetic and courtly graces. Gascoigne presents a series of his poems in *The Adventures of Master F.J.* and embeds them in a background narrative, a rather scurrilous depiction of the development of an affair between two members of an Elizabethan aristocratic household, with the plot revolving around the exchange of manuscripts. The prose narrative that appears around the poems provides a framework and the social structure for the poems. The proto-novel is highly entertaining and also interesting for the insight that it provides into the uses to which lyric poetry was put. It is interesting to see manuscripts being used much in the way that we might use text and email today, as 'as continuous with other forms of communication' (Marotti 1995: 52).

In *The Adventures of Master F.J.* poems are interchangeable with letters in the course of the love affair, and letters are followed by a response written as a poem. At the outset of the story the narrator, Master F.J., wishes to acquaint himself with Mistress Elinor, a married lady. He writes an anonymous letter, then follows this with a love poem-like sonnet, which he 'loses' around the household for her to find. Master F.J. then helps Mistress Elinor recover from a nosebleed, leaving more verses for her to discover in her chamber. Subsequently, Master F.J. catches Mistress Elinor alone in the gallery and manages to kiss her hand. She requests a poem for her to wrap her threads around, a 'bottom for her silk' (Gascoigne 1998: 11) and Master F.J. leaves her with a short sonnet sequence. The sonnet sequence works and 'the flames began to break out on every side' (Gascoigne 1998: 12). The use of another sonnet is employed and Mistress Elinor agrees to meet him. When they meet, they drop their poses and game-playing, and 'fell to plain dealing' (Gascoigne 1998: 28) and very quickly the two rendezvous for a night of passion. Mistress Elinor appears the next morning at breakfast, in full view of the household, in her night attire with the word 'contented' written 'in her hand-writing' (Gascoigne 1998: 34) on her cap. The use of poems has moved now in the narrative from the private sphere of a wished-for relationship, into the public sphere of the whole Elizabethan household.

The next sonnet that is handed over to his mistress is definitely not private in nature. It is one that follows a hunting episode where Master F.J. has been sneering to himself over Mistress Elinor's husband having 'lost his horn' (Gascoigne 1998: 42). In the sonnet F.J. alludes delightedly to cuckoldry. The theme is the planting of seeds to grow horns, which the poet decides to try and plant in Mistress Elinor's husband's brain, the final couplet of which is, 'And as I groped in the ground to grow it/Start up a horn, thy husband could not blow it' (Gascoigne 1998: 42). In a most un-courtly fashion Master F.J. is bragging over the conquest of another's wife and writing lewd, celebratory verse. He composes this sonnet during a hunt 'before the fall of the buck' (Gascoigne 1998: 42) and presents it to his mistress at their return from hunting, in front of the whole household. Thus the composition and exchange is during a very public event, where the whole household would be present.

George Gascoigne has created a series of poems that reflect a whole variety of lyrics that were fashionable in Elizabethan England. He has produced a replica of what he would like to be seen as a manuscript collection of élite, courtly writers, reflecting his aspirations to that position. He has also produced a model of manuscript exchange, where poetry has performed a variety of functions. It has been seen used to bring about actions or suggest desires, as the whole of Master F.J.'s pursuit of his mistress is through manuscript exchange. Poetry initiates Master F.J.'s overtures and, in his sonnet sequence, provides an imaginative model for their relationship. Poems are used physically, as gifts, and materially, in useful places, such as in twists of silk. Manuscript exchange is both private, such as the 'poetry of fruition' (Marotti 1995: 9) and public, such as Master F.J.'s sonnet of cuckoldry. The actual physical exchange is significant, as poems are left where they can be found, or handed over personally and the moment of that exchange exploited. That the poetry is used as part of everyday entertainment is clear, as there is much improvising of poetry to music at social occasions and events. Finally, the way the poetry was circulated comes into the narrative, as we hear of poems being handed round within the household and even into the hands of a courtier. In *The Adventures of Master F.J.* the narrative provides us with a fascinating insight into what the uses and outcomes of manuscript exchange may have been. Whilst creating for the audience a context for his poems and asserting his membership of an élite group, he recreates a model of manuscript exchange and how poems may have been used in Elizabethan, courtly society.

Another very cheerful insight into the 'literary culture' (Palmer 1965: 2) so lively in Elizabethan England is *The Art of English Poesy* by George Puttenham who was a courtier, and related to various élite families. He presents 'the nearest to an aesthetic approach to poetry made in England in the sixteenth century' (Wilcock and Walker, in Puttenham 1970: lii). *The Art of English Poesy* is a lively portrait of the courtly culture that Puttenham observed and it was developed over at least twenty years of his life, very much reflecting a world where poetic action is significant. The conditions for conduct and writing in the work reflect those under which many poets would have been educated and been writing. As a portrait of the highly rhetorical, literary environment of the court, it is a key text providing an insight into courtly, aesthetic culture. The reason for *The Art of English Poesy* that Puttenham gives is to 'make of a rude rhymer, a learned and Courtly Poet' (Puttenham 2004: 147). He stresses that his work relates directly to courtly values,

> for the learning of ladies ... or idle Courtiers, desirous to become skilful in their own mother tongue ... so fit for them and the place as that which teacheth beau semblant, the chief profession as well of Courting as of poesy.
>
> (Puttenham 2004: 147)

The world that Puttenham describes is one in which, 'as far as poetry and the court are concerned, life and art are so closely related as to be, at times, indistinguishable: what works in art works in life, and vice versa' (Silcox 1990: 47).

Puttenham stated that he wrote either for courtiers or those who aspire to master the arts of 'Courting', meaning the arts of courtiership. He equates success at court with skill in the 'mother tongue', the decorum and appropriateness with which language is employed. For Puttenham, 'man is but his mind, and as his mind is tempered and qualified, so are his speeches and language at large' (Puttenham 2004: 139). *The Art of English Poesy* evokes a world where poetry, rhetoric and decorum are as one in the education and comportment of a gentleman. The poetry serves a variety of functions: to advance one's career, to smooth over disputes and to cement relationships, to name but a few, as well as to be given as gifts on particular occasions, such as New Year's Day. Puttenham presents in his book an overview of the history of poetry and the uses to which poetry can be put, with much theoretical discussion of the relationship of poetry to rhetoric. The book explores the significance of style, classical authors, anecdotes from court and vernacular English.

'The Posy' by George Herbert illustrates the sort of courtly activity surrounding poetry that Puttenham describes. Herbert, famous as a writer of devotional verse and as a parish priest, spent his early life at court. He combines aspects of this experience at court with his devotion to God in his poetry. The term 'posy' in the title is a term signifying a bunch of flowers, yet the origin of this well-used term is in 'poesy', as the flowers were originally metaphorical. The word 'posy' is simply a shortened form of 'poesy', meaning a short poem inscribed on a knife or some such surface. The lyric opens with:

> Let wits contest,
> And with their words and posies windows fill:
> Lesse than the least
> Of all thy mercies, is my posy still.
> (Herbert 1991: 186)

Herbert refers to a world of contesting wits and one that very much sees poetry serving a purpose as an object. The world of Puttenham's devices and exchange of poems is present here in 'The Posy', as the wits contest against each other and fill surfaces, such as windows and rings with 'posies'. A posy like this, a motto or a short poem, appears in *Hamlet*, as the prince remarks to Ophelia over the Prologue to the Murder of Gonzago 'Is this a prologue, or the posy of a ring?' (Tobin, in Herbert 1991: 413). Puttenham, in his chapter on posies, describes how they might be 'put upon their banqueting dishes of sugar-plate, or of marchpanes and such other dainty meats as by the courtesy and custom every guest might carry from a common feast home with him to his own house' (Puttenham 2004: 102). These posies are exchanged and taken as tokens or are inscribed on various surfaces. Puttenham observes that 'we … do paint them nowadays upon the backsides of our fruit trenchers of wood, or use them as devices in rings, and arms, and about such courtly pursuits' (Puttenham 2004: 102).

> This on my ring,
> This by my picture, in my book I write:
> Whether I sing,
> Or say, or dictate, this is my delight.
> (Herbert 1991: 187)

The second stanza, referring to the posy of a ring, like the comment of Hamlet's, evokes an image of the creation and performance of poetry as being a public act, 'Whether I sing/Or say, or dictate, this is my delight' (Herbert 1991: 187). The act of creating a poem is depicted as a social activity, like that of singing, speaking aloud or dictating, in an environment where wits compete with each other in the act of creation.

Poetry today: what poets say

And what of poetry today? Poetry is embedded in the National Curriculum, such that all pupils will gain some experience of the poetry from the English literary heritage, from contemporary writers and from different cultures and traditions. Pupils should study some poetry at all key stages. Poetry has become part of the mechanism of assessment at GCSE, such that the pressures on the study of it have become burdensome. So it is important to take a step back and reflect on why we regard poetry as such a significant object of study. Poets themselves are probably the best people to turn to for expressions of the importance of poetry in the twenty-first century.

Together Seamus Heaney and Ted Hughes collaborated on two collections of poetry that they hoped would be used by schools: *The Rattle Bag* and *The School Bag*. In writing about why they did this, Heaney explained:

> We proceeded in the faith that the aural and oral pleasures of poetry, the satisfactions of recognition and repetition, constitute an experience of rightness that can make the whole physical and psychic system feel more in tune with itself. We implicitly believed that a first exposure to poetry, the early schooling in it, should offer this kind of rightness, since it constitutes one of the primary justifications of the art.
>
> (Heaney 2003)

As poets, Hughes and Heaney emphasise the pleasure of poetry and that it is built through sound, by listening and speaking. They believed that poetry has a purpose to entertain, but in that purpose it can make us feel more 'in tune' with ourselves. This is not very far from Arnold's expression that in poetry the human spirit 'feels itself to attain to a more adequate and satisfying expression in poetry than in any other of its modes of activity' (Arnold 2000: 549). Hughes and Heaney also felt that school and the experience of poetry that we get early in life is very important, as did Arnold. Heaney continues to express in his article this belief, like Arnold's, that poetry is related to the spiritual and metaphysical dimension of our lives: 'An experience of words and rhythms like these is arguably more than physical. It represents a metaphysical extension of capacity, an arrival at a point beyond the point that had been settled for previously' (Heaney 2003). As Arnold felt that poetry was a source of spiritual nourishment, so do Heaney and Hughes.

Another very significant figure in contemporary poetics is Michael Rosen. In a lecture delivered in Homerton College as part of the Philippa Pearce Memorial series, he used the ideas of an Early Modern writer, Sir Philip Sidney, to express a plea for poetry. The title of the lecture was 'What is children's poetry for? Towards a new, child-specific "Apologie for Poetrie" (Philip Sidney, 1579)'. In this lecture he traces ideas presented by Sidney in his works *An Apology for Poetry* and *The Defence of Poetry* regarding the significance of poetry. Rosen examines Sidney's defence of the form, firstly because it is 'always derived from "nature", a word which we can take today to mean more like the whole of existence and experience' (Rosen 2009: 2). He then quotes Sidney's analysis of the way that poetry creates nature, in that it is a 'representing, counterfeiting, or figuring forth to speake Metaphorically. A speaking picture, with this end to teach and delight' (Rosen 2009: 3). Poetry then 'teaches' and 'delights' us. Similar to Arnold, Sidney argues that the experiences of poetry can show us emotion in action, and that 'by showing us these emotions in action, the poetry ends up being "memorable" but also ends up by being absorbed into our "judgement" – or as we might call it – our value system' (Rosen 2009: 3). These points, Rosen argues, are all reasons why poetry is on the curriculum, and that it should be an enjoyable, memorable experience. There will be children who do not get experiences of literature and poetry at home, and without these being firmly embedded in their school experiences, they will not get them at all; again, this is a position Arnold would have agreed with.

Rosen is, in the lecture, arguing against what he, and many, see as a reduction in the richness and variety of reading matter in the school curriculum because of pressure on schools to achieve well in league tables, reductive tests and assessments. He passionately argues that:

> What poetry and all fictions do is encapsulate wisdom about human behaviour and they do this, as Sidney implies, by marrying ideas with feeling and putting them into

sequences derived originally from experience and existence but which may also involve creatures and beings that have never been seen or heard of before. And in the process of reading this, we find out what it feels like to be someone facing danger or love or disaster or fun and the like. The poem or the story will do some experimenting for us.

(Rosen 2009: 6)

Poetry provides a forum for play with language, for 'marrying ideas with feeling' and for experimenting with emotions that enlarge our experience.

In *Poetry in the Making*, Ted Hughes discusses ways of getting children to write poetry. He reflects on the experiences that lie behind various poetic moments and looks at ways to write. Hughes equates poetry with expressing something essential about being human:

It is occasionally possible, just for brief moments, to find the words that will unlock the doors of all those many mansions inside the head and express something … of the deep complexity that makes us precisely the way we are … when words can manage some of this … we call it poetry.

(Hughes 1967a: 124)

We hope that some of the ideas presented in this book help us, as English teachers, to enable our pupils to experience some of the joy and possibilities for creative fulfilment that the poets and writers that we have referred to in this chapter have argued for. We also hope that, in these times of burdensome assessment outcomes, the ideas will help your pupils gain the best grades of which they are capable.

Chapter 2

Critical perspectives on teaching poetry

CALIBAN (about Prospero):
  Remember
First to possess his books; for without them
He's but a sot, as I am.
      (*The Tempest*, Act 3, Scene 2, ll.91–3)

In this chapter, we discuss some significant theoretical perspectives on the ways that we teach poetry as English teachers. We look at ideas about the ways that we read and make meaning out of poems, notably those of Louise Rosenblatt and Wolfgang Iser. We touch on how Michael Benton used the ideas of Rosenblatt in the 1980s to examine the ways that young readers deal with poetry and suggest the ways in which these ideas are of significance to the ways that we teach in the classroom today.

When we are teaching poetry, we are subject as English teachers to a whole variety of influences. We have to teach a certain number of texts in a certain amount of time, to fulfil certain criteria. Even at Key Stage 3, where in the past there was time on the timetable to enjoy and have fun with texts, the pressure is ever-present to produce assessable outcomes from what we do in the classroom. So to have a philosophy of teaching English that is our own, to give us a rationale for why we teach as we do, is crucially important for us to remember and reflect on what we do in the classroom, and by extension, with poetry.

Rob Pope in *The English Studies Book* (2002) identifies two polarities that summarise the ways in which ideas about English tend to cluster; see Table 2.1.

Table 2.1 Polarities in English (Pope 2002: 31)

'Traditional'	*'Progressive'*
English for employment	English for 'life'
Vocational training in a specialism	Education of a whole person
Promotion of a single standard language	Recognition of varieties
Emphasis on writing	Attention to speech
Formal written examinations	Mixed-mode assessment
Dictionary definitions and grammatical rules	Flexibility of usage
Canon of 'great works'	Open or no canon
National Curriculum	Local syllabuses
Single dominant identity	Multicultural differences

These ideas recur again and again in discussion on English and the role that it plays, both in policy documents and in the media. There is no doubt that the beliefs that English teachers have relate in a variety of ways to the issues that these polarities raise. In his report of 1989, which introduced the National Curriculum, Brian Cox identified five models that encapsulated the different influences on why people come into the teaching of English and why they remain in it. The five models were defined as: cultural heritage; cultural analysis; personal growth; adult needs and cross-curricular. The report stated about the views that they were 'not the only possible views, they are not sharply distinguishable, and they are certainly not mutually exclusive' (DES 1989: paragraph 2.20) however, they can provide us with some markers against which to judge our own ideas and influences.

Traditional versus progressive

Terry Eagleton states in *Literary Theory: An Introduction* that, 'the fact remains that English students in English today are "Leavisites" whether they know it or not' (Eagleton 1996: 27). That viewpoint is probably as true today as it was when it was written, if English students and by extension English teachers subscribe to the cultural heritage model of the subject of English, which 'emphasises the responsibility of schools to lead children to an appreciation of those works of literature that have been widely regarded as amongst the finest in the language' (Cox 1995: 33). This model had as one of its orginators F.R. Leavis, who has had an enormous influence over the teaching of English and the design of the curriculum, and 'his presence in twentieth century literature and criticism is … inescapable' (Drabble 2000: 550). Writing in the magazine *Scrutiny* for four decades starting in the 1920s, Leavis and others made their case. Leavis believed that the impact of industrialisation, the loss of agricultural communities and the development of the mass media were a danger to modern society and that literature was a force for moral good, humanising readers: ideas reminiscent of those of Matthew Arnold (see Chapter 1). Leavis argued that English tradition could be passed on in universities to an élite capable of understanding and dealing with ideas, who would in turn pass these ideas on to others, maintaining some defence against the encroachment of the mass media and popular culture. For Leavis, some writers possessed the moral qualities which deemed them 'English' enough, and some did not. Eagleton neatly summarises what has come to be termed 'the canon' suggested by Leavis:

> With breathtaking boldness, *Scrutiny* redrew the map of English Literature in ways from which criticism has never quite recovered. The main thoroughfares of this map ran through Chaucer, Shakespeare, Jonson, the Jacobeans and Metaphysicals, Bunyan, Pope, Samuel Johnson, Blake, Wordsworth, Keats, Austen, George Eliot, Hopkins, Henry James, Joseph Conrad, T.S. Eliot and D.H. Lawrence. This was 'English Literature': Spencer, Dryden, Restoration Drama, Defoe, Fielding, Richardson, Sterne, Shelley, Byron, Tennyson, Browning, most of the Victorian Novelists, Joyce, Woolf and most writers after D.H. Laurence constituted a network of 'B' roads interspersed with a good few cul-de-sacs. Dickens was first out then in; 'English' included two and a half women, counting Emily Brontë as marginal case: almost all of its authors conservative.
>
> (Eagleton 1996: 28)

The study of suitable authors, and in a clear, precise fashion, was what Leavis proposed. He and his fellow Cambridge academic I. A. Richards, championing the study of English Literature as a university discipline, advocated a close attention to text, but paid little attention to the historical and cultural contexts within which the texts were produced. Leavis writes, '[The critic] is concerned with the work in front of him as something that should contain within itself the reason why it is so and not otherwise' (Leavis 1952: 224). The text is self-contained and the reader with 'true judgment' (Leavis 1952: 224) will feel and react spontaneously to the quality and life force of a literary work.

In this focus on the autonomous nature of the text, Leavis is also associated with the American school of criticism, New Criticism, a term which originated in 1941 after the publication of Ransom's *The New Criticism*. For these critics too, the text existed on the page, and the critic's role was to read in detail and react to nuances of the language, not to relate the poem to historical or cultural contexts, or indeed to the intentions or personality of the author. The influence of these critical schools can still be well perceived in the design of the curriculum and the teaching of poetry today. The most recent GCSE Literature from AQA includes the analysis of an unseen poem, applying the skills of reading textual detail in language, structure and style, evaluating the success of the writer with little relationship to context. Although, of course, there are other considerations that candidates are asked to consider regarding the analysis of texts in the exam, it is very unlikely that such exam questions would be formulated in the way that they are today without the tradition of close reading that was the dominant mode in English universities until the 1970s and beyond.

Dias and Hayhoe (1988) trace the influences of various critical schools on the teaching of poetry in their survey chapter at the beginning of *Developing Response to Poetry*. They evaluate the impact of the approach of close reading and the New Critics, which became very influential in schools through the critical works and practices at universities, as producing 'a conception of a poem as an object that can and must be closely analysed' (Dias and Hayhoe 1988: 5), which leads into the experiences of students where:

> The apprehension of a poem as a process of close reading, a careful attending to the words on the page, an 'explication' … has led to classes in poetry where the sole object is one of training pupils to read poetry by examining as many aspects as would explain its inner workings.
>
> (Dias and Hayhoe 1988: 5)

I am sure that we have all experienced this kind of poetry class, and indeed given them, but Dias and Hayhoe suggest that the outcome of this kind of approach is that 'the teacher, the keeper of the poem, "owns" the poem, the children merely "rent" it. They live (so to speak) in the poem on the owner's terms; for the poem is not theirs to "mess around in"' (Dias and Hayhoe 1988: 7). In this way pupils regard the teacher as possessing the key to unlock the door of the meaning of the poem; they cannot determine it themselves. This mental image of the poetry class must fall into the 'traditional' polarity that Pope identifies, in which there is a 'canon' of great works, and a poem is an autonomous unit, a problem to which the pupils must find the answer.

In contrast to the 'traditional' vision of English teaching, there is the cluster of ideas that congregate around the 'progressive' notion of English. Cox's 'personal growth' model of English teaching falls naturally into this area, and is one that ' focuses on the child: it emphasises the relationship between language and learning in the individual child, and the role of literature in developing children's imaginative and aesthetic lives' (Cox 1989: paragraphs 2.21–2.27). The 'personal growth' model remains a very powerful influence on why people choose to become English teachers and the factors that influence their pedagogy. Hardman, when researching the influences of the various models on the ideology of PGCE trainees and teachers, found that, 'both teachers and teacher trainees showed that personal growth was perceived as being the most important model and thought to be the most influential on classroom practice' (Williamson *et al.* 2001: 21).

The emphasis on the individual child and the growth of an individual's aesthetic life as a philosophy within the teaching of English came to the forefront in the 1960s, as part of a larger movement towards the liberalisation of schooling, with the founding of comprehensive schools and experiments with mixed ability teaching. In 1966 at the Dartmouth Conference, English and American teaching professionals and academics met to discuss the future direction of English. A report on the conference was written by John Dixon as *Growth Through English* and it championed the voice of the pupil and the significance of children's representational worlds. In a retrospective on the conference, Dixon summarises what the conference felt was the primary concern of English teachers:

> English is about finding personal and social experiences worth sharing, and in the course of doing so, potentially making discoveries. Talking, dramatising or writing become key ways of recapturing experiences in your imagination, selecting key elements and finding how best to articulate them. This process depends on finding a willing, interested audience – including the teacher.
>
> (Dixon 2009: 244)

This conception of English conforms to the 'progressive' model in its attention to speech as central to the curriculum, and in locating the subject in 'personal and social experiences', rather than in a canon of 'great works' or in English for employment. There is an emphasis on writing for real audiences, rather than simply for exams, and on 'making discoveries', such that meaning is constructed, between pupil, teacher or audience. Dixon continues to write in his retrospective on the conference, 'I doubt whether the profession is much further on today than it was in 1966' (Dixon 2009: 244), and cites from *Growth Through English*:

> At their best, teachers are still probably relying on a flow of talk between pupils and teacher, a questing exploratory atmosphere, a sensitive ear to emerging feelings and ideas and a rich sense of the thematic possibilities and connections. ... The point about the teacher's knowledge is that, like the pupil's, it is not static and once for all, but alive and growing through her entering into the experience of others (and her inner self), in reality, and in the imagination.
>
> (Dixon 2009: 245)

There are few in the profession who would not embrace this vision of the classroom, as a place of exploration and emerging meanings, both for pupil and teacher. Our poetry lessons are part of this greater vision of what English teaching is: a classroom that is exploratory, that values the voice of the pupil, and promotes a joy in reading, discussing and writing poetry. The National Curriculum statement regarding 'The importance of English' defines it thus:

> English is vital for communicating with others in school and in the wider world, and is fundamental to learning in all curriculum subjects. In studying English, students develop skills in speaking, listening, reading and writing that they will need to participate in society and employment. Students learn to express themselves creatively and imaginatively and to communicate with others confidently and effectively.
>
> (QCA Programme of Study Key Stage 3, n.d.)

This statement foregrounds the English as 'cross-curricular' and 'adult needs' models of English. The references to creative expression and confident communication relate to personal growth model, although perhaps not directly. The next paragraph refers to English literature:

> Literature in English is rich and influential. It reflects the experiences of people from many countries and times and contributes to our sense of cultural identity. Students learn to become enthusiastic and critical readers of stories, poetry and drama as well as non-fiction and media texts, gaining access to the pleasure and world of knowledge that reading offers. Looking at the patterns, structures, origins and conventions of English helps students understand how language works. Using this understanding, students can choose and adapt what they say and write in different situations, as well as appreciate and interpret the choices made by other writers and speakers.
>
> (QCA n.d.)

The statement seeks to encapsulate both the cultural heritage and cultural analysis model, with reference to 'cultural identity', although it embraces the notion of 'many countries' rather than Leavis' 'Englishness'. It refers to 'experience', but rather as mediated by reading the works of others, than as expressions of personal growth. Writing seems here to be more functional and critical than a mode of self-expression.

So where does this leave us in the poetry classroom? The National Curriculum statement blends the five models, foregrounding 'English for employment', and assessment criteria across all key stages push us as teachers to privilege learning outcomes, preferably assessable ones, over experience and sheer delight in poetry and literary experience. If a poetry lesson is to succeed, we have to come to terms with 'the odd, other-worldly status we seem to afford [poetry]' (Wright 2005: 44) and accept what Wright observes about brilliant English teachers, 'brilliant teachers understand that, while they don't have the author in the classroom, they do have readers, and readers are central to the process' (Wright 2005: 44). In other words, to motivate and really engage young people with poetry, we have to engage with critical ideas about the way that readers respond to texts and bring their own responses to texts, particularly poetic ones.

Texts in readers, readers in texts

Louise Rosenblatt has written much that is influential about the teaching of literature. She has spent a lifetime teaching young people in universities in America, where over her career she observed and reflected on the ways that her students became involved in, and came to their own understanding of, texts ranging from Chaucer to James Joyce. She remarks in her preface to *The Reader, the Text and the Poem* that:

> I presented texts – many of them repeated year after year – to graduate and undergraduate students. … I was able to discover continuities and differences in response with the changing student populations and changing mores, and to analyse the processes and patterns that manifested themselves in the actual movement towards interpretation.
>
> (Rosenblatt 1978: x)

Rosenblatt came to believe that the interpretation of texts is an active process; that the reader is of equal importance in the creation of meaning as the work itself. This puts her in stark contrast to many other literary thinkers of the 1930s and 1940s, where the thinking of influential literary theorists such as Leavis and Brooks placed emphasis primarily in the text itself, with no attention to the reader of the text.

Rosenblatt's first influential work in the field of the response to literature was *Literature as Exploration*, first published in 1938 and rediscovered and republished in 1970. This text reads now as radically ahead of its time. We have come generally to accept these days the idea that the reader of a text has some place in the meaning-making process. However, Rosenblatt's ideas were ground-breaking in their time. In *Literature as Exploration* Rosenblatt argues that, 'a novel or poem or play remains merely inkspots on the paper until a reader transforms them into a set of meaningful symbols' (Rosenblatt 1970: 25). This idea of transformation is key to understanding what Rosenblatt believed was the process that is being undertaken when we read a text, and especially a poem. When we read a text, all readers will have a notion of what, to them, the 'inkspots' or words on the page signify, but this will be different to the meaning and associations that others will have of the same word or groups of words. Perhaps the idea of the meaning of the word 'love' is an interesting one to contemplate with regard to this notion. In teaching 'Ode to a Nightingale' at the beginning of my career, my sympathy for and association with Keats's portrayal of love as a 'drowsy numbness' struck a chord with my experience of romantic love. That perception of love, so keenly felt in all the senses and overwhelming, reads differently now, as the experience of love has changed for me. The personal associations of the word have changed a good deal over the years. Therefore Rosenblatt suggests that, 'the same text will have a very different meaning and value to us at different times or under different circumstances' (Rosenblatt 1970: 35). It is in this way Rosenblatt suggests that a 'live circuit' (Rosenblatt 1970: 25) is set up between a reader and a text.

The formation of a live circuit between reader and text, which Rosenblatt describes, is a process in which 'the reader infuses intellectual and emotional meanings into the pattern of verbal symbols, and those symbols channel his thoughts and feelings' (Rosenblatt 1970: 25). The reader brings their interpretation to the words or 'verbal symbols', and at the same time, by focusing the attention of the reader to the associations of those words, the words 'channel' the reader's reactions. Thus the reading is a two-way process, as illustrated in Figure 2.1.

Rosenblatt discussed specifically this process with regard to the reading of poetic text. She describes this activity of transformation or transaction between reader and text as 'evoking' a poem. The poem acts as both a 'stimulus' for the reader, stimulating the reader's access to their memories and personal associations, and as a 'blueprint' to reorder those associations

Text   Reader

Figure 2.1 Rosenblatt's 'live circuit'

in relationship to what is happening in the text, or to respond to the text. Reading a text is a creative activity; the reader brings 'personality traits, memories of past events, present needs and preoccupations, a particular mood of the moment, and a particular physical condition' (Rosenblatt 1970: 30). The text brings 'into the reader's consciousness certain concepts, certain sensuous experiences, certain images of things, people, actions, scenes' (Rosenblatt 1970: 30). The poem is thus a dynamic interchange between text and reader.

It is this transaction that is the poem. In *The Reader, the Text and the Poem*, Rosenblatt uses the analogy of a musical performance. A musical performance uses the score to guide the musician's actions, but the music does not exist until it is played. Once the performance stops, the music stops. So too with a poem; once the reading by the reader has stopped, the event that is the poem ceases. A poem is an event that happens in a timeframe, within which reader and text come together and 'compenetrate' (Rosenblatt 1970: 12), or to use the words of I. A. Richards that Rosenblatt cites, 'interanimate' (Rosenblatt 1970: 53). However, when that time is over, the event is finished. In 'Ode to a Nightingale', the experience that Keats has whilst listening to the song of the bird, his union through the act of writing poetry, could be seen as a metaphor for this idea of a poem existing in a moment of interanimation between reader and text. The song of the bird is the text and Keats is absorbed in the process of creation whilst listening to the bird, but feels an emptiness when it has departed. The feelings and associations that the song brought to his consciousness are his response to the text that the bird creates. Once the bird has departed, the music stopped, the event is over, and the 'compenetration' of song and Keats's memories and feelings are departed. So a poem exists both in time and space, as characterised by Rosenblatt.

Rosenblatt outlines two types of reading as being central to her philosophy of textual interaction, those of efferent and aesthetic reading. The term 'efferent' derives from the Latin verb *efferre*, 'to carry away' and characterises reading that is undertaken in order to derive information that can be 'carried away' from the text. Perhaps one is reading to derive a solution for something, or to elicit certain points. It is this type of reading that we might undertake in reading a newspaper or a text book. Using this modality of reading, the work could actually be done by someone else for you, if they present you with a summary of a text. By contrast, aesthetic reading is an end in itself. In the aesthetic mode of reading, what is carried away is not the focus, but the process itself. We read using the aesthetic standpoint for the pleasure that a work brings, such as in reading a novel. Rosenblatt refers to Coleridge's famous statement about poetry, that 'The reader should be carried forward … not by a desire to arrive at the final solution; but by the pleasurable activity of the mind excited by the attractions of the journey itself' (Rosenblatt 1978: 28). The aesthetic experience is 'the journey itself' that the reader must attend to fully to be part of. As in performing a musical piece, the individual is participating in the production of the piece of art, be it a poem, a novel or a painting. Both reading standpoints can, of course, be taken on one text. We live through 'Ode to a Nightingale' as we evoke it as a poem, reading it aesthetically, but we can then analyse the effect of alliteration in stanza five in answering a comprehension question. The primary purpose of reading a novel, or a poem, is the aesthetic experience. Therefore, in the theory of reading outlined by Rosenblatt, the process is dynamic, with the reader as much involved in the meaning-making as the text itself.

The German philosopher, Wolfgang Iser, also proposed an interactive role for the reader. In his view a text contains potential meaning. This meaning is only actualised when a reader brings their own interpretation to it. He argued in *The Act of Reading* (1978) that a literary work falls between two poles, with the text created by the author as one pole, the artistic, and the other pole being the aesthetic, which is the 'realization accomplished by the reader' (Iser

1978: 21). The literary work itself must lie in the middle, between the two end points, as the text only lives when it is realised by the reader. This realisation cannot take place without the text itself, so the literary work must be dynamic and it exists virtually. The meaning of 'virtual' here is not cyberspace, but rather in the point of contact between reader and text, in the mind. The virtual existence of the literary work is the product of the interaction between reader and the text. Iser states that 'one should conceive of meaning as something that happens' (Iser 1978: 21).

For Iser, a text guides our interpretation to some degree. Within a text, Iser states that there are sets of shared meanings that are culturally acquired, which he terms the 'repertoire'. This he defines as 'All the familiar territory within the text' (Iser 1978: 21). These will be all the references within the text that are our shared cultural knowledge, and 'may be in the form of references to earlier works, or to social and historical norms, or to the whole culture from which the text has emerged' (Iser 1978: 21). The shared cultural knowledge of the way that reality is represented in the text provides the reader with ways in which the text can be understood. Iser suggests that the repertoire is a meeting point for reader and text. This repertoire, the representation of cultural norms or patterns, is shared, to a greater or lesser extent, by all of us. These patterns, or schemata as Iser calls them, provide a 'hollow form' (Iser 1978: 21) into which the reader can pour their own interpretations. This ensures that to some degree the meaning of a text, our interpretation, is fixed through the patterns or schemata that derive from our shared cultural repertoire. The schemata provide a shape for our interpretations, this 'hollow form' (Iser 1978: 21), and therefore control their form. The 'text mobilises the subjective knowledge present in all kinds of readers and directs it to one particular end' (Iser 1978: 21). However, this is only one part of the reading process. The other aspect is the reader's own subjective standpoint. We have devised an illustration (Figure 2.2) which represents our interpretation of Iser's concept of the literary work.

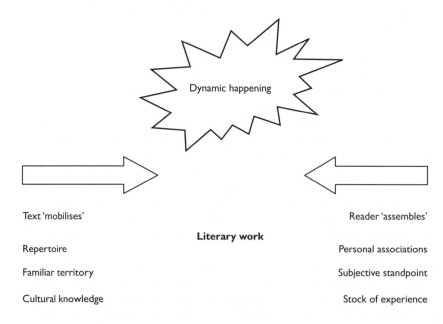

Dynamic happening

Text 'mobilises'

Literary work

Repertoire

Familiar territory

Cultural knowledge

Reader 'assembles'

Personal associations

Subjective standpoint

Stock of experience

Figure 2.2 Model of Iser's concept of the literary work

The reader, according to Iser, 'assembles' (Iser 1978: 38) meaning out of what the text has given her. The schemata in the text provide the framework, the text 'sets off a sequence of mental images which lead to the text translating itself into the reader's consciousness. The actual content of these mental images will be coloured by the reader's existing stock of experience' (Iser 1978: 38). Therefore the text becomes a literary work when the 'dynamic happening' (Iser 1978: 22) occurs between reader and text.

Linked to this concept of reading as a dynamic happening, is Iser's notion of the 'wandering viewpoint'. The process of reading is dynamic, occurring in time as we progress through a text. However, as we read we can only process one bit at a time. As we read sentences, we read them consecutively, one by one. Each sentence puts forward a perspective, on whatever the subject of that sentence is, and the reader takes this in during one moment of time. As soon as the reader moves on and reads the next sentence, the previous sentence's perspective or 'horizon' moves into the background of the reader's consciousness, and the new perspective of the next sentence comes into view. Thus the reading process consists of an interplay between memories of previous perspectives, anticipations of those that are coming, and the horizon, or sentence, currently being the reader's focus. In this sense reading is different to observing other objects, such as admiring a work of art, as with those the reader can at least try to observe the whole object. Reading must be a process, a 'moving viewpoint' (Iser 1978: 109), which can be thought of as being inside the text.

Iser, in the essay 'The reading process: a phenomenological approach', characterises this process of reading as being like a kaleidoscope:

> The activity of reading can be characterized as a sort of kaleidoscope of perspectives, preintentions, recollections. Every sentence contains a preview of the next and forms a kind of viewfinder for what is to come; and this in turn changes the 'preview' and so becomes a 'viewfinder' for what has been read.
>
> (Iser 1988: 192)

The reader is constantly moving between anticipating what is to come, through the 'preview' of the kaleidoscope, and reviewing what has been expressed, through the 'viewfinder' of the kaleidoscope. This progress is not smooth, however. Texts do not progress uniformly, but are full of twists and turns, discontinuities and unexpected avenues. This is where the reader comes into play even more forcefully. The reader must use her faculties to make connections where the text contains 'gaps', areas in the perspectives that are open to interpretation:

> Each individual reader will fill in the gaps in his own way, thereby excluding the various other possibilities; as he reads, he will make his own decision as to how the gap is to be filled. In this very act the dynamics of reading are revealed. By making his decision he implicitly acknowledges the inexhaustibility of the text; at the same time it is this very inexhaustibility that forces him to make his decision.
>
> (Iser 1978: 193)

What are the implications of reader-response theories on our teaching of texts? Of course we need to understand theory, as it is now given an important place in the teaching of A level. Yet it has further-reaching effects than that. There are tensions today in the teaching of English. The pressure to provide guaranteed 'C' grades and above leaves English teachers little room for failure. This means that the freedom for teachers to be creative and innovative is limited, counter-pointed by the absolute requirement to deliver in exams and assessments, therefore playing safe. Yet the criteria for the highest grades explicitly ask for 'original' and 'creative' responses. If we accept that the meaning of a text resides as much in the reader as the text, there are many implications for our teaching.

Readers and texts in the classroom

Peter Benton, in the 1980s, wanted to explore the ideas of Rosenblatt and whether they could be identified in the classroom. In *Young Readers Responding to Poems*, he and three colleagues devised a variety of ways in which poems might be used with school students, which tracked the students' responses, with as little teacher intervention as possible. The results bore out Rosenblatt's ideas in very interesting ways. One of Benton's colleagues, John Teasey, explored the ways in which poems act as both 'stimulus' for the reader to respond using their own experience and references, and 'blueprint' to guide how that reader responds to the poem. Teasey worked with five pupils, looking at the ways in which they interacted with the poems, and how they 'looked at the world of the text, and to the world within him [the reader], generated by the text' (Benton *et al.* 1988: 64). The reactions of one reader, Kristina, are used to trace in detail how she is negotiating the text and responding to it. The activity of text as 'blueprint' is seen to be occurring when Kristina's taped responses, in the study, move between different details at different times; she enters and re-enters the text, attending to different aspects in different ways at different times. She does not read sequentially, but moves around the text backwards and forwards. Kristina is then used to exemplify the notion of the text acting as stimulus, whereby she produces ten responses to the text, two of which relate to the text, and eight of which are 'memories of self' (Benton *et al.* 1988: 67). Benton comments that the diagrammatic studies made by Teasey 'demonstrate clearly that every reading is a unique performance, that entry into the text is idiosyncratic. Each of us makes his own map' (Benton *et al.* 1988: 203). Benton is confident that the findings are consistent with Rosenblatt's view that 'we respond to the work that we are evoking' (Benton *et al.* 1988: 203).

Chapter 4 of *Young Readers Responding to Poetry* presents Hurst's examination of the use of group talk in exploring meaning in poetry. In his study, he looked at the way that students explored 'The Stag' by Ted Hughes, left with no intervention from their teacher. By looking at the ways that the students used questions to construct their understanding of the poem, he suggests that there are various frames through which the students explore their ideas about texts (see Figure 2.3).

These frames will be familiar to anybody who has experience in teaching poetry to young people. They are the source of many familiar questions that we recognise, such as 'what is happening in this poem?' and 'who was Wilfred Owen?' Regardless of how much we as teachers want our students to come to the poetry with their own ideas, we deal endlessly with students using these frames to negotiate some sort of understanding for themselves.

What, then, would taking on these ideas of Rosenblatt's and Iser's contribute to our teaching? How can we, as teachers, balance the pressures between pupil exploration of meaning and our desire, even necessity, to get through the required amount of poetry in a short space of time? There are no easy answers to this question. One of Benton's conclusions is a suggestion for a model as a possible methodology for the teaching of poetry. This model builds on pupils' own encounters with poetry, and therefore their own meaning-making of it, that takes the students from 'apprehending' a poem, to 'comprehending' a poem. He suggests a process that follows in sequence (see Figure 2.4).

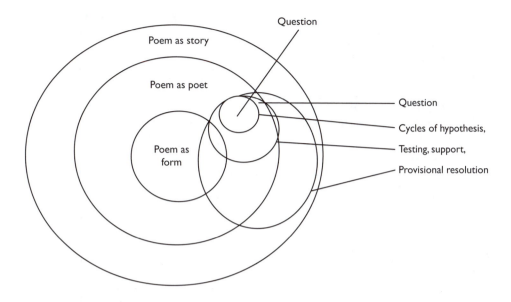

Figure 2.3 Frames of discussion (Benton *et al.* 1988: 177)

This sequence is not definitive, and can be very flexible, as sections may be used independently, or at different points in the teaching cycle. However, Benton wants to acknowledge the principles of Rosenblatt's ideas that a poem is 'an event in time' and that in order for us to 'evoke' a poem, there must be room for individuals to develop their ideas with regard to the poem before sharing them with others. Iser's idea that a text or a poem is a 'dynamic happening', with the text mobilising and the reader assembling, also leads us to the conclusion that poetry is an active construct, not a relic set in stone, and that we as teachers should see it as just that when we prepare our students to make what they will out of poetic texts.

We present here in our book ideas for ways into poetry that we hope will be useful to those of you starting out on your career, or those busy teachers looking for handy ideas for some lively lessons. We feel that the ideas that have come out of reader-response theory, such as the ideas of Iser and Rosenblatt, can help with how we approach teaching poetry, with regard to making poetry fun and empowering pupils to contribute their own ideas with confidence and enthusiasm. There is more relevant critical theory and research than we can possibly cover in this book, however, what we offer are some handy tips that have been hard won over our careers in teaching. We have written a book that we think that we would have found useful at the outset of our careers.

Apprehending

Preparatory context	
Preliminary information	Reading and browsing to create a receptive ethos

First encounter with poems	
Individual commitment to texts	Enabling tasks; sequencing/cloze DARTs Readings silent and aloud

Monitoring own responses	
Attending to and articulating own responses	Jottings around poems

Reflecting on own responses	
Self-assessment of own responses	Preparing notes and ideas for pair/group work

Expressing own responses		
Pair talk Sharing/ comparing	Individual Individual recording/journal writing to record responses	Group talk Sharing/ comparing

Comprehending

Creative involvement with poems via recording, live readings, drama, art
Re-readings and rehearsals of all of parts of the poems

Performances
Individuals/Pairs/Groups

Individual statements
Majking a considered response
Creative responses/Formal writing

Figure 2.4 An adaptation of Benton's methodology (Benton *et al.* 1988: 205)

Chapter 3

Aspects of form

For a rhymer that will be tied to no rules at all, but range as he list, may easily utter what he will, but such manner of poesy is called, in our vulgur, rhyme doggerel, with which rebuke we will.

(George Puttenham, *The Art of English Poesy*)

And now good morrow to our waking souls,
Which watch not one another out of fear;
For love, all love of other sights controls,
And makes one little room, an everywhere.
(John Donne, 'The Good Morrow')

This chapter looks at form as a way into teaching and studying poetry. We discuss the development of the sonnet form from Petrarch to the modern day. We then look at teaching the ballad form at KS3 using 'The Ballad of Charlotte Dymond', introducing free verse at KS4 with Gabriel Okara's 'Once Upon a Time' and looking at blank verse at KS5 using extracts from Marlowe's *Dr Faustus*. We finish with a case study of teaching John Donne's 'The Flea' at KS5.

Introduction: examining aspects of form

Form is integral to poetry. Coleridge stated, 'A poem contains the same elements as a prose composition; the difference therefore must consist in a different combination of them' (Coleridge 2000: 480). Using form as a springboard is to look at a poem using the perspective of Coleridge's 'combination', that is, the order and structure as a way of opening up meaning for the reader. Children enjoy form. Rhyme and rhythm are, to them, natural components of poetry, as they are still deemed so by many adults. Sandy Brownjohn, writing about the teaching of poetry in the 1980s, entitled her first book *Does It Have to Rhyme?* The question of the title mimics the kind of questions asked by pupils about poetry and the form that it takes. This chapter seeks to explore different ways in which form can be used as a starting point to open up poems with pupils. The forms of poetry have a long and colourful history, which can be used to good effect in the classroom.

A rich source for the exploration of form at all key stages is the sonnet. The sonnet has been a highly influential form of poetry, both in English and European literature. Its origins are in thirteenth-century Italy and its greatest early exponent was Petrarch in the fourteenth century, who wrote of his love for Laura in a sequence of lyrical poems and sonnets. Courtly love, originating from French troubadour lyrics, became synonymous with expressions of love in the early uses of the sonnet. Love is depicted as a disease, caught quickly, with dramatic consequences. The man worships the woman, often from afar, and the woman is an object of desire and pursuit. In this tradition love is an ideal, and the poetry is about the experience of love, from a male point of view. This version of romantic love still persists today, although represented now as an experience common to women as well as men, as any survey of films or adverts will show us.

The Petrarchan sonnet form moved from its origins in thirteenth-century Italy, through Spain and France, arriving in England with the work of Thomas Wyatt in the sixteenth century. Here the form became very fashionable for courtiers to express their love, and their ambition, and was used as a mode of expression that was not exclusively private, nor exactly public, between lover and the beloved. Generally they were exchanged within a small, élite group. Sonnets tended not to be written singly, but in sequences, expressing varying aspects of the poet's experience and command of the form. Queen Elizabeth I exchanged sonnets with Sir Walter Raleigh, and Sir Philip Sidney wrote a sequence that, although purporting to be by Astrophel about his love for Stella, is really only veiled flattery for the queen from her humble servant, himself.

The derivation of the term 'sonnet' is from the Italian *sonneto*, or little song. The term *stanza* in Italian can be roughly translated as a 'little room', and the form is indeed like a little room, it is so concise and regulated. In John Donne's lyric 'The Good Morrow', Donne puns on the ability of 'one little room', a stanza, being able to represent an expanse of experience, 'an everywhere'. The Petrarchan sonnet form has fourteen lines, and falls into two sections, the first of eight lines, the octave, and the second of six lines, the sestet. The two sections are divided by their rhyme schemes, the octave having ABBAABBA, only two rhymes for eight lines, and the sestet CDECDE, utilising three rhyming terms. The form naturally suggests that it will explore an idea from two particular angles, with a change in perspective occurring at the break between the two rhyming sections. The change in perspective is called a *volta*, or a turn, where the second part of the sonnet responds to the first part. The Petrarchan sonnet has become the most popular form in English poetry, as noted by Evans (1996) in his introduction to the New Cambridge edition of Shakespeare's *The Sonnets*, 'despite the fact that it is very much more difficult to deal with in English, the Petrarchan sonnet has become the preferred form, used by Milton, Wordsworth, and many more recent poets' (Evans 1996: 6).

One modern poet who has used the Petrarchan sonnet form to express a modern sentiment is Edna St Vincent Millay. Millay wrote at the beginning of the twentieth century, in America, expressing her views of female experience. The origin of Petrarchanism is in an expression of male desire and idealised versions of femininity; Millay reverses this, expressing a completely different vision of female sexuality, using the Petrarchan form. Consider her sonnet.

What lips my lips have kissed, and where, and why

What lips my lips have kissed, and where, and why,
I have forgotten, and what arms have lain
Under my head till morning; but the rain
Is full of ghosts tonight, that tap and sigh
Upon the glass and listen for reply,
And in my heart there stirs a quiet pain
For unremembered lads that not again

Will turn to me at midnight with a cry.
Thus in winter stands the lonely tree,
Nor knows what birds have vanished one by one,
Yet knows its boughs more silent than before:
I cannot say what loves have come and gone,
I only know that summer sang in me
A little while, that in me sings no more.

(Millay 1992: 602)

The voice here is of a woman who has experienced many lovers, who has made her own choices about who to love and when. Although there is much pain here, it is the expression of female sexuality that has had some self-determination. The Petrarchan structure is clear; the octave explores the persona's previous loves, and the sestet revolves around the single image of the 'lonely tree', the remainder of the experience metaphorised as a tree abandoned by birds now that winter has come. There is much here that can be explored with a receptive GCSE group, and most certainly KS5 students. Millay wrote sonnet sequences and used the mode to explore female desire. She utilised the traditional poetic form of the sonnet, including the conventional use of pentameter, yet the voice and experience she represented challenges the accepted male orthodoxy of the form.

The other most influential form of the sonnet is the Shakespearean sonnet. Shakespeare wrote a sequence of 154 sonnets, all exploring love, some for a 'dark lady' and some for a young man. There is much that can appeal to KS3 and KS4 pupils in this sequence. Shakespeare plays with the Petrarchan form; he used fourteen lines, but reorganises the rhyme scheme into three quatrains of four lines (ABAB CDCD EFEF) and finishes with a couplet. The shape then requires more rhyming endings, and suggests that there will be three ideas, related in some way, with a neat ending with a rhyming couplet. Shakespeare can be seen subverting conventional depictions of the courtly lover in the famous Sonnet 130, where he works through a series of negatives of the features that his lover does not have, her hair is 'black wires' and her breath 'reeks'. The relationship between the form of the sonnet, the lover's features, and the content, the play with conventional depictions of love, offer much to explore within the classroom. *Poems from the Past*, by Mary Berry and Alex Madina (Berry and Madina 1997), contains a very wide selection of activities that can be undertaken with pre-twentieth-century poems. Their approach is very much one of using drama and active re-presentation of texts to make the poetry come alive for pupils. For Sonnet 130 they suggest miming and performing tableaux for the different aspects presented of the lady in the sonnet. This activity could feed directly into a discussion of form, as the tableaux would be, in effect, the content of the different quatrains. Another very useful text for ideas regarding specifically the writing of poems is *Jumpstart: Poetry in the Secondary School* (Yates 1999). Written by Cliff Yates, the book describes work in the classroom with different poems and ways to get pupils writing. Regarding the sonnet, Yates writes:

> The sonnet is one of the most useful forms I have used in school; even if the pupils do not manage to write one that satisfies them, the next time they write a poem they will write better for having had the experience of the longer line and the fourteen line structure.

(Yates 1999: 128)

Yates then discusses the use of a particular sonnet by Mick North in the classroom, with extracts of work by the pupils and activities undertaken to produce them. Yates suggests a variety of imaginative approaches to getting pupils writing sonnets, which are practical and demonstrate the rich potential that exploring poetry through form offers us as teachers.

Form at KS3: 'The Ballad of Charlotte Dymond' by Charles Causley

Poetry is rooted in the oral tradition and the ballad is one of its oldest forms, stemming back from medieval times. Ballads were designed to tell dramatic stories in a simple style and form, with straightforward plots and characters, focussing on grand passions like love and death. Inner thought processes and motives were not explored; the function of the ballad was to convey the narrative in an accessible form, often leaving the listener with more questions than answers. Because ballads are often very lengthy, each four-line stanza has the same ABCB rhyme scheme and mostly the same metrical pattern of alternating lines of iambic tetrameter (eight syllables) and iambic trimeter (six syllables), which is known as *ballad meter,* to help the performer remember the story. However, there are many variations on this pattern. Each stanza is a self-contained unit which builds up the story, the last line enclosing that unit.

The combination of the strong rhyme and rhythm, coupled with the action of the story and the multiple voices demands a dramatic reading if pupils are to gain a sense of the ballad's immediacy. In her book *Poetry for Life: A Practical Guide to Teaching Poetry in the Primary School*, Linda Hall discusses techniques for achieving a dramatic reading of the medieval ballad 'Sir Patrick Spens' at KS2, which can be usefully adapted for KS3.

Prior learning from KS2 can be developed in Year 7; for example, knowledge about rhyme can be developed by introducing new ways of matching sounds such as alliteration and assonance. Rhythm can be explored and pupils can learn how to mark stress.

'The Ballad of Charlotte Dymond', written by Charles Causley and first published in 1961, is based on the true story of a girl of eighteen who was murdered on Bodmin Moor by her lover in 1844. In conventional ballad form, the language is uncomplicated and the plot dramatic. Prior to introducing the poem, a very brief recap or introduction to the ballad's purpose in telling stories in the later medieval period is useful. Pupils can be asked to think about which techniques they use when they have to remember something, such as the alphabet, and they will often refer to repetition, chanting and songs as successful ways of learning.

A useful pre-reading task is to download original news reports of the story of Charlotte Dymond, which pupils then read with a focus on highlighting the main facts from the story. Working in pairs, they are asked to decide on the key bits they would put in if they were re-telling the story from memory, and which bits they would leave out, and why.

Each pupil is next given a copy of the ballad to read through to themselves, which they use to refer back to their news report and check the veracity of the ballad; what is included in the ballad that was not in the original news report, and what has been left out? Do they agree with the author's choice or would they have included or left out different facts, and why?

After discussing the story, it is time to hear the poem read out loud. A teacher's dramatic reading allows pupils to hear the sounds and word patterns, developing what T.S. Eliot called the 'auditory imagination' (Eliot 1933: 111) which means in essence to develop a subconscious feeling for rhythm and syllable.

The ballad is 24 stanzas long, so after an initial reading by the teacher it is a good idea to allocate one stanza to each pupil to read out in sequence around the classroom. Allowing time to work out with whose 'voice' they are speaking, to practise their stanza and ensure they are confident with pronunciation prior to reading aloud gives pupils the chance to develop a feeling for the rhythm and rhyme. Different tones will be needed for each speaker so it is important to allow pupils time to decide how their character speaks. This allows the pupil to feel personally involved in conveying meaning. In today's large classes of more than 24 it is important to go back again to the beginning and hear it read a third time. This gives everyone a chance to read and the strong rhythm and rhyme will support reluctant or poor readers.

After hearing the poem read through, ask pupils to decide on conventions or 'rules' for the ballad form. This will entail teaching pupils how to work out the rhyme scheme using conventional ABCB notation and what is meant by the terms 'internal rhyme' and 'half rhyme'. Alliteration and assonance can also be introduced and pupils taught to count syllables to learn how to mark stress. As Veronica O'Brien says:

> Energy should, I suggest, be given to developing the children's natural capacity to respond to rhythm, to identify the effect it has on the reader, and to discover the relationship between rhythm and meaning. Understanding of the rhythm/meaning connection is most easily strengthened when there is a rhythmic surprise, an unexpected turning the pattern.
>
> (O'Brien 1985: 57)

This idea can be applied to 'The Ballad of Charlotte Dymond'; whilst reading the poem aloud, pupils notice the unexpected change to the rhythm in the second stanza:

> It was a Sunday evening
> And in the April rain
> That Charlotte went from our house
> And never came home again.
>
> Her shawl of diamond redcloth,
> She wore a yellow gown
> She carried the green gauze handkerchief
> She bought in Bodmin town.
>
> (Causley 1992: 108)

This metrical bump forces the listeners to notice the 'green gauze handkerchief' and thus to wonder about its significance. There are several other 'rhythmic surprises' throughout the ballad, all of which serve to highlight a particular feature of the narrative which turns out to be important later on.

In order to agree on 'rules' for writing a ballad, pupils will need to re-read the ballad to each other in groups. The teacher thus becomes a guide to the poetic form, not the provider of information. A class spider diagram showing ideas from all groups can be created and pupils' higher-order thinking skills are utilised by asking them to reach a consensus of opinion in their groups by putting the 'rules' in order of importance and to justify their order. The pupils' rules can then be tested by looking at another ballad, such as the traditional medieval ballad 'Barbara Allen' or another twentieth-century narrative poem suggested by Hall which might be attractive to older boys who are also poor readers, such as W. H. Auden's ballad 'O What is the sound', a story of the betrayal of a young man to the military (Hall 1989: 118).

Once satisfied that their rules are sound, pupils are asked to write a class ballad about a current news story, each providing one stanza each which they will memorise and perform to the class. This will reinforce the importance of the regular rhyme and rhythm as an aid to memory. The more able will be able to use the new techniques such as internal rhyme, whilst the less able can satisfactorily adhere to the simple structure and self-contained unit of meaning. As Linda Hall suggests:

> The writing of rhymed, or highly patterned or tightly structured verse can be a boon. It can help such children to express themselves well, probably because of the succinctness of the poetic form and the discipline that the brevity imposes.
>
> (Hall 1989: 118)

This active approach to the ballad will give the pupil a sense of ownership and personal involvement, which is the key to successful learning.

Form at KS4: free verse 'Once Upon a Time' by Gabriel Okara

Once Upon a Time

Once upon a time, son,
they used to laugh with their hearts
and laugh with their eyes:
but now they only laugh with their teeth,
while their ice-block cold eyes
search behind my shadow.

There was a time indeed
they used to shake hands with their hearts:
but that's gone, son.
Now they shake hands without hearts
while their left hands search
my empty pockets.

'Feel at home!' 'Come again':
they say, and when I come
again and feel
at home, once, twice,
there will be no thrice –
for then I find doors shut on me.

So I have learned many things, son.
I have learned to wear many faces
like dresses – homeface,
officeface, streetface, hostface,
cocktailface, with all their conforming smiles
like a fixed portrait smile.

And I have learned too
to laugh with only my teeth
and shake hands without my heart.
I have also learned to say, 'Goodbye',
when I mean 'Good-riddance':
to say 'Glad to meet you',
without being glad; and to say 'It's been
nice talking to you', after being bored.

But believe me, son.
I want to be what I used to be
when I was like you. I want
to unlearn all these muting things.
Most of all, I want to relearn
how to laugh, for my laugh in the mirror
shows only my teeth like a snake's bare
fangs!

So show me, son,
how to laugh; show me how
I used to laugh and smile
once upon a time when I was like you.
                    (Okara 1978: 18)

In the late 1800s the French poets Baudelaire and Rimbaud had been seeking freedom from the constraints of formal versification with their prose poems known as *vers libre*. T. S. Eliot was influenced by his reading of the poems of the French poet Jules Laforgue and sent his *The Love Songs of J. Alfred Prufrock* to Ezra Pound, who was himself seeking a new form of poetic expression. The rest, as they say, is history. For a detailed historical background to the origins and development of free verse see Jeffrey Wainwright's *Poetry: The Basics* (Wainwright 2004) and for a detailed description of the three varieties of free verse see Philip Hobsbaum's *Metre, Rhythm and Verse Form* (Hobsbaum 1996).

In the twentieth century *vers libre* came to be translated to 'free verse', meaning a form of poem that has no recurring metrical patterns and does not use rhyme. It can also avoid all kinds of repetition of stanza pattern and phrases, although Eliot notes that sometimes a rhyme is necessary; 'Freed from its exacting task of supporting lame verse, it could be applied with greater effect where most needed' (cited in Kermode 1975: 36). Eliot argues that there must always be rhythm, 'since even the worst verse can be scanned', a fact agreed with by Philip Hobsbaum who states that free verse proper without any form of scansion can come out like 'chopped-up prose' (Hobsbaum 1996: 92). As Fraser neatly puts it, 'what I recognise as good free verse is verse which does not scan regularly but always seems on the verge of scanning regularly' (Fraser 1970: 74).

One of the key features of free verse is that it can convey lived experience and emotions through naturalness of speech. Using a more casual and colloquial quality of voice, it allows for the personality of the speaker to come through, such as in Eliot's *The Love Songs of J. Alfred Prufrock*.

Linda Hall urges caution in teaching free verse at KS2 and to inexperienced readers of poetry in KS3 and KS4 as it causes much insecurity. She reminds us:

for the very young and the less able of all ages, poetry's earliest and principal appeal is to the ear. It is through such aural pleasure that we will catch the interest of our pupils. The poetry we choose for regular reading sessions should, therefore, display rhythm, rhyme and metre. The use of repetition is very satisfying to young children.

(Hall 1989: 43)

Pupils' lack of confidence in tackling the free verse form can manifest itself in their initial resistance to it, and many have been known to say, 'It's not even a real poem'. Further, there is the expectation that poems contain multiple meanings and this can alarm pupils, as they feel pressure to search for layers of meaning beyond the obvious. Without the formal structures of the traditional poetic form to guide them this becomes a daunting prospect.

Joan Peskin describes a study she carried out based on the assertions of literary theorists Culler (1997) and Fish (1980), that 'poetry reading is animated by a special set of conventional expectations which the reader has assimilated and which form the foundation of a literary education' (Peskin 2007: 22):

The three main conventional expectations are: the expectation of multiple meaning; the expectation of metaphorical content; and the expectation of significance, where the reader searches for the point of the poem. Culler and Fish agree that 'it is readers, with their shared conventions, who produce meaning, that is, when they identify a text as a poem, they creatively add meaning and are responsible for the materialization of poetic characteristics.'

(Peskin 2007: 23)

Peskin found that when presented with a piece of prose in the shape of a poem, students' discussions 'demonstrated their awareness that the poetic genre required that they creatively add meaning to the text, for what is meant is likely to be more than what is said' (Peskin 2007: 25). She discovered that the textual shape of the poem slowed down the reading process and triggered the hypothesised conventional expectations and aesthetic operations. 'The students' minds became active and exploratory, reflecting on the writer's craft and how it adds to the meaning, and they also expressed greater enjoyment' (Peskin 2007: 30).

The poem 'Once Upon a Time' by Gabriel Okara is a good introduction to free verse for KS4 pupils as it creates the colloquial voice and it is relatively easy for pupils to understand the metaphorical meaning, describing as it does an experience common to us all: that of having to put on an act or show a particular facet of the self, depending on the circumstances in which we find ourselves. To overcome pupils' possible insecurity when faced with the free verse form, an initial introduction to the poem can be to set it out as prose.

As Peskin discovered, in the prose form pupils read it and make initial sense of it fairly quickly without delving for any deeper meaning. They will therefore respond to the poem on a fairly superficial level but at least will have grasped the overall meaning: that the poet has changed as he became older and now wants his son to teach him to be happy again. This eliminates pupils' initial fear of not understanding the meaning of the poem. The next step is for pupils to re-write the text in the poetic form, that is, in free verse. This means they have to demonstrate their understanding of the form; the poem exhibits a naturalness of speech without necessarily using rhyme and requires that the students actively engage with the words. Although told there will be no formal rhythm, nevertheless pupils will often write lines that loosely scan. This activity gets pupils to really engage with the language of the poem as by creating the free verse form themselves, they are adding their own layer of meaning to the text. The physical positioning the words on the page forces the emphasis on the ideas that pupils individually want to emphasise.

Finally, pupils are given a copy of the poem in its original form. As they read it, they compare it with their own version which leads to discussion about the words the poet seemed to stress and how this is similar or otherwise to where the pupils created emphasis. As Peskin's study showed, the poetic form triggers the three main conventional expectations which lead pupils to then engage in a close reading of the poem at word level. Exploring the meaning of the metaphors leads to discovery of the wider significance of the poem; essentially that societal expectations make us dishonest.

Form at KS5: blank verse

Blank verse is a highly influential form in English poetry. It was used by Shakespeare, Milton, Wordsworth and Tennyson; more recently by Edward Thomas, Siegfried Sassoon and Robert Graves. The form fell from favour after Ezra Pound and T. S. Eliot mounted a decisive attack on it after the First World War, as representing an old order that was to be dismantled by Modernism.

Old English poetry was driven by alliteration and the use of stress to push forward the sense of the poetry. The poetry used four main accents per line and had a break or caesura in the middle of the line. With its origins in oral performance, this type of line evolved to be memorised. The English language shifted greatly after Old English, with the influx of many influences, most notably Norman French. Chaucer wrote in the new form of English that emerged in the Middle Ages, with consummate success, using iambic pentameter, but his verse was always rhymed. After Chaucer, English verse fell into a sort of 'prosodic anarchy' (Shaw 2007: 33) where, 'in one hapless venture after another, the verse staggers, limps or plunges ahead willy-nilly' (Shaw 2007: 33). To the rescue came Sir Henry Howard, who introduced blank verse into English, in his translation of *The Aeneid* in 1540. Unfortunately, Howard was executed by Henry VIII, but his innovation, influenced by Italian techniques of versification, eventually became a highly popular and influential form.

Blank verse does not rhyme. It possess iambs, or feet, of one unstressed ('×') and one stressed ('/') syllable per foot. The most generally used form is pentameter, in which there are five iambs per line of ten syllables. Perhaps the success of blank verse is its closeness to natural speech. Otto Jespersen observes in his essay 'Notes on metre' that 'Verse rhythm is based on the same alternation between stronger and weaker syllables as that found in natural everyday speech … everywhere we observe a natural tendency towards making a weak syllable follow after a strong one and inversely' (Jespersen 1967: 75). We can detect a contrast between ordered and disordered speech rhythms when we talk and listen to others. This use of contrast in rhythm is used in poetry, and when looked at in the context of blank verse, a clear parallel can be drawn between the form and content of the poetry. This is particularly important at KS5, where it is imperative that students understand the link between meaning and structure in poetry, and are able to articulate that successfully.

Christopher Marlowe uses blank verse to great effect. In *Dr Faustus*, Marlowe depicts the downfall of the scholar Faustus, who contracts his soul to the devil in return for 24 years of what he hopes will be pleasure and enlightenment. The contrast between Faustus' opening and closing soliloquy shows very clearly the differences in his mental state between the opening of the play and the after his 24 years of indulgence. As the play opens we meet Faustus in his study. The language of Faustus' soliloquy is ordered and logical as Marlowe sets out to the audience Faustus' character and concerns. The language of the soliloquy is cohesive and regular, reflecting Faustus' state of mind, the use of iambic pentameter under-scoring this:

```
x  /   x  /   x    /  x   /   x /
Settle thy studies, Faustus, and begin
x    /    x   /    x  /   x    /   x   /
To sound the depth of that thou wilt profess;
x   /   x    /    x / x  / x   /
Having commenced, be a divine in show,
                              (Marlowe 1995: 1–5)
```

In dealing with any long extract of verse, be it a soliloquy or a poem, the main objective is to get the students to interact with the text without feeling that they have to instantly understand it. Yandell and Franks outline a very user-friendly approach to working with a lengthy speech or poem, in *Learning to Teach English in the Secondary School*. The activity commences with the teacher setting the scene and reading the speech for the students, progressing to choral reading of the text by students. This is followed by a game with the words in which students say specific words when pointed at. The text is then read again, with students echoing key words. Finally, the students decide together where to break the text up. This is a particularly useful activity, as it requires a real engagement with the meaning of the text, yet the outcome is totally open-ended, so there is no possibility of students feeling that they might contribute an invalid suggestion.

Using echoes is a very powerful tool for playing with verse. As one person reads, others echo words that they have selected for particular reasons. One option is to leave the selection to the students to echo any words that they feel are important or stand out to them. This requires that the students listen to a piece of text and respond spontaneously to the language without being required to justify their opinions in any way. This technique can also be more focused, in asking students to echo words to do with specific ideas in a text. Any edition from the series Cambridge School Shakespeare of a play by Shakespeare is brimming with ideas for use with verse and drama. An example of the use of echoes in the *Othello* edition can be seen in Act 3. When in Scene 3, Othello is discussing his military career, it is suggested that students can work on the speech in groups, with one member of the group reading the text and the other members echoing any words to do with military activity. In this way echoing can be used to bring out any major themes or ideas in a text.

In the opening soliloquy of *Dr Faustus*, echoing words involved with study and academic success, as the soliloquy progresses in an orderly fashion, could emphasise Faustus' scholarly successes and desire for magic. Contrast this with the use of blank verse in Faustus' final soliloquy in the play, where Faustus is facing the consequence of his choice of magic and consequently his imminent descent into hell. Echoes here might concentrate on time and God. The themes of the play are neatly encapsulated in this one activity.

As the final soliloquy progresses, the rhythm and uniformity of the verse shifts and is unstable. Faustus' language reflects the disturbed state that he is now in:

O, I'll leap up to my God! Who pulls me down?
See, see where Christ's blood streams in the firmament!
One drop would save my soul, half a drop. Ah my
Christ!–
                              (Marlowe 1995: 148–55)

The line lengths are varied. These three lines have eleven syllables, which clearly does not fit with a line of pentameter. Initially, simply asking the students to mark the stressed and unstressed syllables of this section will provoke much discussion, as actually trying to apply the conventional line to the poetry is very tricky. The strikingly emphatic one word line 'Christ!–' indicates a silence where the rest of the syllables in the line should be, is also an interesting talking point. There is much contrast to be drawn between these two soliloquies of the play, as they can be used to parallel each other in terms of the relationship between form and content and are neatly placed at the beginning and end of the play. Brenda Pinder's *Shakespeare: An Active Approach* (Pinder 1990) suggests a method by which students can reflect on the way that the blank verse is deployed as a way of enhancing drama. Her suggestion is that students rewrite the opening of *Macbeth* in the form of a novel. Using this idea of text transformation, and transforming the opening and closing of *Dr Faustus* into the opening and closing of a novel, would indeed provide some very rich interaction with the text and the choices that have been made in the writing of the verse.

Case study: form at KS5, 'The Flea' by John Donne

The Flea

Mark but this flea, and mark in this,
How little that which thou deny'st me is;
It sucked me first, and now sucks thee,
And in this flea, our two bloods mingled be;
Thou knowest that this cannot be said
A sin, nor shame, nor loss of maidenhead.
   Yet this enjoys before it woo,
   And pampered, swells with one blood made of two,
   And this, alas, is more than we would do.

Oh stay, three lives in one flea spare,
Where we almost, yea, more than married are.
This flea is you and I, and this
Our marriage bed, and marriage temple is;
Though parents grudge, and you, we are met
And cloistered in these living walls of jet.
   Though use make you apt to kill me,
   Let not to that self murder added be,
   And sacrilege, three sins in killing three.

Cruel and sudden, hast thou since
Purpled thy nail in blood of innocence?
Wherein could this flea guilty be
Except in that drop which it sucked from thee?
Yet thou triumph'st, and sayest that thou
Find'st not thyself, nor me, the weaker now.
   'Tis true, then learn how false fears be;
   Just so much honor, when thou yieldst to me,
   Will waste, as this flea's death took life from thee.
      (John Donne, in Hollander and Kermode 1973: 534)

John Donne is perennially popular with exam boards and students alike. His work has an energetic and humorous voice that combines with a complexity that can intrigue the reader. In 'The Flea' Donne provides a situation that has a drama that could justifiably be called timeless, as it is the argument of a man trying to persuade the object of his attentions to sleep with him, which may certainly have some resonance with students at Key Stage 5. The poem has three stanzas, and the drama of the lyric advances in three stages. The opening of each stanza is triggered by something that has happened, as it were, in the blank gaps before the stanza starts. As the first stanza commences, the speaker has discovered a flea and is alerting his mistress to its presence, by saying, 'Mark but this flea'. In the second stanza starts, his mistress is in the process of trying to kill the flea, and in the third the mistress has managed to kill the flea.

As teachers, when we start teaching a poem, we often wonder how to start – do we go straight in to reading the poem? What information is needed by the students before we begin, or should they come to it cold? Lynn and Jeffrey Wood suggest:

> If one characteristic of poetry is intensity – language charged with meaning in the exploration of powerful human experiences – then that very intensity is something a listener/reader needs to be prepared for ... There are many reasons why adolescents register discomfort about poetry. Surely one of them is simply embarrassment and confusion on encountering an inexplicable outpouring of joy or desolation. We feel the 'emotional territory' has to be mapped in advance.
>
> (Wood and Wood 1988: 2)

Jeffrey and Lynn Wood suggest various pre-reading activities as starting points for students. These activities can work in two ways: preparing the ground for key images that are to come in the poem, and exploring the 'emotional territory' of the work. John Donne's 'The Flea' is a very powerful poem of seduction. The central metaphor, that of a flea, was a common conceit in the Early Modern period, and the tone of the poem is light and jocular. I decided to start with a pre-reading activity with my students that brought their attention to the central image of the poem. The movement and shape of the flea are important in understanding the central image of the poem, and the actual migration of the flea between the two characters portrayed, feeds into the structure and form of the lyric. Before we looked at the poem, I asked the students to think individually of questions to do with fleas generally and to jot down their ideas. I asked them to consider how a flea moves, where it might live, where fleas might be found on humans and lastly to consider what a flea looks like. I then asked them to do a quick sketch of a flea and surround it with words that might be applied to it. The students responded well to this. The use of a quick sketch enabled ideas to be presented in a visual form, and when we shared our responses as a group we came up with: tiny, black, parasite, blood, hungry, long black legs, hairy, balloon-like, inflated. These words were a fruitful starting point, as the poem's argument advances around the size and colour of the flea, making specific reference to its body being 'jet' (line 15), and an aspect of Donne's rather suggestive image of the flea swelling as it is 'pampered' (line 8) whilst it sucks his mistress's blood, is prefigured in their responses such as 'balloon-like' and 'inflated'.

We moved on to thinking about the emotional territory of the poem, that of seduction. Here I asked them to consider these points:

- In what ways have you tried to persuade someone to go out with you?
- What are the ways that have been tried on you?

Given the rather intimate quality of the questions, I asked them to feed back in smaller groups the outcomes of their discussion. Much hilarity ensued, as we discussed techniques that we might employ to catch someone's interest, such as listening carefully to our targets, laughing at their jokes and feigning interest in topics such as football or clothes. The group were happy to share the outcomes of their discussions.

I then read the poem to the group. As the Woods observe, 'we would urge that, wherever possible, the poems are read to the class, more than once if possible, before the students look at the poems as marks on the page' (Wood and Wood 1988: 2). I deliberately did not ask the students to share their thoughts after hearing the poem, but then asked them to read the poem aloud in groups twice, once sharing the reading out line by line and then reading from punctuation point to punctuation point. This activity is very useful, as it enables groups to discuss and become familiar with a text, without any need to respond, but they can ruminate over the text, if need be looking up words in a dictionary.

Once the students had familiarised themselves with the language, I wanted them to explore the form of the poem. Given that the form of the poem is intricately linked with the drama of the piece, I have found that students need to come to grips with the dramatic qualities of the writing. I set them two alternative activities, both revolving around interpreting the three scenes in the poem. Alternative modes of presenting their understanding enabled the groups to have an element of control over the ways in which they worked. The groups had to figure out what the three scenes in this poem are, select a key line that encapsulates the scene and either devise a freeze frame or sketch storyboards for each scene. It is the discussion that is undertaken to prepare these outcomes that is really the work here, although feeding back and looking at what is presented allows a plenary for their interpretations to be shared. Interestingly, there was an even split in the take-up of freeze frames and storyboarding, and both concentrated on the dynamic between the speaker and his beloved, and the role of the flea within that. One notable freeze frame had the flea as a 'vicar' marrying the speaker and his lady, whilst another saw the mistress victorious with a large flea dead on the ground.

In our plenary we pulled together our understanding of the poem. What distinctly emerged was the very male quality of the voice. This led the group to bring in issues of morality and the way that some in the group saw the historical valuing of virtue as close to extreme, contemporary religious views. We discussed the historical significance of virginity, which led to the group touching upon the royal family and *Romeo and Juliet*. Our final activity was to attempt to redress the balance in favour of the mistress in the poem, and the group were set the task, 'Now you are the mistress. Write an answer back to the speaker, addressing his arguments in the way that you think that she might.' The group came up with some amusing and interesting responses, one which began, 'Is he still going? I'm telling you if he says one more word about getting me into bed, it will be more than that wretched flea that's dead' and one in the form of a short verse, which began, 'To lose my maidenhead is to lose my purity/ False fears perhaps, but real fears to me.'

When teaching poetry from a different time or culture, the temptation is to present students with information regarding context and background before the poem is read. This can have the effect of turning a poem into a historical artefact or curious mystery that needs to be unravelled, rather than as a piece of writing that can speak directly to the reader. That the flea in Donne's poem is a metaphysical conceit is interesting, but the students need to understand the role that the flea is playing in the poem, as a tool for seduction, and relate that to their own knowledge of persuasion and clever argumentation, before they can really understand that the metaphor is the vehicle for the whole argument. The idea is really very simple, and it is the simple activities that allow the complexities of the argument to unravel.

Chapter 4

Words and imagery

POLONIUS What do you read, my lord?
HAMLET Words, words, words.
POLONIUS What is the matter, my lord?
HAMLET Between who?
POLONIUS I mean, the matter that you read, my lord?
HAMLET Slanders, Sir.

> (*Hamlet*, Act 1, Scene 2, ll.191–5)

CLOWN To see this age! A sentence is but a chev'ril glove to a good wit – how quickly the
wrong side may be turned outward!

> (*Twelfth Night*, Act 3, Scene 1, ll.11–13)

In this chapter we explore poetry through the aspect of lexis and imagery. We focus on the importance of word class for teaching, using Ted Hughes' 'Roger the Dog' and Irene McLeod's 'Lone Dog' at KS3. We follow this by looking at teaching through the use of imagery and personification at KS4 with Hughes' 'Thistles'. The next teaching technique addressed is the use of rhyme and rhythm to convey meaning, using Zephaniah's 'It's Work' and Gunn's 'Baby Song' with KS5. The chapter finishes with a case study of teaching Year 9 exploring the use of simile in Wilfred Owen's 'Dulce et Decorum Est'.

Introduction: using words and imagery in the classroom

Shakespeare understood the importance of words. The significance of the single words 'madness' and 'revenge' are pivotal to the plot and action (or lack of it) in *Hamlet*; the word 'nothing' in *King Lear* and 'love' in *Twelfth Night* similarly so. So it is too in poetry. The effect of single words is a fruitful entry into interpreting meaning with pupils, along with the significance of larger clusters of words, which may be linked by imagery or syntactically. The introduction to the Framework for Secondary English states that this is one of the key principles that underlie the thinking of the strategy, in stipulating what should be taught in English lessons:

> Looking at the patterns, structures, origins and conventions of English helps pupils understand how language works. Using this understanding, pupils can choose and adapt what they say and write in different situations, as well as appreciate and interpret the choices made by other writers and speakers.

> (QCA n.d.)

Looking at text at a word level is a significant aspect of the sentiments expressed here. The statement refers to 'patterns' and 'structures', concepts that are of prime importance in the teaching of poetry. The effect of patterning in the use of words is a key to the way that readers perceive texts. The significance of patterning correlates with ideas associated with the way that adults and children learn to read. Two over-arching principles that recur in discussion of reading and the acquisition of language are the 'top-down' and 'bottom-up' principles.

The 'top-down' or 'bottom-up' principles operate in the ways that both adults and children process language. They can be illustrated by reflecting on the ways in which children acquire language. Children use a variety of approaches. They can acquire through learning the smallest units of speech, and begin to put these together, starting to build utterances with small units, or they can utilise large chunks which at first they do not understand other than as a whole unit. Young children can then learn to break these chunks down and start to understand their constituent parts. The top-down approach suggests that young children use clues in the context of a chunk to predict its meaning, while the bottom-up process requires that the smallest units of speech can be understood and manipulated.

In learning to read, there has been much debate in recent years over the merits of using a top-down or bottom-up approach to reading. The top-down view of reading, or whole language approach, is where the emphasis is on creating a rich reading environment for young readers, and in exposing them to many and varied texts, encouraging them to read in an organic way, mirroring the way that we learn to speak. This approach views reading as a system that is context-driven, with the reader predicting meaning through the context that the words are in and looking at the first letters of words. The reader is not necessarily attending to complete words, rather predicting them from the first letter and her knowledge of their context. The 'bottom-up' approach focuses on systematically teaching the smallest units of the writing system, sound–letter relationships and morphemes, such that learners can manipulate these units and understand the formation of written words. Reading regarded in this way, bottom-up, is very systematic, with readers attending carefully to all of the letters in a word, and not relying on prediction and some guesswork. It is this viewpoint that underlies the teaching of phonics that has become prevalent in our primary schools over the last few years. Generally, the best practice is regarded as involving a blend of the two approaches.

Thinking of the processes that we use to learn to speak and read is an interesting methodology that we can use with pupils. We can view all texts through the lens of bottom-up or top-down principles. So too can we look at poems, by apprehending the overall structure, the narrative, and working top-down, or we can work bottom-up, by moving in to examine the meaning through the significance of specific words. Roger Beard, in *Developing Reading 3–13*, analyses the nature of reading via a taxonomy. He characterises reading through a hierarchy of skills. The most skilful reader will deploy all the skills, with the idea of finding pleasure in the act of reading at the top of the hierarchy (see Figure 4.1).

Beard suggests that he adopts a 'top-down perspective' (Beard 1987: 23) on this taxonomy as the actions of the most skilful reader are placed at the top of the diagram, and are mostly characteristic of the endpoint of the process of learning to read. If one views the taxonomy from the perspective of 'bottom-up', starting to analyse the process of reading with the smallest aspects of reading, this might imply that learning to read progresses smoothly in a sequence, from smallest to largest, which it does not. Readers, including young readers, employ a variety of strategies. Thus, in using a variety of strategies as ways into poetry, incorporating both whole-text and word-level work, we exploit what is known about the processes of reading that readers use to interact with texts.

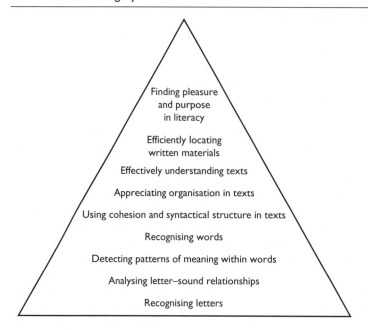

Figure 4.1 Roger Beard's 'top-down' taxonomy of reading (Beard 1987: 24)

The National Literacy Strategy advocated that teachers of English think about three levels of planning, and therefore analysis: word level, sentence level and text level. Working at these three levels features in the primary guidance for poetry teaching. Although the guidance has not been compulsory, it has been utilised by the majority of primary schools, so we can work on the assumption that much of the guidance has been used to plan the teaching of poetry that will have been experienced by our pupils. At word level, the guidance suggests that the pupils will have experienced a number of encounters with decisions to do with word choice for poetry, such as rhyme, alliteration, repetition and patterning in texts. The guidance suggests examining the use of poets' selections of words, such as active verbs, along with key concepts in poetry such as personification, metaphor and onomatopoeia. The specifications for KS3 are much more open-ended, focusing generally on experimentation with form, in both reading and writing.

The sections that follow use a deliberately bottom-up approach to the teaching of poetry. We start with word level, looking at ways to work with lexical choice with Year 7. We move on to look at a variety of approaches to work with imagery with KS4. This approach moves further up Beard's hierarchy as a way into poetry, looking at 'syntactical structure' within texts. In the fourth section, Rhythm at KS5 we explore the effect of patterning and sound as a way in to 'appreciating organisation in texts' (Beard 1987: 24). In the case study, Audrey will present her experiences of teaching metaphor and simile with Year 9. All of these approaches will, we hope, enable all of the pupils to operate at the highest level of Beard's taxonomy, 'finding pleasure and purpose in literacy' (Beard 1987: 24).

Lexis at KS3: 'Roger the Dog' and 'Lone Dog'

Rosenblatt states that it is the individual words and images within a poem that determine what the work communicates to the reader. The poems 'Roger the Dog' by Ted Hughes and

'Lone Dog' by Irene McLeod provide examples of poems that can fruitfully be compared with a focus on individual words. The subject matter and simplicity of form make them ideal for study at Year 7, particularly as at this age children tend to have a shared partiality towards animals.

Ensuring an understanding of word class is important before proceeding, as although pupils will have covered this in KS2 there often remains a degree of confusion, especially over the difference between verbs and adverbs and their function.

A very nice lesson to begin with would be getting pupils to write their own pattern poetry in a modified version of that as described by Hayhoe and Parker in their very useful text *Words Large as Apples*, as below:

Noun

adjective, adjective

verb

adverb, adverb, adverb

(Hayhoe and Parker 1989: 99)

Here is an example:

Cat

black, small

meows

loudly, fearfully, hungrily

Pupils enjoy writing these and presenting them to the class, and an element of peer assessment can be built in to ensure they have in fact used the correct word classes.

To reinforce and build on this knowledge, the structure can be extended to the form of a diamante poem by including synonyms and the use of thesauri as below:

Noun 1

adjective adjective

-ing -ing -ing

synonym 1 synonym 1: synonym 2 synonym 2

-ing -ing -ing

adjective adjective

Noun 2

(Hayhoe and Parker 1989: 99)

Here is an example:

Baby

new-born innocent

crying, weeping, wailing

hungry famished : tired exhausted

caring, loving, feeding

warm comforting

Mother

As suggested by Gabrielle Cliff Hodges (Davison and Dowson 2009: 273), modelling one of these diamante poems by drafting it on the board with input from the students is a good activity for showing how poets draft their work before a final version is reached. I usually start one with the name of the class as the first noun and end it with the name of the teacher as the second noun, which results in much hilarity and enthuses the children to try to create their own. The results are genuinely creative and make pupils focus on individual words at word level.

Roger the Dog

Asleep he wheezes at his ease.
He only wakes to scratch his fleas.

He hogs the fire, he bakes his head
As if it were a loaf of bread.

He's just a sack of snoring dog.
You can lug him like a log.

You can roll him with your foot,
He'll stay snoring where he's put.

I take him out for exercise,
He'll roll in cowclap up to his eyes.

He will not race, he will not romp,
He saves his strength for gobble and chomp.

He'll work as hard as you could wish
Emptying his dinner dish,

Then flops flat, and digs down deep,
Like a miner, into sleep.
                    (Hughes 1995: 97)

A good first encounter with this poem is to present it to the class as a cloze procedure which helps pupils to focus closely on individual words, and thus bring to their consciousness their own personal associations related to old dogs and people. The long vowel sounds in the first line, 'Asleep he wheezes at his ease' sets the calm, lazy tone of the poem. The question, 'What types of people wheeze?' (which might require some explanation or even a demonstration) may bring forth personal associations from pupils who describe their own experiences of old people they know who wheeze, thus making explicit the association between wheezing and old age.

Further probing of the verbs used to describe Roger soon builds up a fuller picture of him. Repetition of the word 'snoring' evokes the image of an old dog that sleeps a lot and can bring to the fore familiar territory within the text: memories of elderly family members snoring in front of the television, or descriptions of old family pets. Roger thus becomes viewed with affection by the pupils, as they 'fill in the gaps' and endow him with the characteristics of a beloved family member.

Figure 4.2 Qualities of similes

Asking pupils to consider the qualities of the similes and metaphors used to describe Roger by creating a Venn diagram will elicit an active response from them as they bring their own responses to the words. An example can be seen in Figure 4.2.

The 'loaf of bread' simile can bring up pleasing associations for pupils and they might comment that the smell of a loaf of bread cooking is very nice, as is the smell of an old, well-loved dog, gently emitting his own particular odour as he snoozes by the fire, presumably before he has rolled in the 'cowclap'. Thus Roger is understood as being brown and cumbersome, having a big square head and a pleasant smell, which enhances their previous associations of him with an elderly relative; pupils sometimes tell you that their granny always smells of powder or cakes or something equally comforting. Consequently Roger is personified by the pupils' associations, illustrating Rosenblatt's 'live circuit'.

Lone Dog

I'm a lean dog, a keen dog, a wild dog and lone;
I'm a rough dog, a tough dog, hunting on my own!
I'm a bad dog, a mad dog, teasing silly sheep;
I love to sit and bay at the moon, to keep fat souls from sleep.

I'll never be a lap dog, licking dirty feet,
A sleek dog, a meek dog, cringing for my meat,
Not for me the fireside, the well-filled plate,
But shut door and sharp stone and cuff and kick, and hate.

Not for me the other dogs, running by my side,
Some have run a short while, but none of them would bide.
O mine is still the lone trail, the hard trail, the best,
Wide wind and wild stars and the hunger of the quest!

(McLeod 1916: 89)

The lone dog is the complete opposite to Roger, and it is useful to draw out the comparisons as you go along. Here, the pupils' first encounter with the poem could be to count up how many times the poet uses the word 'dog' in the first stanza and the use of the first person pronoun, 'I'. Getting pupils to then apply the phrase to themselves and to repeat the refrain several times over ('I'm a boy, I'm a boy, I'm a boy … ') will help them to see that the poem is about the assertion of the dog's identity and individuality. The next focus could be on how the lone dog is described by the use of adjectives in stanza one, initially by highlighting them in the text. The words 'lean' and 'keen' may need some explanation, but 'wild', 'lone', 'rough', 'tough', 'bad' and 'mad' all speak for themselves.

The first impression of the lone dog is further enhanced by study of the verbs in stanza one, which describe how he behaves. Here is a dog that bays at the moon, and again the class will happily join in with a demonstration. This will form the stimulus for them to make the association with wolves, and the lone dog will therefore become much wilder and fiercer in their eyes.

Stanza two tells us what the lone dog will 'never be', and an interesting comparison can be drawn between the long vowel sounds of 'sleek' and 'meek' and those in the first line of 'Roger the Dog'. A focus on the word 'cringing' will encourage pupils to make associations with being somehow weak and pathetic or even being hit, and will illustrate to them the lone dog's disdain for 'lap dogs'. The fact that he will never lie by the fireside or have his plate filled reinforces the idea that he will never be like Roger. The lone dog is asserting his non-conformity and pupils can often relate to this on an individual level, thus endowing the poem with an emotional meaning personal to them. Framing his non-conformity as a positive experience by using the words 'love' and 'best' can stimulate the pupils to identify with that feeling and perhaps consider their own individuality as positive, whilst accepting that those around them might not always appreciate it. The last line of stanza two describes how people react to the lone dog, and the alliteration of the hard consonant sounds coupled with the short vowel sounds of 'shut', 'sharp', 'cuff', 'kick' and 'hate' reinforce the idea of how badly people treat him. Getting pupils to say these words out loud in quick succession, starting with a whisper and ending on a crescendo will help them to evoke the violence behind the words, and for the more able the question, 'What is it the people do not like about the lone dog?' could result in some very insightful comments about human nature.

Imagery at KS4: 'Thistles' by Ted Hughes

Thistles

Against the rubber tongues of cows and the hoeing hands of men
Thistles spike the summer air
Or crackle open under a blue-black pressure.

Every one a revengeful burst
Of resurrection, a grasped fistful
Of splintered weapons and Icelandic frost thrust up

From the underground stain of a decayed Viking.
They are like pale hair and the gutturals of dialects.
Every one manages a plume of blood.

Then they grow grey, like men.
Mown down, it is a feud. Their sons appear,
Stiff with weapons, fighting back over the same ground.

(Hughes 1967b: 17)

The topic of 'Thistles' by Ted Hughes does not, perhaps, appear immediately inviting to a KS4 audience. Hughes describes thistles in a field, but in a way that conflates them with Vikings. The language of the poem is very striking, guttural and harsh, and the main image of thistles as Vikings is a highly effective one. It is the combination of these two elements that makes the poem a rich source of interest in the classroom.

Steiner, in his essay *On Difficulty* (1978), argues that there are four different types of difficulty to be encountered when one reads poetry. One of these difficulties is simply that a poem may deal with something about which the reader has no knowledge and that there are elements of the language or context that, quite simply, 'we need to look up' (Steiner 1978: 19). This is particularly true with young people, who for the most part know less of the vocabulary or the context of a literary work than we as teachers do. Steiner states in the essay that a poem is 'an energized field of association and connotation, of overtones and under-tones' (Steiner 1978: 21) and that difficulty can stem from unfamiliarity with this 'field'. We need to support pupils accessing the 'association and connotation' of the words in what Steiner terms the 'corpus' (Steiner 1978: 22) or nexus of associations that constitute a poem. Preparing the ground, then, for a poem, in a way that is engaging and interesting to the pupils, can be a way of supporting them access the 'corpus' of a poem.

As a starting point for a poem such as 'Thistles', some preparatory work with pupils is effective. This is a principle utilised to great effect by Jeffrey and Lynn Wood in their Cambridge Poetry Workshop series. For every poem that they present in their helpful series, they have devised what they call a 'preamble', which they suggest is 'mapping the themes and/or emotional territory of the poem' (Wood and Wood 1988: 1). For Hughes' poem 'Rain', they suggest this as a pre-reading activity:

Picture a cold, wintery afternoon of pounding downpour.
Imagine yourself working outside – gardening, trying to fix a car, building something or working on a market stall.
How would your clothes feel, your hair, your hands?
What would make the jobs so difficult?
What mood would you be in?
Jot down a few words or phrases to set such a scene.

(Wood and Wood 1988: 34)

The strength of such an approach is that the pupils are beginning to create some aspects of the experience of the text that is to come. They are exploring the imaginative territory that the poem will present to them. It is important that this experience is imaginative, so that the poetic landscape is opened up to them, first of all by reference to their own thoughts, experience and feelings. The imaginative territory of 'Thistles' could be prepared through ideas around associations with Vikings. Pupils could think through the stereotypes of tough, resilient fighters that Hughes draws on in the poem. Some suggestions for a 'preamble' in the mode used by Wood and Wood are: What pictures go through your head when you hear the word Viking? What sort of man do you think of? How does this man dress? How does he move? What might he carry? What sort of language do you imagine this man to speak?

Once some work on the 'preamble' has been undertaken, the poem can be read. Different types of reading suit different poems, and there is no one-size-fits-all approach to this; however, it is important that the pupils both read the poem themselves and also hear an expert reading, either from a teacher, from a recording or even from a real live poet. Pupils can be very resistant to reading and then rereading texts, as we have all experienced, but this is an activity that they must undertake. As O'Brien notes:

> A great deal of the reading a secondary pupil does across the curriculum demands the ability to read with the eye, not the ear, and much energy is naturally given to helping pupils to increase their skill in rapid eye-reading. But this skill is useless for reading poetry. It is impossible to skim read a poem. The organization of the language there demands the slower attention of the ear, an attention learned through hearing poetry read aloud.
>
> (O'Brien 1985: 26)

In our teaching of poetry, we need to develop the skills needed for reading that poetry. O'Brien identifies the crucial aspect of listening with the ear. One effective method that I have used repeatedly is to ask the pupils to read a new poem aloud, in groups or pairs, twice. The first time they are to divide the poem line by line between them, sharing the lines between them as they like, and the second time they are to read from punctuation point to punctuation point. The groups have to decide where the segments start and finish, but the instruction is that each segment must make some sense on its own, being guided by the punctuation. The discussion that follows, in which the students discuss where the segments begin and end, promotes valuable dialogue about the shape and structure of the poem, which the pupils do not realise that they are doing. Pupils are happy to embark on reading in this way, as they are reading privately amongst themselves and can use the time to become familiar with the poem.

Having read the poem, we are still in what Benton (1988) would term the 'apprehending' (Benton 1988: 205) stage of our work with it. We work with the pupils, giving them 'enabling tasks' (Benton 1988: 205) or 'jottings around poems' (Benton 1988: 205). The poem 'Thistles' revolves around one extended image, that of the tough, resilient thistles that grow up again and again, whose roots are in the same ground in which the memories of Vikings remain as an 'underground stain' (line 7). The comparison is between the thistles and the Vikings. Here a very useful activity to ensure that the pupils start to interact with the imagery and the specific lexis, is to ask them to sketch in outline, side by side, a thistle and a Viking. They can use whatever stereotypical notions they like to draw the Viking – with a large sword and pointy helmet – as these are the aspects that Hughes draws on in creating the comparison. Labelling both sketches with words and phrases from the poem soon brings out the clear parallel between prickly plant and much maligned Viking.

This activity can be developed by looking at the sound quality and word derivations of the lexis of the poem. Steiner's discussion of difficulty with regard to lexis looks at the degree to which words operate singly and in unison to create effect. He suggests that we have to 'look up' (Steiner 1978: 19) definitions and work to understand the context in which they operate. He states that 'poetry is knit of words compacted with every conceivable mode of operative force' (Steiner 1978: 21). To move towards understanding the 'operative force' of this poem, some work on the morphology of the vocabulary can be most enlightening. Hughes deliberately avoids words that derive from French or Latin, but focuses on words from Anglo-Saxon or Old Norse, to evoke the tough, blunt nature of the thistles and the Vikings. These words tend to be monosyllabic and guttural, in the way that Hughes describes the language of the Vikings as 'gutturals of dialects' (line 8). For a very clear discussion of the nature of the

Anglo-Saxon influence on English, and on this poem, look at Shirley Russell's *Grammar, Structure and Style* (2001). Russell notes about the lexis of this poem that 'Only ten words … – hoeing, blue, revengeful, resurrection, pressure, pale, gutturals, dialects, plume and appear – are from Latin or French' (Russell 2001: 81). With access to some reasonably good dictionaries, pupils could spend some time fruitfully looking up definitions and origins of words, compiling a table or a diagram to represent the origins of the words and in discussing the impact of the sound of the words. These activities would go some way towards the pupils understanding the 'operative force' (Steiner 1978: 21) at work in the crafting of the poem.

The focus of this section was the impact of words and images at KS4. With reference to George Steiner's essay *On Difficulty* consideration has been given to the ways in which, using imagination and visual images provided by pupils, we can look at a poem through the lens of 'bottom-up'. Through a detailed examination of word textures and origins, we can construct with the pupils a means for them to articulate the ways in which a difficult poem has 'operative force' (Steiner 1978: 21).

Rhythm at KS5: 'It's Work' by Benjamin Zephaniah and 'Baby Song' by Thom Gunn

It's Work

I could hav been a builder
A painter or a swimmer
I dreamt of being a Rasta writer,
I fancied me a farmer
I could never be a barber
Once I was sure about de future,
Got a sentence an I done it
Still me angry feelings groweth
Now I am jus a different fighter,
I sight de struggle up more clearly
I get younger yearly
An me black heart don't get no lighter.
I will not join de army
I would work wid malt an barley
But here I am checkin me roots,
I could work de ital kitchen
But I won't cook dead chicken
I won't lick nobody's boots,
Yes I could be a beggar
Maybe not a tax collector
I could be a streetwise snob,
But I'll jus keep reciting de poems dat I am writing
One day I'll hav a proper job.

> (Zephaniah 1997: 45)

Students today are surrounded by sound in a way previous generations never were; the furtive use of mobiles and iPods is the bane of the modern classroom. Ask any child the lyrics of their favourite song, and most will be able to repeat long passages verbatim: a fact particularly true of boys and rap. Ask students what it is that draws them to a particular song and the vast majority will reply that it is the rhythm more than the words. With rhythm so central to their culture, it makes sense to utilise it as a way into poetry where students might initially be put off by studying the words on the page. An active approach, allowing students to find the rhythm for themselves, will bring to life patterns of intonation, pace, pitch and tone, all of which contribute to the students' understanding and enjoyment of the poem.

An adaptation of Oliver Bernard's technique described by Hayhoe and Parker (1989: 117) is summarised below, and is a valuable way of getting students to explore and discuss the sound of poetry as read by their peers. Different readers and groups will select from a range of stress patterns which will enable different interpretations of the poem's meaning, and lead to discussion of how meanings are altered by placing the emphasis on different words.

This approach is particularly useful when applied to much of the poetry available from other cultures, like those of the Caribbean, which include new rhythms which do not conform to English versification rules. Benjamin Zephaniah's 'It's Work' contains a variety of imperfect rhyme and has a flexible rhythm which appears to follow his thought processes rather than conform to a fixed metrical pattern. Group exploration of the sound of the poem as described below will lead to a variety of emphasis as the students discuss and make meaning of it.

- Students are given their own copies of a poem with the instructions they are going to perform it to a small group. They read it individually and annotate it as they might a script, for example which words they will emphasise, where they will get louder, softer, faster or slower, pauses, intonation and so on.
- They get into groups of four and each student performs the poem to their group. The others in the group respond by saying what they liked about the reading, for example, 'I liked the bit where you got louder at the end because … '. Thus the group hears the poem several times over and becomes aware of the different possibilities for interpretation. The group next decides on the ideal interpretation of the poem, using the best bits from everybody's reading, and decides who has the best voice for that reading.
- The group trains that person for a set amount of time, rehearsing and adjusting the reading until it is what the group wants it to be. Similar to how a script or a musical score becomes an entity in performance, the poem itself becomes an event: a group version of Rosenblatt's compenetration.

The exploration of the sound of the poem can be left at this point, or it can be taken further:

- Each group's chosen reader reads the poem out loud to the rest of the class, who then comment on which words were consistently emphasised and what the main differences were between the interpretations.
- There follows a discussion of what they consider to be the particular thoughts and feelings the poet is trying to express through his poem, based on the different interpretations.

The performance of the poem enables what Iser calls a 'dynamic happening' (see Chapter 2). The performances will all be different and students will realise that meanings in poetry are never fixed but are open to individual interpretation. Crucially, they will see that their own interpretation is as valid as anybody else's.

Baby Song

From the private ease of Mother's womb
I fall into the lighted room.

Why don't they simply put me back
Where it is warm and wet and black?

But one thing follows on another.
Things were different inside Mother.

Padded and jolly I would ride
The perfect comfort of her inside.

They tuck me in a rustling bed
– I lie there, raging, small, and red.

I may sleep soon, I may forget,
But I won't forget that I regret.

A rain of blood poured round her womb,
But all time roars outside this room.
(Gunn 1976: 28)

At KS5 students are expected be able to be able to use technical vocabulary to say how the structure and form of the poetry have influenced their personal response, so they will need to develop the skills required to write in an academic way. (For a very clear definition of technical terms and how to apply them see Eric Boagey's *Poetry Workbook* (1978).)

The active approach previously described can be used to help the students to notice the subtle changes in rhythm which inform meaning, which they can then write about using technical terms. Here is an example as applied to Thom Gunn's 'Baby Song':

For most of the poem the recognisable meter is tetrameter, which is coupled with a regular pattern of stresses and syllables known as stress-syllable verse. The rhyming couplets and regular rhythm mimic the sound of a nursery rhyme, which is appropriate for expressing a simple idea: that the baby was happier in its mother's womb. Onomatopoeic rhythm, the poetic technique where the rhythm of the verse corresponds to the movement that is being described, is used here as the rhythm could be said to mimic the comforting, regular beat of the mother's heart, which the baby was accustomed to before it was born. This emphasises the difference from the loud and unpleasant sounds of the reality of life which 'roars' outside the womb. In stanza six there is a subtle change to the rhythm with an extra syllable on the second line of the couplet, forcing emphasis on the drive word, 'But' (line 12). The syllables and stresses do not evenly match, which causes a sense of discomfiture in the reader; they feel uneasy but do not know why. Reading the poem aloud reveals both the end rhyme and the internal rhyme of 'forget' and 'regret', two even-stress words. The combined effect of the irregular rhythm and the rhyme is to emphasise the central idea of the poem: that whilst the baby may forget the trauma of birth, the grief of this first separation from his mother will remain with him for life.

Perhaps because of this universally shared first experience of sound as the rhythmic beat of our mother's heart, we are all receptive to rhythm. When the poem becomes a dynamic happening and students actively discover the rhythms and cadences of poetry for themselves, it becomes a much more meaningful and enjoyable experience for them, which in turn can lend itself to the higher-level personal responses required in examinations.

Case study: the poetry of the First World War at KS3

The poetry of the First World War has long been on the English curriculum, and is particularly useful for boys who 'don't get poetry' but do 'get war'. The Great War inspired a huge variety of poetry and as such it can be daunting for the beginning teacher to know what to choose, particularly if it is not an area they themselves have studied. It is helpful to remember that the poetry developed as the war continued through four main stages: the patriotism of the early days as espoused by Rupert Brookes and his famous sonnets ('The Soldier' being perhaps the most widely read); the propaganda such as that of Jesse Pope and Harold Begbie's repellent 'Fall In'; the angry satire of Sassoon and Graves; the paternalist care for the troops as demonstrated by Owen and finally poetry that expressed a desire for change. However, it is important to note that although we may expect the early poetry to be patriotic, there were some poets who had a more realistic view of the conflict right from the start.

In his beautifully illustrated anthology, *The War Poets: The Lives and Writings of the 1914–18 War Poets*, Robert Giddings argues against the traditional view that First World War poetry can be divided neatly into two halves: that before the battle of the Somme the poetry was patriotic and concerned with the righteous and heroic battle of right against wrong, whilst the later poetry illustrated a sense of despair and disillusionment brought on by being involved in a senseless war of attrition. As Giddings says, 'Signs of disquiet exist in much of the poetry written in the earliest days of the war' (Giddings 1998: 8).

Another anthology that is recommended is Martin Stephen's *Poems of the First World War: 'Never Such Innocence'*, a collection notable for its extensive selection of well-known and also unfamiliar poetry. Stephen states that after twelve years of studying First World War poetry he has found that the voice we actually hear is that of 'outraged middle-class protest' (Stephen 1993: xiv). He argues that the voice of the infantryman is hard to find and so includes in his anthology poetry by barely-known poets on the grounds that it will, 'go some way towards re-creating the feel and atmosphere for those who fought in it' (Stephen 1993: xvii). His method is to give factual, historical information and to then explain the effects on the poetry. This is most useful background reading for those of us who are not historians but nevertheless believe that poems are products of their time and do not exist in a vacuum.

At KS3, the poetry of the First World War is perhaps most usefully introduced in Year 9, as this is typically when pupils will have studied the First World War to some extent in history, and there could be opportunity here for cross-curricular working. The key ingredient is that in order for the imagery of the poetry to be grasped, the students have to be able to start to imagine for themselves the reality of war in the trenches.

I taught a Year 9 class of middle ability Wilfred Owen's 'Dulce et Decorum Est', the final outcome of which was a written analysis that was to be assessed against the renewed National Curriculum reading criteria. The focus of the lessons was how imagery is created in the poem and what the poet was trying to achieve by using those images.

I ascertained what pupils already knew using a simple collaborative starter activity of producing a useful spider diagram, which I saved on the interactive whiteboard for future reference. A common mistake was that pupils confused the two World Wars. Gas, trenches and barbed wire appeared on the diagram and it seems to remain true that the mud of the Somme battlefields is the image of the First World War that still pervades our national consciousness. However, in today's multicultural classroom we cannot take anything for granted and some pre-teaching was required to ensure the whole class grasped the key ideas and images associated with trench warfare. 'Going over the top' is a phrase that came up, although pupils were not completely confident about what it meant and tended to translate it into modern-day idiom, to mean over-reacting. To aid further explanation I drew a simple diagram illustrating the key features of trench warfare on the board with input from the more knowledgeable members of the class who offered explanations as I drew. A pre-prepared diagram on the electronic whiteboard could be used, or indeed some well-selected photographs, but the outcome will be the same, namely that the pupils will have some understanding of the characteristics of trench warfare before attempting to tackle the poetry.

To appeal to visual learners, prior to teaching any poetry I presented a selection of images via Moviemaker. Whilst my own grandfather had indeed 'gone over the top', pupils are now several generations removed from the First World War and to them it is ancient history (and for those new to the country it may not be their history at all). I therefore felt it was important to spend as much time as necessary on the context and reality of trench warfare, as I hoped that by the end of the study pupils would reach the conclusion that Owen was aiming to convey his lived experience through his poem.

Once I was satisfied that the pupils had a grasp of the main features of trench warfare, I started with Owen's wonderful poem 'Dulce et Decorum Est' as it contains much of the imagery that the pupils themselves had already identified in the spider diagram, thus allowing them to approach it with a feeling of confidence. The authors recommend *Out in the Dark* (1999) edited by David Roberts, which provides the context and basic notes on this poem and Roberts' website (www.warpoetry.co.uk) which will give you both the text and explanatory notes.

I explained to the pupils a little about Owen's life and that he was what is known as a 'trench poet'. They appreciated the fact that he was writing from his own personal experiences and the boys especially were therefore more willing to listen, although initially they seemed to find the concept of a soldier writing poetry somewhat hard to grasp. I made a mental note to return to this point later with study of more modern wartime poetry.

I read the poem to the pupils whilst they made notes on plain paper of whatever images sprang to mind, which could be in the form of words or sketches. I explained that they did not need to worry about the exact meanings of the words, as it was the images that were important at this stage. After I had read the poem through twice, pupils fed back their ideas initially to each other in groups, then volunteers from each group shared the main ideas with the class.

The pupils were then given their own copies of the poem to annotate, with strict instructions to name and keep, as they would need them later on for a piece of assessed work. Annotation was a skill that was new to them, so it was useful to have the poem printed centred on the page with wide margins for their notes, and several spare copies as invariably some children made mistakes and demanded to 'start again'. Here, as before, the interactive whiteboard was an invaluable tool for modelling annotation to the pupils.

The first stanza begins with the imagery of the soldiers. I asked pupils to highlight the similes, with a brief reminder of what a simile actually was. I then got them to describe a beggar and a hag in their own words, and discuss in their groups why they thought Owen had chosen those particular images and what he was trying to show us about the soldiers. One boy wrote: ' … saying they look like beggars shows us they are so worn out and dirty and that's just the first line of description alone.'

I next asked the pupils to highlight the words Owen had used to show how the soldiers moved; 'bent double', 'knock-kneed', 'trudged', 'limped', 'lame' and 'blood-shod', asking them what the effect was when these words were combined. Another boy responded, 'It makes a picture of four years doing the same thing, over and over again. It shows us they limped on blood, sweat and tears.'

The words 'blood-shod' in particular bore closer scrutiny. Connotations of bloodshed and bloodshot allowed pupils to make their own meaning and imagery, typically that the soldiers' feet were bleeding so it looked as if they were wearing shoes of blood, whilst one quiet, average-ability boy drew the connection with shoeing horses, and said, 'it is as if the soldiers were being forced to walk on in the way an animal might be made to.' I was able to use this example to show pupils that all their contributions were valid, no matter how unsure they were about their opinions.

The second stanza opens with the dramatic warning shout of 'Gas! Gas! Quick, boys!' The pupils had already put gas on the class spider diagram so we referred back to that, and I asked if any of them really knew what the effects of gas were. Some of the boys were relatively knowledgeable about this and we agreed that it was like breathing in something that burns and causes the lungs to melt and fill up with fluid. I suggested this could feel a bit like drowning. We discussed Owen's use of simile 'like a man on fire' as a means of conveying the utter agony the soldier must have been in as it felt he was being burned alive. The pupils were confident about the idea that a soldier who had not got his gas mask on in time was now yelling and stumbling and 'drowning' in his own fluids.

However, they missed the importance of the narrative voice and I had to point out to them that the voice of the speaker was now 'I' and therefore possibly Owen himself describing something he had actually seen. Closer analysis enabled them to realise that this episode subsequently became a recurrent nightmare for Owen:

> As under a green sea, I saw him drowning.
> In all my dreams, before my helpless sight,
> He plunges at me, guttering, choking, drowning.
> (Owen 1984: 188)

The Latin translation that ends the poem had to be explained in full, that it is sweet and right to die for your country. Pupils are familiar with the notion of patriotism and we had a discussion about whether or not we thought Owen really believed this, given the preceding poem. Pupils were unanimous in their belief that he didn't, because he referred to it as an 'old lie'. We next considered to whom Owen was referring in the final stanza as 'you' and 'My friend'? At this point they didn't know, but one girl made the observation that 'It could be anyone who says it is a good thing to go to war but doesn't really know what it's like themselves.' This led us rather neatly back to one of the main foci of the lessons, which was what we thought Owen was trying to achieve by using the images he had in his poem. The pupils concluded that he was trying to get people who didn't know what it was really like, to imagine it, and agreed that this was the effect that studying the poem had had on them.

Chapter 5

Voice in poetry

BOTTOM (AS PYRAMUS) I see a voice; now will I to the chink,
                     To spy, and I can hear my Thisby's face.
                     (*A Midsummer Night's Dream*, Act 5, ll.192–3)

In this chapter we explore teaching poetry through the aspect of voice. In the introduction we consider Eliot's ideas about three voices in poetry, which is followed by considering the use of the third-person voice in teaching Shelley's 'Ozymandias' at KS3. We follow this with an exploration of teaching through the first person using Maya Angelou's 'Still I Rise', and the possibilities of exploring poetry through multiple voices at KS5 with Eliot's *The Waste Land*. The case study recounts the use of the Socratic Seminar as a means of exploring the dramatic monologue with KS5 using Robert Browning's 'My Last Duchess'.

Introduction: voice in poetry

What is voice in poetry? If we think of the origins of poetry, it is linked to song. *The Odyssey*, one of the oldest and most influential works of epic poetry, starts with:

> Sing in me, Muse, and through me tell the story
> of that man skilled in all ways of contending,
> the wanderer, harried for years on end,
> after he plundered the stronghold
> on the proud height of Troy.
>   (Homer 1996: 1–2)

The narrative is equated with singing. *The Odyssey* was an oral epic, sung by a bard, who accompanied himself with a lyre. We still retain the association between this tradition and poetic terminology in our term 'lyric', which is defined in the OED as 'of or pertaining to the lyre. ... Now the name for short poems ... directly expressing the poet's own thoughts and sentiments' (Onions 1973: 1253). In the opening lines of *The Odyssey* we are plunged directly into a story about a 'harried' wanderer and want to know more. The inspiration for the song is told 'through me', the bard, but derives from the Muse, in modern terms perhaps a personification of the imagination. The poet here is presented as the voice of the imagination, the channel through which ideas are formulated and expressed. The poetic voice is that of one who is passing on to us, using his creative talents, the essence of the great epic.

According to the *Princeton Encyclopedia of Poetry and Poetics*, to speak of voice in a poem is to:

> attempt to identify the voice or combination of voices that are heard in the poem ... and then to characterize the tonal qualities, attitudes, or even the entire personality of this speaker as it reveals itself directly or indirectly (through sound, choice of diction, and other stylistic devices). The concept of voice reminds the reader that the meaning of what is said is qualified by who says it and by the attitude that the speaker takes toward his subject and audience.
>
> (Preminger 1965: 991)

As teachers, we know that when presented with a poem, pupils delight in speculating on the story around a poem. One study that looks at the ways in which young readers of poetry do this is described in Benton *et al.* (1988). Keith Hurst researched two groups of pupils who studied the same poems; however, some were taught the poems by their teacher, the others were left to discuss the same poems by themselves with no intervention. Hurst noticed that the pupils in the second group 'engage in cycles of exchange ... initiated by questions ... [which] could come from a "problem" set by any part of the text at any time' (Benton *et al.* 1988: 176). Hurst then continues to suggest three areas that prompt these questions and describes three ways in which the students viewed the text: either as a narrative, as the product of the poet and the voice of their opinions, or as form. He suggests that:

> It seems that the students' concern to construct a story from the text and, on occasions, to gain some perception of the poet, overrides conscious considerations of many other aspects of form unless they impose themselves strongly on the reader.
>
> (Benton 1988: 195)

That pupils want to construct a narrative around the text and understand what the concerns of the poet are is frequently encountered in the classroom. What and who the voice might be, then, is a potential means for pupils to find a way into a poem that ties in with pupils' inclinations towards making sense out of texts. However, voice is not a simple concept. T. S. Eliot suggested that there were three voices in poetry in his essay 'The Three Voices of Poetry'; that of the 'poet talking to himself' as the first type of voice; the second being 'the poet addressing an audience' and the third, found in poetic drama or dramatic monologue, 'the voice of the poet, who has put on a costume and make-up of some historical character, or one out of fiction' (Eliot 1957: 95). These voices can be found separately or together. The way in which these different voices can be constructed is the starting point for the discussions in this chapter.

An example of Eliot's second voice, of the poet addressing an audience, that could be used as starting point for examining voice with pupils is William Carlos Williams' 'This is Just to Say'. It is a poem of startling simplicity. The poem opens with:

I have eaten
the plums
that were in
the icebox

and which
you were probably
saving
for breakfast
    (Williams in Bayn 1998: 1224)

The choice of diction here is simple, conversational, with a direct address by the 'I' of the speaker, to the 'you' of the person addressed in the poem. There is an indication of intimacy, as the 'icebox' seems to be shared. There is no punctuation to delineate the thoughts here, it is free verse and has no regular rhythm, but the organisation of the lines and space regulate the ideas. The poem could be presented as a piece of prose to pupils, and working out where the lines of the poem might be placed would provide an interesting starting point for discussion. Also, very much worth investigating is the 'Wordle' program, free to use via Google, into which you can paste any text and the programme will provide a myriad of different ways of reorganising the words in the text, using different size fonts for repeated words. This is a very stimulating starting point for any discussion of a piece of poetry. The final stanza concludes:

Forgive me
they were delicious
so sweet
and so cold
    (Williams 1996: 1274)

Apparently, Williams had come home from his work as a doctor, ate the plums that were in the fridge and left this poem as a note for his wife, so in the first instance the audience for this poem is just one person. Analysing the constituents that indicate the audience is one person, and what makes the poem intimate, from the language used, is a process that reveals the use of voice in the poem. Is the speaker really sorry? The tone indicates, probably not. The juxtaposition of the refreshing adjectives, 'delicious', 'so sweet' and 'so cold', repeated in three consecutive lines, seems to suggest otherwise. The repetition of the adverb 'so', and placing these lines as the last three, creates a wry humour which suggests the attitude of the speaker.

In 'Medusa', Duffy uses the third of Eliot's voices, where the poet adopts a persona. The voice is of Medusa, bitter in her transformation from beautiful maid to fearful gorgon. The diction is tightly constructed, full of angry adjectives that evoke her sense of dismay, and powerful verbs that portray her actions and behaviour as she 'laments her fate as a woman' (Mechelis and Rowland 2003: 26). Hints at her previous state of beauty and desirability are contrasted with her present state as 'foul mouthed now, foul tongued,/yellow fanged' (Duffy 2004: 175). Repetition is a key technique used here to evoke the bitterness of Medusa. The destruction of her stare is repeated as she relates the live creatures that have been turned to stone by her, again and again. The once beautiful bride, at whom people would have stared, now uses her eyes to kill and destroy, until she stares at the mirror and contemplates what she has become, 'I stared in the mirror./Love gone bad/showed me a Gorgon' (Duffy 2004: 175). The significance of gaze and looking is repeated throughout the poem. The final line, 'Look at me now' (Duffy 2004: 175), where Medusa asks Perseus to look directly at her, is 'a sorrowing cliché of the once beautiful woman' (Mechelis and Rowland 2003: 53). The poem is a meditation on female beauty, with Duffy exploring the complexity of loss of beauty, male regard and self-loathing through the voice of the persona, Medusa. The AQA digital anthology provides a rich source of activities arranged around this poem with a variety of accessible and engaging ICT activities.

Edward Thomas's 'Rain' is a very moving poem which does seem to belong to Eliot's first classification, the poet talking to himself. Thomas wrote this poem whilst training in England before leaving for the war in France in 1916, and in it he seems to be writing for himself, contemplating his probable death:

> Rain, midnight rain, nothing but the wild rain
> On this bleak hut, and solitude, and me
> Remembering again that I shall die
> And neither hear the rain nor give it thanks
> For washing me cleaner than I have been
> Since I was born into this solitude.
>   (Thomas, G. 1978: 87)

The pronouns 'I' and 'me' are repeated in practically every line, as Thomas emphasises his 'solitude' alone in the bleak hut. The rain has cleansing properties and blesses those that it rains upon, dead or alive. The rain links, as Thomas contemplates, himself with the dead:

> Blessed are the dead that the rain rains upon:
> But here I pray that none whom once I loved
> Is dying tonight or lying still awake
>   (Thomas, G. 1978: 87)

The poem resembles a prayer that Thomas makes for himself and those he has loved; it is as if he is preparing to leave them. Thomas uses the phraseology of the bible, referring to the beatitudes of the Sermon on the Mount in stating 'Blessed are … '. This was prophetic indeed as he was killed in action very soon after he was deployed to France. In a prose work published in 1913, Thomas writes a very similar passage of prose, where 'a ghostly double' (Thomas, G. 1978: 157) speaks to him. Speaking as seemingly part of a split personality, Thomas' doppelganger says:

> I am alone in the dark still night, and my ear listens to the rain piping in the gutters and roaring softly in the trees of the world. Even so will the rain fall darkly upon the grass over the grave when my ears can hear it no more.
>   (Thomas, G. 1978: 157)

That Thomas has adapted 'a fine introspective passage' (Motion 1980: 35) and used it again as a piece of poetry provides a lot of scope for investigating what it is about the construction of voice in 'Rain' that makes it a fine example of 'poet talking to himself' (Eliot 1957: 95).

Writing in the third person: 'Ozymandias' with KS3

Ozymandias

> I met a traveller from an antique land
> Who said: Two vast and trunkless legs of stone
> Stand in the desert. Near them, on the sand,
> Half sunk, a shattered visage lies, whose frown

And wrinkled lip, and sneer of cold command
Tell that its sculptor well those passions read
Which yet survive, stamped on these lifeless things,
The hand that mocked them and the heart that fed.
And on the pedestal these words appear:
'My name is Ozymandias, king of kings:
Look on my works, ye Mighty, and despair!'
Nothing beside remains. Round the decay
Of that colossal wreck, boundless and bare
The lone and level sands stretch far away.
(Percy Bysshe Shelley)

Shelley's 'Ozymandias' has an appeal for KS3 pupils, as it is a short sonnet that has the effect of opening up a whole array of possibilities. Shelley's use of voice is part of that appeal. Although the opening line is in the first person, Shelley invents a traveller to recount what he has seen in the desert. The details that the traveller relates are all significant, as they build up a picture of a vast statue that is now in ruins. They also reveal the character of the ruler that commissioned the statue, each one adding to the layers through which emerge the portrait of an arrogant and unkind man. The use of the voice of the traveller, and the narrator, ensures that the reader gets a third-hand account of what has become of Ozymandias. His power is now gone, and the very indirectness of the account of what remains of him underlines the temporary nature of his strength and dominion.

To prepare the ground, before reading the poem, there are a whole variety of possible pre-reading activities that can be undertaken. Looking at the connotations of key phrases, using the interactive whiteboard (IWB) with the whole class, is one starter activity. Suggestions for this are 'antique land', 'shattered visage' and 'sneer of cold command', as the adjectives are particularly effective and also the archaic expressions will need some introduction. In the very useful book *Cambridge Poetry Workshop: 14+*, Lynn and Jeffrey Wood suggest pre-reading activities which focus on mapping the emotional territory of the poem, speculating over what the qualities of a great ruler may be. They suggest that the pupils think about the questions, 'What sort of person does the phrase "king of kings" make you imagine? What qualities do you think The Ruler of the World would need?' (Wood and Wood 1989: 79). This encourages the pupils in to draw upon their own ideas of power, and draw on their associations with key words and concepts in the poem.

For the pupils' first encounter with the poem, Mary Berry and Alex Madina, in *Poems from the Past*, suggest that pupils 'divide the poem into three voices and read it aloud several times' (Berry and Madina 1997: 98). The three voices could be those of the first person, 'I', the traveller and the words of Ozymandias inscribed on the pedestal. If given the choice, however, this is not necessarily what the pupils will decide or how they will want to divide it. The discussion of the possible readings and the speculation over what voices the pupils will choose is what is of interest here to us as teachers, as we want the pupils to negotiate the text themselves.

Of central interest is the character of Ozymandias, and the way that the poet has presented this through the various voices of the poem. After reading the poem several times in a group, the pupils can explore character by looking at the details in the poem for themselves; one way is to ask them to draw a picture or sketch of the poem, labelling key parts with phrases from the poem. This encourages the pupils to engage with the details through which Shelley has evoked the character of Ozymandias but is not asking them to formulate any definitive response to them, by representing the details visually; the vast legs with no body; the huge face that is 'half sunk' in the sand, with its 'sneer of cold command' and the carved pedestal. What a sketch or picture really brings out well for the pupils is the contrast between the dislocated remnants of the statue, and the sands 'boundless and bare' that 'stretch far away' into the distance. Drawing a desert can be very simple, but allows the imagination to play with the ideas of emptiness and vast spaces. In discussing the various details selected for the sketch, the pupils' ideas can be drawn out over the qualities of the language that led them to select the phrases as being significant, such as alliterative elements or the way in which Shelley balances phrases and lines within the sonnet. What discussion of this activity can also bring out is the form, that of a sonnet, and the way that information has been telescoped and so much is created by inference.

To work further with the character of Ozymandias, there are many writing or speaking and listening activities that can be derived from the poem. A letter home from the traveller, describing what he has seen and the thoughts that it prompts for him is a relatively simple one, using the skills of text transformation from poetry to prose. A more imaginative approach is suggested by Berry and Madina, whereby the pupils imagine that they are one of Ozymandias' subjects and 'Write a diary entry about the day the statue was finished. Include a description of the statue and your opinions of the ruler' (Berry and Madina 1997: 98). Wood and Wood suggest a variant on these ideas, asking the pupils to imagine that they are a sculptor, Ezra, living in the kingdom of Ozymandias, and they 'Write an account of the day you were summoned to the king's palace and given instructions for the monument' (Wood and Wood 1989: 80). They guide the writing around the palace, the character of the king, the sketches, the construction of the statue and the feelings of the sculptor. Speaking and listening activities could derive from the ideas of the different voices in the poem, interviewing the traveller or the narrator. Other voices could be invented, such as one of the workers who built the monument or perhaps Ozymandias' wife. Pupils could write and perform playscripts of scenes from Ozymandias' palaces; the permutations are manifold.

Shelley wrote the poem 'Ozymandias' inspired by tales of the huge statue of Rameses II, famous throughout Europe and acquired for the British Museum, arriving in London in 1818. He submitted his sonnet to the magazine *The Examiner*, and it was published within a month of another version of a sonnet with the same name, written by his friend Horace Smith, with whom Shelley was having a friendly competition. Smith's version was later published under the snappy title of 'On A Stupendous Leg of Granite, Discovered Standing by Itself in the Deserts of Egypt, with the Inscription Inserted Below' and is available on the Romantic Circles website (http://www.rc.umd.edu/rchs/reader/smith.html). There is little doubt that Shelley's version is a more finely-crafted work, however, for able classes or for extension work for specific groups of pupils, a comparison of the two versions and an investigation into what the differences are and what the effect of these is can be a fruitful activity.

Poetry in the first person: 'Still I Rise' at KS4

Still I Rise

You may write me down in history
With your bitter, twisted lies.
You may trod me in the very dirt
But still, like dust, I'll rise.

Does my sassiness upset you?
Why are you beset with gloom?
'Cause I walk like I've got oil wells
Pumping in my living room.

Just like moons and like suns,
With the certainty of tides,
Just like hopes springing high,
Still I'll rise.

Did you want to see me broken?
Bowed head and lowered eyes?
Shoulders falling down like teardrops,
Weakened by my soulful cries.

Does my haughtiness offend you?
Don't you take it awful hard
'Cause I laugh like I've got gold mines
Diggin' in my own back yard.

You may shoot me with your words,
You may cut me with your eyes,
You may kill me with your hatefulness,
But still, like air, I'll rise.

Does my sexiness upset you?
Does it come as a surprise
That I dance like I've got diamonds
At the meeting of my thighs?

Out of the huts of history's shame
I rise
Up from a past that's rooted in pain
I rise
I'm a black ocean, leaping and wide,
Welling and swelling I bear in the tide.

Leaving behind nights of terror and fear
I rise
Into a daybreak that's wondrously clear
I rise
Bringing the gifts that my ancestors gave,
I am the dream and the hope of the slave.
I rise
I rise
I rise

(Angelou 1978: 41)

Maya Angelou's poem, 'Still I Rise', is an example of Eliot's second voice, the poet directly addressing an audience: the 'I' of the poet addressing the 'you' of the listener. Unlike W. C. Williams, who addresses a single listener, his wife, it could be argued that the 'I' of this poem speaks for all black Americans, and particularly women, whilst the 'you' represents white racist society. In order to fully understand the concerns of the poet, it is important to do some preparatory work on the history of the struggle of black Americans to overcome racism.

Suzanne Scafe, in her essay 'Teaching Black Literature' reminds us of the importance of acknowledging that all texts are contextualised:

> We consciously need to acknowledge that we place all texts in the world, and that in our classification of literary production and our approaches to teaching we signal the historical, social and cultural context of its making ... The task for teachers and educationalists is to ensure that Black writing is valued critically; that is read as it defines itself, as a cultural and artistic whole reflecting and a reflection of the political and cultural struggles which are its context.
>
> (Scafe 2004: 133)

Angelou's poem does indeed reflect the struggles which are its context. Taught at KS4, the exploratory phase could include some class discussion of what students already know about Black American history. Most will know about the history of slavery but it is possible that they will not have fully grasped the full horror of it as time distances us from the grim reality. This important poem gives us the opportunity to challenge prejudiced ideas and encourage genuine exploration of racial prejudice and current attitudes.

David Stevens and Nicholas McGuinn endorse a culture of creative learning in the English classroom, and recommend a structural pattern to lessons as summarised in Figure 5.1.

This is a very useful structure to use when teaching Angelou's 'Still I Rise'. Exploring personal reactions and responses to the subject of racism *per se* is a useful way of encouraging students' expression of their own perceptions. This can be done by providing a recent newspaper article describing racially motivated crimes either locally or nationally, or by

---

- The first stage is the exploratory stage, to which reactions to a given stimulus or theme are tentatively elicited and offered. The teacher's role here is to stimulate a broad range of responses, opening up to learners' experiences and perceptions, and providing the necessary texts and contexts to encourage their expression.
- The second stage focuses on various possibilities for understanding, interpretation and broader contextual exploration. The development of a phase of 'intensification' of meaning through rigorous questioning and negotiation, and, if appropriate, the judicious introduction of further texts to stimulate deeper thought.
- The third stage is the making, sharing and critical evaluation of artefacts as appropriate.
- Critical evaluation, pertinent reflection and celebratory creativity all have a part to play throughout the sequence of activities – which may span one or more lessons depending on the nature of the teaching and learning taking place.

Figure 5.1 Structured pattern for creative learning (Stevens and McGuinn 2004: 22–3).

downloading information about the murder of the Year 11 student Stephen Lawrence who was stabbed to death while waiting for a bus. The purpose is to show that unprovoked racist attacks are still happening. This can be a sensitive area of discussion and you might be shocked at some of the comments that students make, often related to things they have heard their parents say. In these cases it is crucial to remember Edward de Bono's words, 'if our perceptions are wrong then no amount óf logical excellence will give the right answer ... Logic will not change emotions and feelings. Perception will' (de Bono, cited in Stevens and McGuinn 2004: 13). It thus behoves the teacher to try to change those narrow-minded perceptions.

The second stage of learning is to go on to consider three contrasting but thematically linked texts: an excerpt from the Steven Spielberg film *Amistad* (1997) which is based on the true story of a slaves' revolt on the ship *Amistad*. An eight-minute clip showing the most powerful sequence of the film, where the chained slaves are dragged over the side to drown because the crew miscalculated the amount of supplies required for the journey, is extremely harrowing and enough to show students the cruel reality of the slave trade; an extract from chapter 19 of Maya Angelou's autobiography, *I Know Why the Caged Bird Sings* (1969) which describes a boxing match she saw as a child and expresses the racist ideas she had grown up hearing; and finally an excerpt from Louis Theroux's documentary, *Louis and the Nazis* (2003), where Theroux visits neo-Nazis in California, who show themselves to be ignorant beyond belief. These sources will allow for a more intense exploration of the theme of racism and will stimulate much discussion, and the hope is that any previously expressed prejudiced perceptions will begin to change.

The third stage of learning is the critical evaluation of the poem, 'Still I Rise'. Having already learnt a little about Angelou's background, students will have some perception of the poet and her concerns so the focus will be how her personality reveals itself through an examination of the linguistic features of the text and how the poem is structured.

As always, it is crucial for students to hear the poem read aloud. The poem has a regular rhyme and rhythm for the first seven stanzas while the final two build up like a crescendo, giving the poem a musical quality as if written for performance. It is therefore an extremely good activity to get students to perform the poem, perhaps as a choral reading. John Taylor reminds us:

> For a group of pupils to consider how they are going to read a poem aloud means they become closely involved with meaning and the expression of meaning; they experience the power of alliteration, hear assonance, rhyme and rhythm at first hand and absorb in the most obvious and common-sense way what are often taught as remote technical features.
>
> (Brindley 2004: 214)

As students prepare their performances, they will necessarily examine the language and notice the use of colloquialisms and abbreviations that reveal the 'real' voice of the poet. Through repeated questioning Angelou expresses her bafflement that people would want to see her suffer. Her questions suggest a tone of confusion at the mentality of such people. Students will also focus on the verbs as they perform the actions to go with the poem, verbs that express a real sense of character; we learn that the poet is cheeky (sassy), haughty, she laughs, she's sexy and she dances. Her tone is not bitter or accusatory but assertive; the refrain 'I rise' is repeated eleven times and creates a sense of her indomitable spirit.

The performances will lead to a reflection on the character of the poet and how her personality is expressed through her 'voice'. Following the students' own performance, a clip from YouTube of Angelou reading the poem herself can be shown, which will confirm their impressions of her as a remarkable, inspirational woman.

Multiple voices: T. S. Eliot's *The Waste Land* with KS5

The Waste Land is a challenging, and fruitful, poem to study with KS5 students. It is the quintessential modernist poem, in which 'traditional notions of culture and society have been – literally and metaphorically – blown apart by recent experiences' (Selby 1999: 7). The fragmentary nature of the form compiled of various voices and literary references is puzzling, but also provides many 'gaps' and discontinuities over which students can speculate. Wolfgang Iser suggested that it is the gaps in a text that draw the reader in (see Chapter 2) and there are plenty in *The Waste Land*. Looking at the multiple voices that Eliot uses in the poem is a way of opening up speculation about the poem, encouraging students to 'hear' and connect with their auditory imagination. Eliot defined this type of imagination as 'the feeling for syllable and rhythm, penetrating far below the conscious levels of thought and feeling, invigorating every word; sinking to the most primitive and forgotten' (Eliot 1964: 118–19). These qualities in the language of the poem can be explored through the different aural qualities, encouraging students to respond to voice and sound in the poem, in whatever way they are able.

Considering the setting of the poem as a cityscape is an entry into the poem. Before reading the poem, ask the students individually to visualise floating about a city at night listening to sounds. Their answers will set the scene for the poem, conjuring up specific moods or atmosphere, and they may well imagine hearing people talking or moving around the streets at night. Ask them then to imagine standing, invisible, outside someone's house, this time in the suburbs. What might they hear? Their answers can easily prefigure the sort of scenes in *The Waste Land*, such as arguments between lovers or domestic conversations. T. S. Eliot was very interested in drama, and *The Waste Land* draws on many dramatic sources and conventions, including dialogue, monologue and references to soliloquies.

Before reading any poem, particularly longer ones, much important preparatory work can be done with one or two key lines as a way in to certain themes or aspects of the poem. The form of *The Waste Land* resembles a collage of lines and scenes from other works of literature, edited and linked in a certain way, to create the impression that Eliot wanted. Indeed, Ezra Pound radically edited the poem for Eliot, enhancing the dislocated quality of the verse. Written in 1922, the poem portrays a civilisation that has wrought destruction on itself, 'Whether waste land or no-man's land, the poem's imagery of sterility, drought and death is grounded in the trenches and battlefields of the First World War' (Selby 1999: 7). Eliot strives to produce an art form that reflects this destruction. A line from the ending of the poem that encapsulates the dislocated quality of the poem is 'These fragments I have shored against my ruin' (Eliot 1963: 79). To project just this line on the IWB and simply speculate over what it might mean opens many options for musings on the poem; what are 'these fragments', who is 'I' and what is 'my ruin'? All such inroads lead to exploratory discussion, laying the groundwork for the poem and some openings for the students to engage with. The enigma triggered by these lines draws in the students. The lines might stimulate such topics as the fragmentary nature of the form, the voice of the speaker, the 'ruin' or waste land vision of the city and the possibility of redemption embedded in the verb 'shored'. How have these fragments prevented the ruin of the speaker? In this way all sort of questions regarding redemption and faith can naturally emerge, which are significant aspects of the poem's imagery.

Having spent some time beginning to explore the foothills of the poem, how does one start to climb the mountain of *The Waste Land* and read the poem with a class? There is a recording of Eliot reading the poem, but this might induce a certain lethargy in adolescent students; a better first step is for students to read the poem in groups, not asking for any particular comprehension of the poem. Identifying various voices in the poem and producing a dramatic reading of the different sections is one way of approaching this. Fiona Shaw can be found on YouTube discussing her sell-out dramatic reading of *The Waste Land* and performing a reading of some characters from section two, which immediately brings these characters alive and models a professional dramatised reading (Shaw 2008). Another way in is to produce a collage of the different sections, with images from paper or electronic sources representing the different voices, or characters, placed with lines cut from the printed text. This could be done as a Wiki, with images, a poster for display, or as a PowerPoint with images, lines and possibly music as well. For example, in section two, 'A Game of Chess', we have references to Cleopatra, the voices of strained anonymous lovers and a scene from a London pub with two women discussing their husbands and their sex lives. Much could be done with finding images of rich, bejewelled women and characters that might be found in a London pub. In selecting images to represent the lines, the students need to decide their interpretation of the context of the lines in the poem, who the characters seem to be, what they might wear and how they imagine them to look. This opens up a lot of potential exploration of the lines and examination of small, linguistic detail. This may also bring to the fore discussions of the historical context of the poem, with regard to what the appearance of the characters might be and the setting they are in.

Again and again we come across the issue in teaching poetry of encouraging students to be independent in their responses to poetry, and not relying on the points of view of teachers. Individual relationships with the poem are fostered by working on aspects of the poem in groups before coming to a detailed examination of the poem in class. Asking students to read the poem individually, as part of independent study, over a period of a few days, and recording their responses, enables them to spend time familiarising themselves with the text before any classroom analysis intervenes between their own interpretation and that of the teacher. They could record their responses in the form of a diary, blog, notes or even in text message format. Whichever format is chosen, two areas can be emphasised. One is the personal response of the students to the text; perhaps they can record what the poem made them think about, or any connections with what might be happening to them or texts they were reading. Second, they might try to set up a connection between the characters in the text and themselves; ask them if they relate the voices in the text to anyone they know, have read about, or have seen depicted. If you as the teacher also undertake this activity in parallel with the students, much extended dialogue could be undertaken in class, where all opinions of the poem have equal validity and students feel confident with their own responses.

The Waste Land is a challenging text to study. The form can be opened up by exploring it as a compilation of voices from different places and different times. As a modernist text, like all texts, it offers no definitive meaning, but also has a history of multiple meanings. As teachers we aim to ensure that students feel confident in starting to form their own interpretation and navigate the text with confidence.

Case study: Robert Browning's 'My Last Duchess' at KS5

The Greek philosopher Socrates believed that the best way to inspire students' interest and curiosity was to answer their questions with more questions, thus forcing them to question the validity of their beliefs and consider other possibilities. The Socratic Seminar is a method by which students can be encouraged to question each other, and as such is a particularly useful tool for teaching poetry at KS5. By this stage students are familiar with poetic conventions and therefore more confident in describing their experience of a poem to their peers. It allows students to gain a sense of the basic situation of the poem; what Hurst calls the 'simple construction' (Benton *et al.* 1988: 178) encourages independence of thought and helps students to achieve a deeper understanding by thinking aloud and examining ideas in a rigorous, thoughtful manner. They will also focus on the aspects of the poem which seem most significant to them, which avoids reinforcing the idea that studying poetry is just an academic exercise.

The teaching context for this case study was a mixed-ability class consisting of 24 students of both genders, in the first week of their second half term at the school. Coming from a variety of secondary schools they had had varying experiences of being taught poetry. Prior questioning had revealed to me the depressing truth that many students had only chosen to do English Literature A level because they had reasonable grades at GCSE, and not because of any great love of literature, and that they had chosen to come to our school in particular because it has an attached football academy of some renown. I had not taught any poetry to this class before and hoped the Socratic Seminar would reveal to me any individual strengths and weaknesses in accessing poetry *per se*. However, I considered the class size to be too big for the traditional format of the Socratic Seminar which consists of one inner and one outer circle, so I divided the class into halves, each with their own inner and outer circle. This meant that there were six students in each inner and six in each outer circle, which I hoped would yield better results, as the smaller group sizes would result in greater engagement with the poem under consideration.

To facilitate a successful Socratic Seminar, it is important that students have already read and thought about the poem in question, and have prepared open-ended questions that will encourage discussion. Benton emphasises the importance of allowing opportunity for the reader to reflect on his own responses before participating in group discussion:

> It is in the private talking to oneself and in the spaces behind public talk that the poem will be evoked and at this stage, the demands of group work may well push aside what the reader is trying to grasp.
>
> (Benton *et al.* 1988: 206)

I therefore set the class homework to read the poem on the Monday before the Wednesday lesson, emphasising how important it was that students should do the preparation. As a pragmatist I knew that not all students would actually do the required reading, but the beauty of the Socratic Seminar is that it can still work well as those who have not done the preparation can be seated on the 'outer circle' and still gain from the discussion.

The room was set out with two conference tables in the middle, and desks were placed around them (see Figure 5.2). Those who had prepared the reading of the poem were sat around the conference table, in what is known as the 'middle circle'. The others sat at desks around the outside of the conference table, in the 'outer circle'. A 'Hot Seat' was placed at the head of the conference table.

All students had copies of the poem to refer to and the rules were explained to them using PowerPoint, as in Figure 5.3.

My role as teacher was to allow the students to run the discussion. Naturally they tried to involve me when certain points were unclear, and I had to remind them to ask their fellow

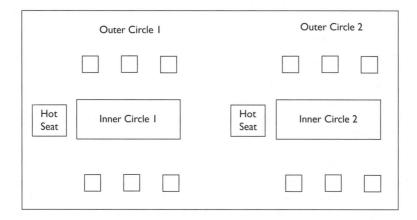

Figure 5.2 Classroom layout for the Socratic Seminar

Inner Circle
- Students in the inner circle are to have an open discussion about the poem. It is not a debate; there are no right answers.
- Be civil and polite. Address each other by name and use good eye contact.
- Encourage discussion from quieter members; do not dominate the conversation.
- Be respectful and do not interrupt each other.
- It is acceptable to 'pass' when asked to contribute.
- The goal is to become an active participant.

Outer Circle
- Students on the outer circle are partnered with those on the inner circle.
- Listen, observe and take notes as you evaluate your partner's participation in the discussion.
- If you wish to make a comment or observation you may go and sit on the 'Hot Seat' for the duration of your comment.
- Take turns to question members of the inner circle.
- The inner circle cannot question you.

Figure 5.3: Student guidelines for the Socratic Seminar

students in the inner circle. I found it useful to keep my head down and avoid eye contact, as several times students tried to engage in dialogue with me.

The discussions that ensued were fruitful and interesting. Hussein opened the discussion by stating that the title gets straight to the point of the poem. 'Because she's the "last" wife, we already know she's dead.' This stimulated some discussion over whether this was actually the case, or did it mean that she's his 'last' wife because he is never going to marry again?

A significant area of difficulty was in identifying the listener. It was suggested that the Duke was talking to the father of his next wife or possibly a servant, or someone who was going to come and work for him who was being shown around. Discussion focused on this for a while until James, who was on the outer circle, at this point sat on the Hot Seat, and suggested that the listener was the servant of the 'Count', who was presumably the father of the next intended wife.

Grace asked what the names of the characters within the poem were, and what the status of the speaker was. Students in the inner circle answered that he was a duke, which they knew because the wife was a duchess. The fact that he had a 'nine hundred years old name' implied he was of high status and came from an aristocratic family. There was then some discussion on why the name of the painter was given and nobody else's. The idea was postulated that Frà Pandolf was a very famous artist at that time and therefore the Duke was boasting because he had the painting; it was a way of showing the importance of the painting and because he owned it, he now had control over the duchess. Pippa joined in with the observation that the curtain shows the poem is all about control; 'He keeps her behind the curtain so no one else can look at her. Does that mean he killed her out of jealousy?'

The other circles focused on the reliability of the narrator. It was agreed the poem was a dramatic monologue, as he was speaking all the way through to an unknown listener, but the question arose as to whether he was an unreliable narrator, as it is only his viewpoint that is voiced. Students suggested an alternative viewpoint, that 'the Duchess was actually a nice person and he was just paranoid.' Compton asked, 'Do you think he's just accusing her because he's not in control of her?' Further discussion focused on the fact that the duchess liked the simple things in life, 'she gave other people the exact same smile as she gave to the Duke. He wanted her to himself. She likes the simple things but he's upset that she doesn't appreciate his materialism.' Then referring back to the curtain, Compton remarked, 'She's hidden but she's there; she'll always be in the back of his mind,' which is reminiscent of Stefan Hawlin's comment, '[The Duke] seems undermined by her continuing presence and vitality' (Hawlin 2002: 70).

This initial exploration of the basic circumstances of the poem using the Socratic Seminar reinforces Patrick Dias' research findings which showed that when left to discuss poetry uninterrupted, 'groups will in any case make reference to most of the points teachers see as significant but in a framework of their own choosing' (Hayhoe and Parker 1988: 43). The importance of the psychological impact of the open agenda allowed by the Socratic Seminar cannot be over-emphasised; it allows students to take ownership of the poetry and become committed to it. In this particular case, my footballers who were reluctantly studying English to fulfil their timetable obligations participated fully in subsequent lessons where we moved on to a deeper analysis of the poem at word level.

Chapter 6

Settings as mirrors

Be not afeard; the isle is full of noises,
Sounds and sweet airs, that give delight and hurt not.
Sometimes a thousand twangling instruments
Will hum about mine ears, and sometime voices
That, if I then had waked after long sleep,
Will make me sleep again: and then, in dreaming,
The clouds methought would open and show riches
Ready to drop upon me that, when I waked,
I cried to dream again.
　　(Caliban in *The Tempest*, Act 3, Scene 2, ll.135–43)

In this chapter we explore how setting has been used in poetry past and present. We consider the pastoral mode, which is developed through providing approaches to the teaching of Marvell's 'The Garden' with KS5. Exploring poetry about growing up in the countryside environment uses Heaney's 'The Barn' at KS3 and the modern urban setting is considered through Hayhoe's 'City Blues' with KS4. The case study examines teaching Blake's 'London' at KS4.

Introduction: the use of setting in poetry past and present

In many poetry anthologies, poems are grouped together under headings to do with where they are set. This approach is mirrored in examination syllabuses at GCSE, which often have poetry selections under titles such as 'place' or 'landscape'. Setting has long been used by poets to either emphasise aspects of their ideas, or to contrast elements of their thoughts with the landscape present in the poem. Settings have been used over time in different ways, and in English poetry, the way that the rural landscape has been utilised has ranged from the highly artificial and conventional to the naturalistic. This chapter will explore how settings can be used in teaching as a way in which to explore poems from various time periods and open up the texts for pupils.

The oft-anthologised poem 'The Passionate Shepherd to His Love' by Christopher Marlowe was a hit in its time, and exemplifies the pastoral idiom that was the height of fashion in the Elizabethan period. The first three stanzas provide the quintessential ingredients of a pastoral poem:

Come live with me and be my love
And we will all the pleasures prove
The hills and valleys, dale and field,
And all the craggy mountains yield.

There will we sit upon the rocks
And see the shepherds feed their flocks
By shallow rivers, to whose falls
Melodious birds sing madrigals.

There will I make thee beds of roses,
And a thousand fragrant posies
A cap of flowers, and a kirtle
Embroider'd all with leaves of myrtle.
    (Marlowe in Hollander and Kermode 1973: 408)

All the ingredients of the pastoral are here: shepherds, the rural landscape, harmony and, most importantly, romance. The pastoral tradition in poetry has classical origins, with Theocritus and Virgil writing before the birth of Christ. Virgil used the pastoral setting as a means of expressing an image of rural harmony, looking back to a Golden Age that was free from the trouble of contemporary life. The perceived tranquillity and purity of the rural setting, as viewed by a town-dwelling poet, contrasted with the reality of life in Rome. These classical ideas re-emerged in Italy in the fourteenth century and then developed in England as part of the flowering of Elizabethan literature in the Early Modern period. Shakespeare used the pastoral in *As You Like It*, in which the Duke is usurped and retreats to the forest of Arden, away from the corruption of the city. Here in the rural setting there are shepherds, and love can flourish. The characters are away from the reality of their city lives, but eventually they will have to return. In the pastoral genre, the setting was used as a backdrop, as a means of exploring ideas, rather than as an examination of nature or the countryside itself, 'a way of not looking at the country' (Barrell and Bull 1974: 4).

The artificiality and conventions of the genre are acknowledged in Sir Walter Raleigh's 'Answer to Marlowe' in which he responds to 'The Passionate Shepherd':

If all the world and love were young,
And truth in every Shepherd's tongue,
These pretty pleasures might me move,
To live with thee, and be thy love.

But the speaker acknowledges that youth and an eternity of pleasure are not the case, that what the shepherd has offered her is illusory:

The flowers do fade, and wanton fields,
To wayward winter reckoning yields,
A honey tongue, a heart of gall,
Is fancy's spring, but sorrow's fall.

Thy gowns, thy shoes, thy beds of Roses,
Thy cap, thy kirtle, and thy posies
Soon break, soon wither, soon forgotten:
In folly ripe, in reason rotten.
  (Raleigh, in Hollander and Kermode 1973: 338)

Raleigh adopts the poetic persona of the nymph replying to the shepherd, speaking of the reality of this proposal to her. Life is not sitting by rivers, listening to birds, and for a young woman, 'A honey tongue' offers danger and sorrow. Youth fades and fortunes are changeable. The poetic exchange is clearly artificial – both writers are adopting personas within an imaginary pastoral landscape, playing with the conventions of the form. Raleigh is taking a cynical view of the pastoral form, in contrast to Marlowe's well loved and joyous lyric. Raleigh's response can be categorised as 'anti-pastoral satire' (Gifford 1999: 138) which exposes the artificiality and escapism of the form and use of setting.

The use of poetic exchange, of poems and answers in the same style, is one that can be exploited in the classroom. Pupils can take a poem and respond to the poet in exactly the same style, which is certainly a challenge but requires a real engagement with the language, form and tone of the original poem. Or classes could exchange poems between themselves, responding to each other's poems in the same style, on a theme or to do with particular festivals or times of the year. That this was a common practice for centuries, in manuscript form, could be updated to text or email poems and responses. The instability of the manuscript texts, their shifting natures through the use of handwriting and the audiences they were aimed at, relates directly to the more chameleon production of electronic texts in the world that pupils now inhabit.

Gifford suggests in *Pastoral* the use of the term 'post-pastoral' to categorise the way in which rural settings have been used after the eighteenth century and the revolution in poetry that the Romantics brought about. Rather than using the rural setting as a means to idealise nature and as a device to contrast the complexities and problems of urban living, which the pastoral tradition did, many of the Romantics had an 'awe in attention to the natural world'. The pastoral tradition held an 'anthropocentric position', in which the rural setting was a backdrop to human activity and interaction, whilst the 'post-pastoral' (Gifford 1999: 152) world of the Romantics and others utilise setting to explore 'the truth of human interrelatedness with nature' (Gifford 1999: 147). What nature is, and how it is perceived and constructed, is a complex philosophical discussion, but for this chapter we will be using one of the three aspects of the definition of nature proposed by Raymond Williams in *Keywords*, 'the inherent force that directs either the world or human beings or both' (Williams 1976: 184).

In their utilisation of setting, many of our most well-loved Romantic poets muse on the 'interrelatedness' of man with nature. In 'Daffodils', Wordsworth explores the relationship of nature with man's spirit, which he associates with poetry and imagination. The use of setting here is not as a backdrop to the concerns of the poet, as with the pastoral, but the setting is the wellspring of the poetic experience. In a sense the setting is the poem, and is central to it. As with Keats's 'Ode to a Nightingale', where the moment of union with nature is the central experience of the poem, so too with 'Daffodils'. Responding to an inspirational moment whereupon he and his sister came across 'A host, of golden daffodils', Wordsworth recollects his joyous delight at the sight of the daffodils, 'Fluttering and dancing in the breeze'. They dance and sparkle in their crowds:

Continuous as the stars that shine
And twinkle on the milky way,
They stretched in never-ending line
Along the margin of a bay:
Ten thousand saw I at a glance,
Tossing their heads in sprightly dance.

The waves beside them danced, but they
Out-did the sparkling leaves in glee;
A poet could not be but gay,
In such a jocund company!
I gazed—and gazed—but little thought
What wealth the show to me had brought:
(Wordsworth 1998: 383)

At this point in the experience, Wordsworth is in harmony with nature, he experiences a transcendent moment, in unison with the setting, 'I gazed – and gazed'. It is later, when he experiences 'emotion recollected in tranquillity' (Preface to the *Lyrical Ballads*: 361), that Wordsworth understands the significance of this moment and can recreate it in his imagination and his poetry:

For oft, when on my couch I lie
In vacant or in pensive mood,
They flash upon that inward eye
Which is the bliss of solitude;
And then my heart with pleasure fills,
And dances with the daffodils.
(Wordsworth 1998: 383)

Wordsworth is viewing nature as crucially linked to his experience and poetry. The setting is integral to the poetic work, as it is to human experience. Setting, used as a literary device in previous generations, has moved away from 'the anthropocentric position of the pastoral' (Gifford 1999: 147) to one that views nature as more interlinked with humanity. Other poets that can be explored fruitfully with students in their use of nature and natural settings are John Clare, Ted Hughes and Seamus Heaney. Gerard Manley Hopkins explores the magnificence of nature and its relationship with God, 'The Windhover' being an accessible and extremely interesting sonnet to examine with KS4 or KS5 pupils.

This chapter sets out a variety of approaches to poetry through setting. Marvell's 'The Garden' is the earliest example, and relates to the classical literary tradition of pastoral. Blake's 'London' is an example of anti-pastoral in which:

The immediate environment offers up images of tyranny, punitive law and corrupted church. Those things in life that are normally associated with creation and regeneration, love and children, are blighted by the moral pollution that surrounds them … you might see this view as essentially anti-pastoral.

(Beard and Bunton 2008: 42)

Seamus Heaney's 'The Barn' is used as an example of how, like Wordsworth, Heaney has developed 'a poetry that thinks through images of nature' (Gifford 1999: 97) and Mike Hayhoe's 'City Blues', as a contrast to Heaney, where in twentieth-century poetry, 'the natural – and human – world is conceived as shattered, fragmentary, painful' (Preminger 1965: 822).

Pastoral setting at KS3:'The Barn' by Seamus Heaney

The Barn

Threshed corn lay piled like grit of ivory
Or solid as cement in two-lugged sacks.
The musty dark hoarded an armoury
Of farmyard implements, harness, plough-socks.

The floor was mouse-grey, smooth, chilly concrete.
There were no windows, just two narrow shafts
Of gilded motes, crossing, from air-holes slit
High in each gable. The one door meant no draughts

All summer when the zinc burned like an oven.
A scythe's edge, a clean spade, a pitch-fork's prongs:
Slowly bright objects formed when you went in.
Then you felt cobwebs clogging up your lungs

And scuttled fast into the sunlit yard –
And into nights when bats were on the wing
Over the rafters of sleep, where bright eyes stared
From piles of grain in corners, fierce, unblinking.

The dark gulfed like a roof-space. I was chaff
To be pecked up when birds shot through the air-slits.
I lay face-down to shun the fear above.
The two-lugged sacks moved in like great blind rats.
(Heaney 1980: 14)

Like many of Heaney's poems, 'The Barn' is set in rural Ireland, drawing on his childhood experiences and memories of growing up on the family farm, Mossbawn, in County Derry. In his essays Heaney describes how as a young boy he had freedom to explore his natural surroundings and he depicts his observations in detail throughout his poetry. As such, the setting of this poem can at first seem most unfamiliar to our pupils, unless you do happen to teach in a rural school. Generally pupils' experience of farms will be limited to visits when they were a small child, sometimes not even that, and certainly not at night. It is therefore important to do some preparatory work to get pupils receptive to the imaginative territory of the poem prior to reading it.

'The Barn' describes Heaney's experience of being a young boy whose imagination gets the better of him, causing him to be afraid in his father's barn. As such it is ideal for encouraging pupils to bring their own experience of fear to the poem. Prior to reading the poem, a discussion on phobias can be had, starting with a definition of the word 'phobia'. At KS3 pupils are usually familiar with the term, and will be able to name several phobias. They could start with a matching activity, where they have a list of phobias with their meanings mixed up on opposite sides of a work sheet. Working in pairs, pupils match the word to the meaning. They might know arachnophobia, and some will know other more common fears such as claustrophobia and agoraphobia. Creating a list including some less familiar ones will generate much discussion. (A personal favourite is arachibutyrophobia which means a fear of peanut butter sticking to the roof of the mouth!) For those who need some extra support (such as pupils with EAL) pictures can be included. As an extension pupils can be asked to create names for modern phobias, for example 'textophobia'. The end result of this activity is that pupils will have engaged with the idea of phobias and naturally, during the course of the activity, will have discussed their own phobias and fears. This will lead on to a productive discussion about what makes these fears worse. Pupils are being guided to the recognition that usually being alone or in the dark stimulates the imagination and intensifies the sense of fear.

A very good way into the poem is make a line drawing of the barn together on the board; the teacher draws it and pupils copy it on to plain paper as you go along on (see Figure 6.1) Label the drawing with quotations from the poem as you go, explaining certain words. For example, 'two-lugged sacks' is usually understood by pupils as meaning there are only two sacks, whereas it describes the two knots at the corners of the sacks. 'Gilded motes' is also an unfamiliar phrase but it is very easy to illustrate if you can leave a gap in your curtains for the light to come through on a sunny afternoon. Typical of Heaney's style, every aspect is minutely observed leading to an intense feeling of claustrophobia. The words used sound menacing and dangerous. The barn itself is described as an 'oven' and the sharp farmyard implements within are described as an 'armoury'. The personification of inanimate objects makes them seem more threatening, such as the secretive dark hiding its weapons.

Each stanza develops the idea of the fear of the child, increasing the tension. As the poem progresses the scene gets darker; pupils have already recognised that darkness will magnify the child's fear. The poem takes on a nightmarish quality. As his imagination gets the better of him, the child lies on the floor in the way that children do, as if closing their eyes will make the object of their fear go away. At this point it is unclear whether the child is in the barn at night or whether he is dreaming, a sense of confusion which serves to emphasise the child's extreme terror.

Once the pupils have the labelled diagram in front of them, it is straightforward to discuss the setting of 'The Barn'. One way of doing this is to pick apart the similes in a similar way to that described in Chapter 4 on 'Roger the Dog', by asking pupils, for example, what the qualities of grit are (hard, sharp, cuts you when you fall onto it), or of cement (heavy, unwieldy, difficult to move).

Heaney describes his memories in such a way that a child would experience them, by appealing to the senses, so the reader can vividly imagine the experience for themselves. 'The Barn' appeals mainly to the sense of touch; the 'smooth, chilly concrete', the heat and the 'cobwebs clogging up your lungs' all serve to stress what an unwelcoming place the barn was. Note that Heaney doesn't mention his family at all in this poem, which accentuates his sense of being alone and therefore magnifies the fear. Having done the preparatory work on phobias, pupils are in a position to remember how it feels to be alone in a dark, scary place, and therefore the poem elicits a powerful emotional response from them.

The VAK model of learning styles suggests that all pupils learn through visual, auditory and kinaesthetic modes of perception. Individuals are said to differ in their preferences for one or more of these modes and in their ability to process information received through

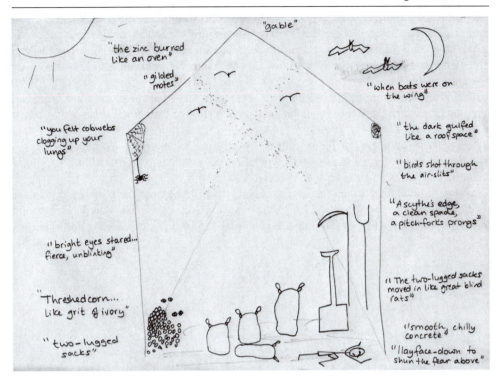

Figure 6.1 Line drawing of the barn

them, so can be classified as visual, auditory or kinaesthetic learners. Although not without its critics, it is a model widely known in schools and is seen as an important aspect of good practice in lesson planning and delivery. (For a useful summary see Mike Hughes' *Closing the Learning Gap*.) This activity appeals to visual learners.

Nicholas McGuinn tells us Heaney believes that poetry and place are inextricably linked, and that the poet 'listens' for his poems which somehow 'rise out of the earth like some strange gift from the natural world awarded to the poet for his patient homage' (McGuinn 1986: 18).

Through the poems in his first volume of poetry, *Death of a Naturalist*, Heaney describes his loss of childhood innocence as he grows up. It is clear that his rural upbringing and the observations he made as he dawdled to school had a profound effect on the poetry he went on to write. Heaney believed that 'When a poet is cut off from his roots and can no longer "listen" to the landscape, he is cut off from the source of his inspiration' (McGuinn 1986: 18). Though not pastoral poetry in the traditional sense of the word, Heaney uses his Derry landscape to explore his childhood emotions and fears: fears familiar to us all whatever our own 'natural roots'.

Urban setting at KS4: 'City Blues' by Mike Hayhoe

It is well known that poets such as Blake and Owen redrafted their poems several times over in order to accurately convey the images and emotions they had in mind when writing. This is a useful point to make to pupils, particularly when embarking on a close reading of a poem for examination purposes. Mike Hayhoe suggests printing a brief poem with optional words at key points as a means of getting pupils to become aware of how a poet chooses words, and gives the first four lines of Hardy's 'I Look Into My Glass' as an example of how this might be done (see Figure 6.2).

This is a useful exercise in raising pupils' awareness that a change of even one word can alter the tone of the entire poem, and is an approach Hayhoe further develops with his own poem, 'City Blues'.

'City Blues' is a poem that lends itself to the multi-modal approach, its title conjuring up as it does both a variety of shades and a type of music, thus making it a useful starting point for enriching pupils' broader cultural experience.

In order to make the poem relevant to pupils, it is of paramount importance to explore their own experience before introducing the poem, and asking the class what they know and feel about the two words of the title is a good place to begin. A quick brainstorm of each

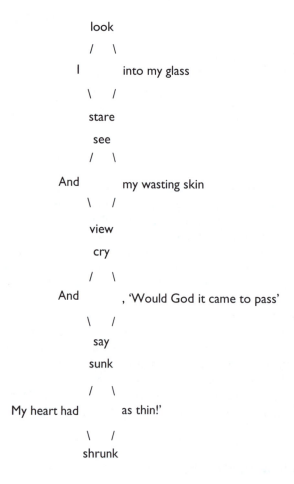

Figure 6.2 Thomas Hardy's 'I Look Into My Glass' (Hayhoe 1988: 112)

word, followed by class feedback, will have pupils sharing ideas and recreating their experiences. The word 'city' will provide a variety of sights, sounds, smells and memories, usually involving crowded streets and lots of traffic, depending on where your pupils live, whilst the word 'blues' will yield both a variety of colours, such as aqua, baby blue, navy and so on, and that ubiquitous teenage depression with which pupils at KS4 are so familiar. To add some variety to the lesson and to appeal to aural learners, play an extract from a classic blues track such as 'Need Your Love So Bad' by Peter Green's Fleetwood Mac (easily found on YouTube), asking pupils to jot down their emotional responses to the music whilst listening and add them to their 'Blues' brainstorm. Their next task is to consider the idea that if this track were to represent the sound of the city, then what time of day do they imagine it to be, and what would the inhabitants be doing?

Following this, a PowerPoint showing examples of Whistler's 'Nocturnes' with a brief contextual explanation will engage them visually. Ask pupils as they look to decide which of the paintings they think could illustrate the emotions expressed in the Fleetwood Mac song.

Then play an example of a more jazzy style of blues, such as Michael Brecker playing 'Delta City Blues', and again as they listen ask pupils to jot down the images they get, what they think is happening in the city and what time of day it is. Finally, ask them choose the Whistler painting they think goes best with this track. Their feedback and the ensuing discussion will allow pupils to crystallise their thoughts about the city, and realise that it is a constantly changing environment, the sounds and sights changing depending on the time of day or night, the day of the week, the season and even the mood of the inhabitant.

Following this initial exploration of ideas and associations, pupils are ready to be introduced to the poem. The poem itself offers a vision of a city at dawn on a Sunday in November. That much is not negotiable; however, within the poem the word options create a variety of interpretations of the city, and show quite clearly the sort of choices poets have to make while writing. Hayhoe suggests that initially pupils work individually on deciding which word they would have chosen at which point and then work in pairs, comparing ideas and seeing where they agreed and disagreed (Hayhoe et al. 1990: 48).

Pupils read their version aloud and discuss how their word choices affect their impression of the city, eventually deciding which version they like best and giving their reasons. They will see that the whole tone and therefore the description of the city depends upon their choice of words; for example, the choice of 'sky-spoilers' as opposed to 'skyscrapers' implies the faceless 'corporations' (as opposed to the more friendly 'companies') do not care about the look of the city and will spoil the landscape just to make money. Pupils will realise that by choosing particular words the city becomes a more hostile environment; for example, 'chased' is more aggressive than 'followed'.

Next, pupils are asked to underline the lines that are not optional and to read them aloud, noting which words or phrases catch their attention and considering what the poet seems to want the reader to feel. The words have largely negative connotations, and phrases such as 'knows its place/as the less fortunate should' seem to be making a comment not about a particular city, but about society in general. The fact that the sun is described as 'lousy' is also negative and challenges our expectations; normally we are pleased to see the sun. Asking pupils to discuss why the poet might not be pleased to see the sun will encourage them to think about how the city looks at night as opposed to during the day, and they will probably conclude that the poet might have preferred the look of the city in the dark because he couldn't see the buildings and the litter. Pupils should then be encouraged to contrast the poet's vision of the city with their own; do they agree that it looks better at night?

Finally, pupils are asked to return to the title of the poem and to consider to what it refers. Does it mean the sorts of blues associated with depression or the grey/blue tones of the buildings and pavements? And how does the choice of optional words affect the impact of the title? Ultimately, even if the 'softer' options were chosen, the overweening impression is one of negativity because of the connotations of the non-optional words, which leads us to question whether there is any real choice in our interpretation or if the layout of the poem is merely a construct to make us think we have a choice.

Pastoral at KS5: 'The Garden' by Andrew Marvell

The Garden

How vainly men themselves amaze
To win the palm, the oak, or bays;
And their uncessant labors see
Crowned from some single herb or tree,
Whose short and narrow-vergèd shade
Does prudently their toils upbraid;
While all the flowers and trees do close
To weave the garlands of repose.

Fair Quiet, have I found thee here,
And Innocence, thy sister dear!
Mistaken long, I sought you then
In busy companies of men:
Your sacred plants, if here below,
Only among the plants will grow;
Society is all but rude,
To this delicious solitude.

No white nor red was ever seen
So amorous as this lovely green;
Fond lovers, cruel as their flame,
Cut in these trees their mistress' name.
Little, alas, they know or heed,
How far these beauties hers exceed!
Fair trees! wheresoe'er your barks I wound
No name shall but your own be found.

When we have run our passion's heat,
Love hither makes his best retreat:
The gods who mortal beauty chase,
Still in a tree did end their race.
Apollo hunted Daphne so,
Only that she might laurel grow,
And Pan did after Syrinx speed,
Not as a nymph, but for a reed.

What wondrous life is this I lead!
Ripe apples drop about my head;
The luscious clusters of the vine
Upon my mouth do crush their wine;
The nectarine and curious peach
Into my hands themselves do reach;
Stumbling on melons as I pass,
Insnared with flowers, I fall on grass.

Meanwhile the mind, from pleasure less,
Withdraws into its happiness:
The mind, that ocean where each kind
Does straight its own resemblance find;
Yet it creates, transcending these,
Far other worlds, and other seas;
Annihilating all that's made
To a green thought in a green shade.

Here at the fountain's sliding foot,
Or at some fruit-tree's mossy root,
Casting the body's vest aside,
My soul into the boughs does glide:
There like a bird it sits and sings,
Then whets and combs its silver wings;
And, till prepared for longer flight,
Waves in its plumes the various light.

Such was that happy garden-state,
While man there walked without a mate:
After a place so pure and sweet,
What other help could yet be meet!
But 'twas beyond a mortal's share
To wander solitary there:
Two paradises 'twere in one
To live in Paradise alone.

How well the skilful gard'ner drew
Of flowers and herbs this dial new;
Where from above the milder sun
Does through a fragrant zodiac run;
And, as it works, th' industrious bee
Computes its time as well as we.
How could such sweet and wholesome hours
Be reckoned but with herbs and flowers!
                    (Marvell in di Cesare 1978: 112)

Teaching an Early Modern poem, such as 'The Garden', and avoiding the perception that 'poems are puzzles to which the teacher holds the key' (Benton *et al.* 1988: 2) is a challenge which few of us manage to overcome. There are endless commentaries and question and answer sheets to be found on the internet about Metaphysical poetry, and very useful they are too, but using this approach with students turns poems into dusty museum pieces. The 'art of English' (Pike 2003: 6) is to enthuse and inspire students, while giving them enough context within which to understand a difficult poem. No mean feat.

In his essay 'Poetry teaching in the secondary school: the concept of "difficulty"' Fleming states that 'expectations of what poetry should mean and how it should function have changed over time. ... Reading poetry from the modern movement is a different matter from reading a Shakespeare sonnet' (Fleming 1996: 40). This is undoubtedly the case, and Fleming suggests that

> One of the decisions which the teacher has to make pertains to the appropriate lexical, syntactical, contextual or historical details which need to be supplied in order to provide enough clarity for the reader to be able to make an authentic response.
>
> (Fleming 1996: 38)

What the teacher has to decide is what information, contextually or otherwise, needs to be given regarding the poem, and most crucially, at what time.

Where should one start with 'The Garden'? This would depend on whether the poem is being taught as part of a sequence of poems by the poet, or perhaps as a larger study of genre. The poem is one of Marvell's most well known and a good place to commence a study of his work, after looking at 'To His Coy Mistress', which rarely fails to please (see Chapter 7). That the poem belongs to the pastoral tradition is a key element to understanding it, and the idea of retreat from activity is certainly something that students can relate to. The deliberate withdrawal from activity is one of the main ideas about 'The Garden' students will need to grasp. This will need to be part of preparing the thematic or 'emotional territory' (Wood and Wood 1988: 1) that the students will encounter in the poem. One piece of pre-reading work for the poem is to ask the students to consider and/or discuss their weekends. What do they like to do? Among the responses might be some reference to rest and recuperation, and the discussion could then be extended to holidays: why do people take them? Where do they go and why? The hope is that the discussion will lead towards ideas of rest, escape and probably rural settings. Images of beautiful, green bucolic destinations on the IWB could be used here. Certainly the students may well be familiar with the phenomenon of people moving to the countryside when they have made their money in the city amid the hustle and bustle of city life.

The theme of escape can be extended into the second main idea that can help students prepare the ground for the poem, which is the idea of greenery and gardens, of rest amongst greenery. Some visualisation work, where students imagine themselves in a peaceful garden, imagine what they might see and be able to feel, will encourage them to inhabit the imaginative space of the poem. Working on the phrase 'a green thought in a green shade' could produce some very interesting responses. Alison Ross has worked extensively on creative writing with A Level students, and one idea that she uses is to write quickly, with a limited amount of time, in order to get students to respond openly and freely, without any planning or prior thought. Asking the students to respond individually and spontaneously to the idea of 'green thoughts' and 'green shade' could lead to very interesting avenues to explore.

Given that the poem is a complex one, it is preferable that students have an initial encounter with the poem that allows them to read the text without being required to respond immediately. The students will already have some ideas of the imaginative spaces that the poem will inhabit, those of retreat and greenery, and this will ideally have aroused their curiosity. Sequencing the poem, that is, jumbling up the stanzas and asking the students in pairs to put them in the correct order, can be done as a paper-based activity or using ICT. This could be difficult, as the measured rhyme scheme and stanza organisation give no structural clues as to links between the stanzas, such as a sentence that runs over from one verse to another. Some of the lexis will also be challenging, but the resemblance of sequencing to a game allows the students to respond to the text on a surface level. Steiner argues that the first level of difficulty in poetry is that the words may be 'archaic' (Steiner 1978: 20) and undertaking this activity enables students to use contextual cues to meaning, rather than needing to understand all the vocabulary. It also allows time for them to look up or discuss any lexis that they do not understand and to get to grips with this first level of difficulty. In order to sequence the poem correctly, the students will have to work out the progression of the poem, where the argument starts and finishes, and what seems to be the central experience of the poem. Before discussing the outcome of the sequencing activity, asking the students to write a sentence or two, again in pairs, about each stanza, justifying its position in their chosen sequence, will ensure that they begin to look in detail at the language of the text to articulate their choices.

Discussing the logical progression of the text should bring to the fore the structure of the poem, that the experience is like that of 'An Ode to a Nightingale', whereby the speaker is drawn in to and out of an experience. In 'The Garden', the speaker delights in the withdrawal from activity to the peace of the garden, and in the central section of the poem his soul departs his body, as a bird, in perfect peace. Before progressing to more detailed discussion of the poem, at this point the students may well spot the reference to the Garden of Eden, which Marvell points out was much happier before the creation of Eve. There are also classical references to Ovid's *Metamorphoses*. This would be the point at which, with KS5 students, it would be appropriate for them to research various elements that feed into an understanding of the literary context for the poem. Fleming observes:

> It is perhaps more appropriate to think of poetry as being potentially 'bewildering' rather than 'difficult' because the barriers to understanding are more to do with having inappropriate expectations or not quite knowing the 'rules' which apply. Pupils therefore will be helped by some attention to the genre itself, not to pursue strict definitions of poetry but to examine the way different texts require different types of reading.
>
> (Fleming and Steven 1998: 72)

That the students are becoming more familiar with the text and have already thought through some thematic areas, means that their research will be of more interest and relevance to their studies. Allotting pairs or groups to research and feedback on the pastoral tradition; the Golden Age; the Garden of Eden and Ovid's *Metamorphoses* at this point would enable them to build upon the 'different types of reading' that Fleming points out are so important with poetry of this period. Using artistic images here, such as Lucas Cranach's *Adam and Eve in the Garden of Eden*, as the basis around which students build their presentations could be a good starting point.

The visual elements of the poem are those around which the next stage of work can be built. Leishman comments that in 'The Garden' Marvell 'is arguing in images' (Leishman

1966: 296) and the regularity of the form through which the argument is made lends itself to a sequential analysis. Using a series of storyboards to depict each stanza would involve students further with the language and imagery of the text, thinking for example how they would represent the personification of 'Quiet' and 'Innocence', or the lusciousness of stanza five, where fruits press themselves upon the speaker, onto his lips or into his hands. Depicting these scenes would be a great deal of fun but also require serious engagement with the language and imagery of the text. In following up the storyboards and sharing the varying interpretations of the text, the representation of the speaker's soul as a bird, and the curious Early Modern belief that the 'oceans contained counterparts to all earthly creatures' (di Cesare 1978: 113) would entail investigating further the Platonic dualism that underpins Marvell's discussion of the separation of body and soul.

Having worked through the text in such detail, and researched the main ideas without which a poem from this period cannot be understood, the students should be ready to engage in a serious critical exploration of their own. The poem works through a series of binary opposites, such as action and contemplation, mind and body; it presents ambiguities in attitudes and is certainly witty. We want our students to arrive at some apprehension of this themselves, and bring their own understanding of the meaning of the text, before they then go on to read and absorb what other critics have written about the poem, which they most assuredly need to. If the students have enjoyed their first encounters with the poem and found that it has some meaning for them, they are more likely to take away a desire to know more, which is our desired outcome as English teachers.

Case study: 'London' by William Blake at KS4

London

I wander through each chartered street,
Near where the chartered Thames does flow,
And mark in every face I meet,
Marks of weakness, marks of woe.

In every cry of every man,
In every infant's cry of fear,
In every voice, in every ban,
The mind-forged manacles I hear:

How the chimney-sweeper's cry
Every black'ning church appalls,
And the hapless soldier's sigh
Runs in blood down palace walls.

But most through midnight streets I hear
How the youthful harlot's curse
Blasts the new-born infant's tear,
And blights with plagues the marriage-hearse.
(Blake 1992: 46)

The immediate teaching context was that we spent half a term on Blake, based on two sessions a week of ninety minutes, culminating in an assignment written under controlled conditions for GCSE. Students had some experience of responding to poetry but were very much schooled in the idea that the teacher has the magic key to the meaning, a myth I was keen to dispel as I wanted to encourage their own individual responses.

Before we even started to study 'London', I set the students some homework to independently research William Blake's views on education. They were able to do this well using the internet, and in the next lesson we discussed their findings: that Blake believed children should not have to go to school in summer and that 'children are like birds trapped in a cage'. One boy suggested that Blake felt formal education caused the children's 'minds to be caged' and another boy coined the rather beautiful phrase 'free-range children' which we agreed summed up Blake's view of a perfect childhood rather nicely. This had the desired effect of causing students to view Blake positively and to be sympathetic towards his ideas before we began to tackle the poetry.

From my prior experience, I knew that students generally lack awareness and knowledge of the cultural and historical context in which Blake worked, and therefore needed some kind of formal teaching about Blake and the conditions in London at the time. As Boden points out, 'creative thinking cannot happen unless the thinker already possesses knowledge of a rich and/or well structured kind' (Boden 2001: 95). I therefore prepared a PowerPoint presentation for them, giving details of Blake's life and times, carefully adding points which I felt were crucial to the understanding of the poem, such as the French Revolution and the American War of Independence. I also added some detail about the practice of selling young children to be sent up chimneys to sweep and the conditions in which they lived, and the fact that there were some forty thousand prostitutes working in London at the time. Students were asked to jot down anything they thought to be interesting or important whilst they watched the presentation.

Interestingly, students chose mostly to write down the more non-conformist elements of Blake's behaviour and declared him insane, which was the view Wordsworth held, and which somehow endeared him to them (see Figure 6.3).

I next showed the class musical examples of Tavener's version of 'The Lamb' and Ginsberg's version of 'The Tiger' via YouTube as a means of illustrating how popular Blake's poems remain, and that many of them have been set to music. We then looked at a variety of Blake's illustrations, which were deemed to be 'weird' and reinforced the view of pupils that he was somewhat mad. I finished by showing the class an example of 'Jerusalem' sung at the Proms; many recognised the tune but had not realised the words were Blake's. My intention here was to simply introduce the class to the wide variety of Blake's work as poet and artist, and to reinforce the idea of his enduring popularity.

Next students were given copies of the poem and after my initial reading of it they re-read it together in groups and discussed their initial responses to it. They bullet-pointed the images they got and wrote down any questions they had. Questions were usually based on the meanings of specific words, such as 'chartered', 'blighted', 'harlot' and 'hapless'. I was keen not to give my own interpretation of the poem and wanted pupils to make their own meanings based on the images they had, so handed out dictionaries to look up single words, whilst reiterating to them that if they come across an unfamiliar word in a poem it is still possible to understand the overall ideas of the poem without getting bogged down in the meanings of single words. However, I still had to explain some of the words as the school dictionary definitions were unsatisfactory. Whilst I believe that pupils do not need to be able to understand every word before making a

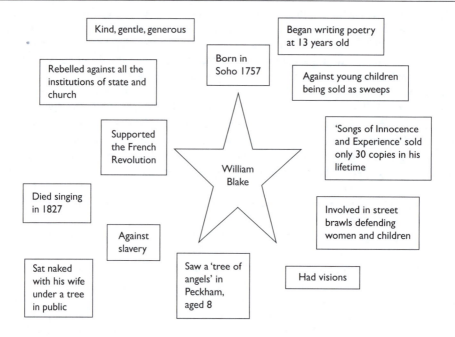

Figure 6.3 Students' responses to presentation on Blake

response to a poem, sometimes their lack of comprehension may present barriers which prevent further engagement with the work.

Several of the groups were receptive and did make a good attempt at responding to the poem, their initial bullet-pointed images being of:

- Young prostitutes, swearing
- Soldiers being killed
- Night-life
- Men crying
- Chimney sweepers
- Plague
- Fear and sadness of children and men
- Repetition of 'every'
- Everyone is sad
- Gloomy and dark city
- Diseases.

I could see from these responses that pupils were responding to the poem on a literal level and the next task would be to unpick the poem for a greater degree of understanding, in the hope of exploring the possible connotations of these images and their metaphorical meanings.

In order to achieve this level of deeper understanding, I decided that focused discussion on particular parts of the poem was necessary, and so used a de Bono-style discussion as my template for organising group work and focusing on particular aspects in depth (see de

Bono 1985 for further information). I created a grid using some questions taken from Blake's *Selected Works* (Blake 1995:72) and some of my own.

Each pupil was allocated a colour and a number from one to five. In colour groups, they discussed the aspect of the poem on the grid (see Table 6.1), writing down the group's responses in the box.

After about ten minutes of focused discussion on the requisite aspect, pupils where then instructed to change groups, this time into number groups. This time each person fed back to the number group the results of their colour group discussion, and the rest of the group added their own thoughts. The ultimate aim was for all pupils to have a completed grid they could then use to write a focused respose to the question, What is the deeper meaning behind Blake's 'London'? The organisation for this activity can be seen in Table 6.1.

This approach enabled a greater focus on modes on interpretation and therefore a much more interesting level of discussion ensued, for example whilst discussing the picture:

TARIQ The old man symbolises weakness and the little boy is guiding him.

ALICE How do you know it's a boy? It isn't necessarily a boy.

TARIQ OK, a child then. What does that matter?

GEORGIE Because the child symbolises youth. The old ways are crumbling and new ideas are leading the way.

TARIQ The old man is blind and crippled which means the old ways aren't working.

GEORGIE That's what I said.

ALICE But what's it got to do with the poem?

TARIQ Because Blake is saying that people need to open their ears and listen to what's going on around them.

ALICE How do you work that out?

TARIQ Because he keeps repeating the word 'hear'.

GEORGIE Because he says they have mind-forged manacles which means they aren't thinking for themselves.

ALICE So the old man in the picture is like the old London then?

TARIQ Could be, I hadn't thought of that.

It can be seen from the above dialogue that pupils were engaging with the complexities and possibilities without my explicit guidance, and were able to reach their own interpretations. Pupils agreed that following this activity a deeper, more satisfying exploration of the poem had been achieved and they were able to go on to comment on what they thought Blake was criticising about his society and its institutions as part of their controlled assessment.

Table 6.1 Template for organising group work based on de Bono's Hats (de Bono 1985)

Colour	Focus of discussion	Group's response
Red Stanza 1	What does Blake seem to be saying about the Thames and the streets of London? What is the significance of the word 'every' in stanza one? 'Mark' may mean notice and remark, or a physical mark. Which meaning fits better? What is the effect of the long vowel sounds?	
Yellow Stanza 2	What is the effect of the repetition of the word 'every'? Which sense is Blake appealing to in this stanza and how? 'Ban' means swearword or marriage vows. Which meaning fits better? In what sense are the manacles 'mind-forged'?	
Black Stanza 3	New churches quickly turned black in the polluted atmosphere of London. What else may 'black'ning'imply? 'Appalls' suggests 'filling with dread' but refers also to the dark cloth used at funerals. How appropriate is this? What does the metaphor ' … hapless soldier's sigh … palace walls' mean?	
Green Stanza 4	'Plagues' are sexually transmitted diseases, known to affect victims' babies. What symbolic meaning is there also? Which sense is Blake appealing to and how? What is the effect of the oxymoron, 'marriage hearse'?	
White The picture	Concentrate on the details of the picture. What can you see and what does it seem to symbolize? Does it help your understanding of the poem?	
Blue The poem overall	Are there any signs of hope in this poem? What are the links between sweep and church, soldier and palace, and harlot and marriage? How many times can you find the word 'hear' in the poem? What does Blake seem to be criticising?	

Chapter 7

Constructions of character through time

HAMLET What a piece of work is a man! How noble in reason, how infinite in faculty, in form and moving how express and admirable, in action how like an angel, in apprehension how like a god! The beauty of the world, the paragon of animals – and yet to me, what is this quintessence of dust? Man delights not me – no nor woman neither, though by your smiling you seem to say so.

(*Hamlet*, Act 2, Scene 2, ll.286–92)

Here we explore how we can use in the classroom the way that poets create character in their work. We include an introduction on the development of ideas about identity from medieval to postmodern times. We look at ways of exploring the construction of a female character with KS3 using Duffy's 'Mrs Midas'. Then we look at the construction of a male viewpoint in Marvell's 'To His Coy Mistress', with KS4. Blake's 'The Chimney Sweeper (Innocence)' is used to examine the way Blake created a child's voice to critique society. Our case study is on teaching Chaucer's 'The Miller's Tale' at KS3.

Introduction: constructions of character through time

Character is often conflated with voice in poetry. The Assessment and Qualifications Alliance (AQA) has a section of its GCSE anthology *Moon on the Tides* entitled 'Character and voice', in which the two aspects are indistinguishable. In Chapter 5 on voice we took Eliot's definitions of voice as the ways in which the poet constructs the address of the poem: 'to himself', to 'the audience' or as another character from history or 'fiction' (Eliot 1957: 95). We have followed through these definitions with ways into poetry through authorial address: first, second or third person. In this chapter, we suggest ways to explore poetry through constructions of character. We will look at the representations of self in poems and seek to explore ways of teaching how character is constructed in a short piece of poetic text.

When working with young people on poetry, we have to keep at the forefront of our minds that we are always dealing with 'a constructed subject' (McManus 2005: 211) in a text. The representation of character, and the idea of identity, is always 'the self forged under the pressure of historical, social and discursive circumstance. Among the forces working on the subject are class, gender, nationhood, race and sexuality' (McManus 2005: 211). We have selected examples of the construction of a male's, female's and child's perspective from different historical periods, to sample different approaches to the creation of character in poems. We make brief reference to the historical perspective on the definition of 'character', as this provides a framework on which to build up perspective on how the poems are positioning us as readers. It is always important to remember that our modern perspective on consciousness or identity is very different to that of those writing in different periods, especially as we all have a post-romantic, and even post-modern, consciousness in the twenty-first century.

Using Chaucer's *Canterbury Tales* in the classroom is a highly rewarding occupation: his characters are lively, humane and vibrant in their language and antics. However, as characters they are positioned very clearly within a hierarchy of social and religious affiliation. What we believe about the medieval mindset will influence how we teach poetry of this period. A very influential thesis on our thinking about the history of how individuals perceive themselves is that of Jacob Burckhardt, writing in 1860, who argued that until the Renaissance in Italy, 'Man was conscious only of himself as a member of a race, people, party, family or corporation – only through some general category' (as cited in Hebron 2008: 103). Burckhardt was only referring to Western culture and probably just men, and there has been much discussion over this topic, but the essence of his argument still holds, to a large degree: within the confines of the feudal system in Western Europe, people saw themselves less individualistically than we might see ourselves today, and more as bound by affiliation to family, guilds, religion and class. In the case study at the end of this chapter, teaching Chaucer at KS3, we look at teaching 'The General Prologue' and how far this aspect needs to be addressed with younger pupils. In order for pupils to grasp Chaucer's characterisation some attention needs to be paid to the hierarchical positioning of the characters and the way that they are related to each other in the social structure.

The Early Modern period has been traditionally viewed in literature and art as a period where a consciousness of 'self' emerged, traced in all the changes that occurred in the arts and religion in Western Europe in the Renaissance period. The thought of the period 'added a new discourse about human nature, mind and subjectivity. This new discourse stressed self-reflection and self-control, it individualized refined social values and it laid the basis for modern subjective sensibility' (Smith 1997: 57). Characters such as Hamlet and Faustus express their struggle with their 'self-reflection' and the rigid structures of religion and social expectation, although perhaps self means more to them in terms of how we might understand soul today, than in the modern understanding of 'self'. Greenblatt argues that, 'in the sixteenth century there appears to be an increased self-consciousness about the fashioning of human identity as a manipulable, artful process' (Greenblatt 1980: 2) and that 'self-fashioning acquires a new range of meanings … it suggests representation of one's nature or intention in speech or actions' (Greenblatt 1980: 2). Andrew Marvell's 'To His Coy Mistress', with which we have chosen to explore ideas for KS4 pupils, certainly exemplifies the representation of a self in speech and wished-for actions, as the male speaker is constructed as attempting to exert his power and rhetorical force upon his unwilling mistress.

The speaker in 'To His Coy Mistress' seeks to enact power by the force of his rhetoric and logic. It is not a poem to be taken too seriously, as it utilises humour and Marvell is clearly positioning his speaker as part of the popular *carpe diem* tradition; however, we can see in this poem the issue that:

> The creation of identity, then, is bound up with the circulation of power through society and its negotiation by those who have it (e.g. men, monarchs, colonists, military leaders) and by those upon whom it is imposed (e.g. the poor, women, the colonised).
>
> (McManus 2005: 211)

That the woman is silent in the poem, and that Marvell is writing as the member of an élite, for an élite audience, poses particular issues in the teaching that we can contemplate while organising our activities. What are the rhetorical traditions that influence the ways in which such a poem was written? The reception of the poem at the time, and the ways in which it was written can never be reproduced, so how much of that do we have to teach? This is, as Steiner discusses, 'the operative distinction between surface-understanding or paraphrase on the one hand, and penetrative comprehension on the other' (Steiner 1978: 29). How far can we go to provide the 'penetrative comprehension' or 'the rationale of the poem's being' (Steiner 1978: 29) for our pupils? We as teachers have to decide this based on our own personal context, the outcomes desired from the reading of the poetry and the contexts within which we and our pupils together find ourselves.

Whilst in 'To His Coy Mistress' the woman is silenced, in 'Mrs Midas' a female character is given a voice and personality to allow her to counter her silence and challenge patriarchal assumptions underlying most of our Western myths and cultural legends. We suggest approaches to teaching this poem at KS3, in order to look at how Duffy creates the character of Mrs Midas and how the 'creation of identity' (McManus 2005: 211) in the poem is directly associated with the 'circulation of power' (McManus 2005: 211) in mythology. Mrs Midas in Duffy's poem expresses a female perspective on her husband's greedy desire for wealth. Mrs Midas observes how her husband has lost his life, and also, as a consequence, lost the chance for them both to have a child and live as a family. His decision to wish for gold, with no consultation with her, leaves both of them forlorn.

In our section on Blake's 'The Chimney Sweepers', from *The Songs of Innocence*, we have selected to look at the work of a Romantic poet with KS5. The poem uses the character of a child to express the relationship of those who have no power with those who possess it: the church and the political establishment in this case. In the eighteenth century, 'the individual moved centre stage' (Porter 1997: 5) and the influence of Descartes and Locke are significant here. Locke argued in his *Essay Concerning Human Understanding* that 'the mind is not like a furnished flat, prestocked with innate ideas, but like a home gradually put together from scratch out of ceaseless mental acquisitions. The self is thus the product of experience and education' (Porter 1997: 4) operating in a rational fashion. The child, as a *tabula rasa* depicted in Blake's poem, is innocent and uncorrupted by Original Sin. It is society and its corrupt institutions that threaten its innocence.

This notion of identity has changed again by the nineteenth century; Romantic thinkers were embarked on an 'odyssey of self-discovery' (Porter 1997: 5) which is summed up very neatly by Cardinal:

> The hallmarks of Romantic thought were its accentuation of unconstrained impulse and its de-emphasizing of rationality as the shaping principle of art. Romantic writers, painters and musicians placed ever greater store by the individual imagination, cherishing those peak experiences wherein the creative spirit sheds the fetters of humdrum circumstance.
>
> (Cardinal 1997: 135)

In two sections in our next chapter, on narrative, we look at the possibilities offered by the ideas of two Romantic writers, Wordsworth and Keats, while this chapter offers approaches towards constructions of character from four different periods from the history of English literature.

The female voice at KS3: 'Mrs Midas' by Carol Ann Duffy

Mrs Midas

It was late September. I'd just poured a glass of wine, begun
to unwind, while the vegetables cooked. The kitchen
filled with the smell of itself, relaxed, its steamy breath
gently blanching the windows. So I opened one,
then with my fingers wiped the other's glass like a brow.
He was standing under the pear tree snapping a twig.

Now the garden was long and the visibility poor, the way
the dark of the ground seems to drink the light of the sky,
but that twig in his hand was gold. And then he plucked
a pear from a branch – we grew Fondante d'Automne –
and it sat in his palm like a light bulb. On.
I thought to myself, Is he putting fairy lights in the tree?

He came into the house. The doorknobs gleamed.
He drew the blinds. You know the mind; I thought of
the Field of the Cloth of Gold and of Miss Macready.
He sat in that chair like a king on a burnished throne.
The look on his face was strange, wild, vain. I said,
What in the name of God is going on? He started to laugh.

I served up the meal. For starters, corn on the cob.
Within seconds he was spitting out the teeth of the rich.
He toyed with his spoon, then mine, then with the knives, the forks.
He asked where was the wine. I poured with shaking hand,
a fragrant, bone-dry white from Italy, then watched
as he picked up the glass, goblet, golden chalice, drank.

It was then that I started to scream. He sank to his knees.
After we had both calmed down, I finished the wine
on my own, hearing him out. I made him sit
on the other side of the room and keep his hands to himself.
I locked the cat in the cellar. I moved the phone.
The toilet I didn't mind. I couldn't believe my ears:

How he'd had a wish. Look, we all have wishes; granted.
But who has wishes granted? Him. Do you know about gold?
It feeds no one; aurum, soft, untarnishable; slakes
no thirst. He tried to light a cigarette; I gazed, entranced,
as the blue flame played on its luteous stem. At least,
I said, you'll be able to give up smoking for good.

Separate beds. In fact, I put a chair against my door,
near petrified. He was below, turning the spare room
into the tomb of Tutankhamun. You see, we were passionate then,
in those halcyon days; unwrapping each other, rapidly,
like presents, fast food. But now I feared his honeyed embrace,
the kiss that would turn my lips to a work of art.

And who, when it comes to the crunch, can live
with a heart of gold? That night, I dreamt I bore
his child, its perfect ore limbs, its little tongue
like a precious latch, its amber eyes
holding their pupils like flies. My dream-milk
burned in my breasts. I woke to the streaming sun.

So he had to move out. We'd a caravan
in the wilds, in a glade of its own. I drove him up
under cover of dark. He sat in the back.
And then I came home, the woman who married the fool
who wished for gold. At first I visited, odd times,
parking the car a good way off, then walking.

You knew you were getting close. Golden trout
on the grass. One day, a hare hung from a larch,
a beautiful lemon mistake. And then his footprints,
glistening next to the river's path. He was thin,
delirious; hearing, he said, the music of Pan
from the woods. Listen. That was the last straw.

What gets me now is not the idiocy or greed
but lack of thought for me. Pure selfishness. I sold
the contents of the house and came down here.
I think of him in certain lights, dawn, late afternoon,
and once a bowl of apples stopped me dead. I miss most,
even now, his hands, his warm hands on my skin, his touch.

                                        (Duffy 1999: 11)

In her collection *The World's Wife*, Duffy constructed identities for the female partners of male characters from a variety of fairy tales, myths, history and so on who form part of our cultural identity. In an interview with Barry Wood, published on the Sheer Poetry website, Duffy explains how she came to write a poem which offers a female perspective the Midas story:

> I was asked to contribute to Michael Hoffman's collection of translations of Ovid and was asked to do the story of Io. But my favourite was the story of Midas. I used to love that as a child, I used to imagine what it would be like if everything you touched turned to gold, not only your food but people you loved, so I really did want to do Midas. And this is a poem about the failed love, autobiographical – if you like, another take on the man in Little Red Cap, but done more lovingly. It's a poem about leaving someone.
>
>   (Duffy, www.sheerpoetry.co.uk)

An interesting way into teaching this poem is via an exploration of gender stereotyping and feminist theory, as suggested in Barbara Bleiman and Lucy Webster's English and Media Centre workbook, *Studying The World's Wife* (2007). Although aimed at A level students, the teaching ideas presented can be manipulated to be accessible to younger students. Certainly from Year 9 onwards pupils should be able to grasp the basic feminist argument that a patriarchal society assumed women should be subservient to men. Until the emergence of feminism, it was argued, women were treated almost as objects: passive agents in a male world. If you show pupils some examples of old advertisements from YouTube, such as the Folgers Coffee advertisements from the 1950s where the sole *raison d'être* of the female characters seems to be to make a decent coffee for their husbands, pupils will soon see what feminists were protesting about. Informing pupils of Aristotle's snail metaphor for the perfect woman (silent and always in the home) should have the desired effect of arousing sympathy for the feminist movement, the fruits of which are too often taken for granted nowadays.

Feminist writers, historians and critics felt that women's voices were often missing from history, literature and culture, and re-wrote what they saw as 'sexist' representations of women. An excellent way of introducing these notions to the class, as suggested by Bleiman and Webster, is to show the children's book *Princess Smartypants* by Babette Cole (1986) which subverts the typical fairytale in order to give the story a feminist slant. This approach can be seen in Figure 7.1.

A follow-up activity is for pupils to create a revised version of Little Red Riding Hood (or in a multicultural classroom, any similar folk tale) in a similar way to Babette Cole, either by using illustrations or writing it in prose or as a poem. This will consolidate pupils' learning about classic gender stereotypes and how to subvert them.

Prior to reading the poem a quick review of the myth of King Midas is important; most will know the story from primary school but some may not, particularly if they are new to this country. This can lead to some interesting debate about what pupils would wish for if they were given one wish. Asking pupils to write down what they think the message of the Midas story is will often result in some comment about the importance of thinking things through.

Bleiman and Webster suggest giving A level students fragments of the poem before reading it in order to focus on voice, imagery, word groups, implied audience and register, and this also helps pupils to focus on character. Fragments such as those suggested in Figure 7.2 which show Mrs Midas' use of idiom and dry humour can be read through by pupils in groups who then discuss what they reveal about the character of Mrs Midas.

Class or paired discussion could focus on:

- the roles the characters play;
- the pictures and how the female and male characters are presented in them;
- the use of names;
- the way language is used and what effect this has;
- the way in which conventional fairytale events are turned on their head;
- the way in which the tale ends.

Figure 7.1 Deconstructing a fairytale (from Bleiman and Webster 2007: 5)

| I'd just poured a glass of wine, begun/to unwind, while the vegetables cooked. |

| I thought to myself, Is he putting fairy lights in the tree? |

| You know the mind; I thought of/the Field of the Cloth of Gold and of Miss Macready |

| I said,/What in the name of God is going on? |

| I poured with shaking hand,/a fragrant, bone-dry white from Italy |

| It was then that I started to scream. |

| I locked the cat in the cellar. I moved the phone./The toilet I didn't mind. |

| Look, we all have wishes; granted./But who has wishes granted? |

| At least,/I said, you'll be able to give up smoking for good. |

| He was below, turning the spare room/into the tomb of Tutankhamun |

| And who, when it comes to the crunch, can live/with a heart of gold? |

| What gets me now is not the idiocy or greed/but lack of thought for me. |

| I miss most,/even now, his hands, his warm hands on my skin, his touch. |

Figure 7.2 Fragments from 'Mrs Midas' for discussion

Following this discussion, pupils are ready to hear the poem. There is a reading by Miranda Harris on the very useful website People Reading Poems, which is excellent in the absence of an Irish voice, which Carol Ann Duffy was trying to recreate:

> the rhythm of the poem comes very much from my own family, my mother and my grandmother, which were actually Irish, so it is in an Irish voice, 'What in the name of God is going on?' and 'Look, we all have wishes; granted; /But who has wishes granted?' etc. I wanted to bring into the poem some of the rhythms of the exasperation of women. Jesus!
>
> (Duffy, www.sheerpoetry.co.uk)

During the second reading, pupils are instructed to follow the text and annotate as it is read, using a question mark for any word, image or line they have questions about, an asterisk for parts they like and an exclamation mark for parts of the poem that remind them of experiences they have had. At the end of the reading they write down any questions they have.

In their groups pupils then compare which parts they had annotated similarly or differently, explaining their reasons and trying to answer each other's questions. This way pupils undertake a systematic analysis of the poem, engaging closely with the text and discussing it at length with their peers without asking for the teacher to provide answers. Simple misunderstandings of word meanings can easily be rectified with the use of dictionaries. Following this discussion, pupils are asked questions which develop their idea of the character's fictitious background: where and when they imagine the poem is set, what sort of people the Midases are, to which class they belong, and what gives them this idea.

The tonal shifts in the poem give a real sense of the character of Mrs Midas; an excellent way of making these changes in tone obvious to a younger class is to ask them to read the poem around the classroom, stopping at the full stops. The use of different voices really brings out the short sentences and emphasises the shifting feelings of Mrs Midas as the poem progresses. She starts off relaxing in her kitchen as she cooks the evening meal, and is then confused by what is happening, expressing her exasperation with, 'What in the name of God is going on?' (l.18) Her confusion turns to fear as she realises that she may be next to be turned to gold, but at the end the mood changes to nostalgia and regret as the narrator recalls how the thing she misses most is her husband's touch. As Duffy points out:

> although she's annoyed and exasperated with him, she's also in love with him – 'we were passionate then … unwrapping each other like presents'. And his selfishness has ended their love. So this is what this poem is about: selfishness destroying their marriage.
>
> (Duffy, www.sheerpoetry.co.uk)

As often happens when left to their own exploration, pupils can sometimes make surprising responses. When I last taught this poem, pupils responded that they thought the poem reinforced traditional gender roles, in that it was the woman who was at home cooking the dinner, waiting for her husband to come home. Further, they contradicted Duffy's view that '*his* selfishness has ended their love' (my italics) and concluded that in fact they were both equally culpable, as Mrs Midas had done nothing to try to help her husband to get a cure for his 'illness' but instead was only worried about herself.

The male voice at KS4: 'To His Coy Mistress' by Andrew Marvell

To His Coy Mistress

Had we but world enough, and time,
This coyness, lady, were no crime.
We would sit down and think which way
To walk, and pass our long love's day;
Thou by the Indian Ganges' side
Shouldst rubies find; I by the tide
Of Humber would complain. I would
Love you ten years before the Flood;
And you should, if you please, refuse
Till the conversion of the Jews.
My vegetable love should grow
Vaster than empires, and more slow.
An hundred years should go to praise
Thine eyes, and on thy forehead gaze;
Two hundred to adore each breast,

But thirty thousand to the rest;
An age at least to every part,
And the last age should show your heart.
For, lady, you deserve this state,
Nor would I love at lower rate.

But at my back I always hear
Time's winged chariot hurrying near;
And yonder all before us lie
Deserts of vast eternity.
Thy beauty shall no more be found,
Nor, in thy marble vault, shall sound
My echoing song; then worms shall try
That long preserv'd virginity,
And your quaint honour turn to dust,
And into ashes all my lust.
The grave's a fine and private place,
But none I think do there embrace.

Now therefore, while the youthful hue
Sits on thy skin like morning dew,
And while thy willing soul transpires
At every pore with instant fires,
Now let us sport us while we may;
And now, like am'rous birds of prey,
Rather at once our time devour,
Than languish in his slow-chapp'd power.
Let us roll all our strength, and all
Our sweetness, up into one ball;
And tear our pleasures with rough strife
Thorough the iron gates of life.
Thus, though we cannot make our sun
Stand still, yet we will make him run.
             (Marvell in di Cesare 1978: 104)

There is no doubt that 'To His Coy Mistress' is a *tour de force*, 'one of the finest lyrics of an age of great lyrical poetry' (Young 1985: 39) and is unquestionably the voice of a man, speaking to a woman. The woman is silent throughout, and she is the recipient of the argument of the speaker, at times seducing her and at times haranguing her to accede to his demands. The poem belongs to the *carpe diem* tradition, along with other poems such as Herrick's 'Gather Ye Rosebuds' (properly titled 'To the Virgins, to make much of Time') and many of Shakespeare's sonnets, particularly numbers one to six. That the poem belongs to this tradition is important, but this is not necessarily the place to embark upon the study of it.

Before discussing the literary tradition and historical context, we need to allow the pupils to find a way to relate to the content of the work for themselves, as Fox and Merrick commented in their invaluable *Thirty-Six Things To Do With a Poem*, 'poetry … needs to have its way prepared' (Merrick and Fox 1987: 28). Preparing the way can be thematic or emotional.

Thematically, 'To His Coy Mistress' is about seduction, and the pupils may well have points to contribute here. One way to start is to ask the pupils to think through experiences of chatting up or being chatted up by a member of the opposite sex. As in the case study on 'The Flea' (see Chapter 5) pupils could consider such questions, if they were appropriate, as: In what ways have you tried to persuade someone to go out with you? What are the ways that have been tried on you? An emotional area of the poem that the pupils may be able to engage with is the fear of death, and any experiences of death that they might have. This will take careful handling, but the presence of death is an important theme in 'To His Coy Mistress', and the speaker himself seems fearful of its presence.

Preparing the 'emotional territory' (Wood and Wood 1988: 1) is one lead into the poem; the other is prefiguring the imagery. Wood and Wood, in their preparatory work for the poem, suggest thinking through some ideas regarding the image of time as it is revealed in the poem by asking the pupils to consider such questions as: If time had a face, what do you think it would look like? And if time was a worker, what work would he/she do? (Wood and Wood 1988: 53).

Having prepared some of the areas that the poem will cover, the pupils benefit from hearing an expert reading of the poem before they come to read it themselves. Speculation on the title, and picking up on the adjective 'coy', will give away a few clues about what is to come, but at this point saying nothing more about the content should be whetting the pupils' appetite. Ideally a really strong performance reading by the teacher is the place to start, as it is important that pupils see that poems from this period can be read easily by expert readers, and they can hear that the language is not too far different from our own. Ask the pupils to listen carefully to the poem as it is read to them and to note down initially, in silence, their reactions to it. They may well react to the masculine quality of voice immediately, which could instigate an opening discussion about their initial reactions to the poem.

A strong reading of the poem will bring out the difference in tonal quality of the different sections. Eliot commented on the 'syllogistic relation' (Eliot 1975: 164) of the three verse paragraphs of the poem, in that the lyric advances an argument in three sections. A syllogism, part of the classical tradition of philosophy and logic, is a logical argument in three parts; a major premise (e.g. all humans have mothers), a minor premise (I am human) and a conclusion (therefore, I have a mother). The three sections in the poem are opened by three statements: 'Had we but world enough'; 'But at my back ...' and 'Now, therefore ...', indicating a logical argument that readers of the period would certainly have recognised. A first paired activity on the text, then, that identifies this structure and responds to the forward movement of the lyric, will build on an expert reading and the pupils' first responses to the poem. O'Brien suggests that the pupils devise an 'identifying heading' (O' Brien 1985: 90) for each section. The discussion amongst the pupils to decide on the main thrust of each verse paragraph will familiarise them with the tone and movement of the poem, and also with the vocabulary. It is always handy to have dictionaries on the desks and to train pupils to be self-reliant when encountering unfamiliar lexis.

Low and Pival argue that in 'To His Coy Mistress' Marvell uses the 'emotional power of images in support of his logical pattern' (Low and Pival 1969: 415) for the speaker to cajole and persuade his mistress. The pupils need to engage next with this 'emotional power' of the imagery. The opening section is highly visual, with the male speaker creating a vision of the ideal world in which his mistress could be coy. Pupils could storyboard the scenes from this first section, and quite naturally the humour could emerge as the speaker is seen grumbling and complaining by the banks of the Humber with nothing else to do, whilst his lady dawdles by the Ganges picking up rubies. Following this scene, Marvell then employs the literary technique popular in the Renaissance period of 'blazon', whereby the male lover lists the various parts of his lady and praises their qualities. How the pupils storyboard this could be interesting. The blazon uses 'extravagant yet ludicrously specific length[s] of time' (Young 1985: 42), and the pupils will have to render the masculine gaze as it moves down the mistress' body and uncover the humour in the allocation of time to specific body parts. The use of pronouns is a telling aspect of this first section, the movement from 'we' in the opening lines, to 'I' and 'you', serves to underline the clearly masculine viewpoint as the speaker pursues in his seduction and the comic, phallic qualities of 'My vegetable love' have caused much amusement over the years in English classrooms.

The first verse paragraph of 'To His Coy Mistress' is premised on the conditional 'Had', the tone of the second is shifted immediately by 'But'. The 'emotional power' of the imagery here is very different. Referring the pupils back to how they imagined a personification of time before reading the poem and looking at the image of 'Time's winged chariot' would be a discussion point. Images around the idea of *tempus fugit* can be researched on the internet by the pupils, as this image is one with a long classical heritage. Freeze-framing various moments from the poem can bring the language alive, and this moment particularly is one that is highly dramatic: the imminent arrival of an unseen but always heard assassin is very frightening. The marble vault that the speaker depicts is also one that can be drawn or explored within a freeze-frame. The reading of 'To His Coy Mistress' by Damien Lewis on YouTube dramatises this resounding and empty space very effectively, and he chooses to end the reading at this point. This filmed dramatisation of the poem brings out very markedly the masculinity of the text and the passivity of the lady in the whole experience. The quality of the lady who is the one who is enacted upon is underlined by the parallel phallic imagery here of worms that take the lady's virginity. This all serves to enhance the darkness of the argument at this point.

The final section is presented as the logical conclusion from the syllogistic argument: that the lady should indeed succumb to the speaker's requests. The images are of unity, of energetic life and movement. The pronouns have changed to those of 'us' and 'our' while the speaker urges that the two of them beat Time at his own game and outrun him with their own strength and pleasure. The extraordinary reversal of the imagery, the opposition of the deadly marble vault with the life force of birds of prey and the explosion of active verbs and vivid adjectives, could be the basis for some games with the language. Constructing three word syllogisms using lexis from the poem's three sections, for example love + time = fire, and then explaining or illustrating them, or drawing up lists of binary opposites from the poem, would require a detailed yet playful reading of the poem.

Having completed a detailed investigation of 'To His Coy Mistress', the poem can be put into its historical perspective; there are a number of follow-up activities. Imaginative exploration of what has happened before the poem, such as what is the mistress being 'coy' about, could be used for scriptwriting or improvisation. Is this just a poem of seduction, or has the poet asked the mistress to marry him? The English and Media Centre in *The Poetry Pack* suggest arguing back to the speaker and provide Lady Mary Montagu's 'An Answer to a Love Letter', both of which activities provide the forum for giving a woman a voice and arguing back to the male seducer. For an extension activity, very able pupils might be given the Haward version of 'To His Coy Mistress' from a manuscript of the late seventeenth century, which could arguably be from an earlier version of the poem (see Appendix A, The Haward version of 'To His Coy Mistress') and investigate the difference between the two versions and the impact made by the changes between the two drafts.

The child's voice at KS5: 'The Chimney Sweeper' by William Blake

The Chimney Sweeper

When my mother died I was very young,
And my father sold me while yet my tongue
Could scarcely cry, 'weep weep weep weep'.
So your chimneys I sweep and in soot I sleep.

There's little Tom Dacre, who cried when his head,
That curled like a lamb's back, was shav'd, so I said:
'Hush, Tom, never mind it, for when your head's bare,
You know that the soot cannot spoil your white hair.'

And so he was quiet, and that very night,
As Tom was a-sleeping, he had such a sight:
That thousands of sweepers, Dick, Joe, Ned and Jack,
Were all of them locked up in coffins of black.

And by came an angel who had a bright key,
And he opened the coffins and set them all free.
Then down a green plain leaping, laughing they run,
And wash in a river, and shine in the sun.

Then naked and white, all their bags left behind,
They rise upon clouds, and sport in the wind.
And the angel told Tom if he'd be a good boy,
He'd have God for his father and never want joy.

And so Tom awoke, and we rose in the dark,
And got with our bags and our brushes to work.
Though the morning was cold, Tom was happy and warm.
So if all do their duty, they need not fear harm.
                    (*The Songs of Innocence* 1789, in Blake 1992: 12)

In his *Songs of Innocence* and *Songs of Experience*, William Blake uses the character of the child as a means of critiquing aspects of eighteenth-century British society. Through 'The Little Black Boy', spoken as if by a black child, Blake uses the character of the child to draw attention to the collusion of the established church in the practice of slavery, with the suggestion that if black people were to accept their unjust treatment then they would be rewarded by God in heaven. 'The Chimney Sweeper' poems in both *Songs of Innocence* and *Songs of Experience* have a similar theme, this time with Blake using the character of the young chimney-sweep to express his views that the established church seemed to condone the practice of selling children as young as five to be sent up chimneys to sweep them, and certainly did nothing to protect them.

In their study, 'Poetry immersion: reading, writing and performing with secondary students', Schillinger, Meyer and Vinz argue that because many English teachers are required to teach poetry that leads to 'high-stakes assessments', in many cases the teaching of poetry becomes a 'fast-paced, skills oriented trend of broad but shallow coverage' (Schillinger *et al.* 2010: 114). They describe Arthur Applebee's three distinctive aspects of teaching poetry at work in the English classroom: the 'classical tradition' which values historical movements and figures, the 'aesthetic tradition' which values art as it enriches the reader's inner life and encourages imaginative and emotional connections to the text, and the 'moral/ethical tradition' which regards the teaching of poetry as a vehicle for character development and social progress. Schillinger *et al.* suggest that while all three traditions have much to offer, they are rarely used simultaneously in the classroom; because of pressure from the curriculum, teachers are compelled to work within the tradition which 'will best prepare his or her students to do well on a test' (Schillinger *et al.* 2010: 114).

Schillinger, Meyer and Vinz created an experimental poetry class where they were able to consciously blend the boundaries of Applebee's traditions, and this approach has much to recommend it at KS5 where a more sophisticated level of understanding is required. The study of 'The Chimney Sweeper' from *Songs of Innocence* provides us with an example where the combined approach can be utilised to good effect.

The classical tradition

At KS5 students need to know and be able to write about the historical and literary context of poetry. Working out of Applebee's classical tradition, an obvious place to start would be focusing on a biographical study of Blake as a first-generation Romantic poet and what that means. The case study on 'London' (see Chapter 6) describes how Blake's poetry can be introduced at KS4 but at KS5 greater detail will be needed about the social, economic and conceptual changes of the Enlightenment and Blake's reaction to them, as well as the influence on Blake of the unorthodox religious thinker, Emanuel Swedenborg. Crucial to the understanding of the poem 'The Chimney Sweeper' (*Innocence*) is some teaching or independent research into the practice of selling young boys to master sweeps. They were badly treated, having to sweep the chimneys in the early morning before the fires were lit, and some did burn to death. After the morning's sweeping they were put out onto the streets to beg. They suffered from a range of diseases of the eyes and lungs and often from cancer of the scrotum; early death was common. In order to respond to the verse with the depth of understanding required at KS5, students will also need to know that Blake was angry at injustice, cruelty and oppression, and saw the established church as a hypocritical institution which supported a corrupt and unjust status quo.

The aesthetic tradition

Working in the aesthetic tradition invites students to connect with a poem on their own terms, drawing on their experiences and imaginations. In order to stimulate students' imaginations, supplementary texts can be introduced prior to reading the poem, such as the opening section of Charles Kingsley's children's novel *The Water Babies*, which describes a little chimney-sweep (also named Tom): how he cries when he has to climb the chimneys, is beaten by his master and is hungry every day. This will enable students to empathise with the little chimney-sweep, described here in very simplistic language as the story is written for children, compared to that which Blake uses in his poem. Similar to the speaker in Blake's poem, Kingsley's character also accepts his fate without question.

In *Oliver Twist*, by Charles Dickens, there is a passage where Mr Gamfield, a master sweep, describes the practice of lighting fires to make the boys in the chimney come down again as he endeavours to persuade Mr Limbkins at the workhouse to allow him to have Oliver as his apprentice. Reading this will enable students to appreciate the callousness of adults in dealing with the child sweeps. Both extracts will reinforce how widespread the practice of selling unwanted children was, and that for the children there was no choice in the matter as no one was trying to protect them.

Following an exploration of the subject matter, the poem can be introduced. A deeper investigation of Blake's two child characters, the speaker, who tells us his history in the first stanza, and 'little Tom Dacre', who seems to be a new sweep who 'cried ... when his head was shaved', can be achieved by using paired role play with a focus on extending the dialogue between the two boys. This will reveal the speaker's acceptance of his fate and that Tom's dream of the angel who released the boys from their 'coffins of black' leads to Tom's feeling 'happy and warm' the next morning. This exploration will also lead students to realise that not only is the speaker trying to console Tom, but he is also trying to convince both Tom and himself that it does not matter if they suffer in this life because what matters is going to heaven, where everyone is equal. By using the character of the child to express this, Blake makes his point even more forcefully: what kind of society allows children to suffer to such an extent that all they have to look forward to is death? The cruelty which Blake's chimney-sweepers endure seems to the speaker of the poem to be the normal state of affairs. Teaching in the classical tradition prior to aesthetic response enables students to understand Blake's views and therefore to read the final line ironically.

The moral tradition

Working in Applebee's moral tradition means using poetry to help students question and critique social problems, just as Blake himself did. In this case, we are expected to question our own integrity; the poem presents a direct challenge to readers as the speaker says, '*your* chimneys I sweep' (my italics). Although we no longer have child sweeps, we benefit from other examples of modern-day exploitation of children, as some of the harrowing videos on YouTube or the Unicef website will reveal. Asking students to do some research and create their own poem in the style of 'The Chimney Sweeper' is a good way of driving home Blake's message, especially if written in a similar way to Blake's so that the speaker justifies the exploitation.

A close textual analysis of how Blake creates the character of the child speaker will help students to produce their own versions, as well as being invaluable for 'high-stakes assessment'. Nicholas Marsh offers an extremely accessible explanation of how Blake creates the character as deeply fatalistic. He tells his story as 'plain statements of fact, without emotive content' and repeats the conjunction 'so' which connects each stage of the story, thus encouraging that sense of fatalism. As Marsh says, 'Each stage in this grim story is thus presented as an inevitable consequence of the last: the speaker shows no consciousness that the ghastly train of events could be altered or avoided in any way' (Marsh 2001: 110).

The dream is also presented as a 'fact': the angel represents the church and its moral blackmail with the speaker reinforcing the message, 'submit to misery and poverty without complaint. Then, in return, you will be given an optimistic dream' (Marsh 2001: 112).

To successfully write their own poems, students will need to engage with the fatalistic acceptance by the child speaker, the sense of inevitability and some form of religious black-mail. Tom is 'happy and warm' because of the dream of heaven and the speaker cannot imagine any other life. Thus Blake uses the character of the child to highlight the role of the established church in colluding with the unjust treatment of the very people whom it was supposed to protect; by using the character of the innocent child who accepts this fate uncomplainingly, he makes it seem all the more obscene.

Case study: teaching Chaucer's *Canterbury Tales* at KS3

When focusing on character, there is no poetry better than *The Canterbury Tales* for a rich illustration of how character can be brought to life through description, actions and possessions. Written in Middle English in around 1387 the poetry can at first seem impenetrable to the modern ear, however, reading it aloud can aid understanding. Although the spellings are different a modernised pronunciation will lead to an approximation of the word. As Gail Ashton says:

> The easiest way to understand it is by common sense and by informed guesswork for most words sound like our own … If you are embarrassed to read Chaucer aloud, then just modernise it; nine times out of ten the meaning will remain consistent with modern usage, as in words like 'werkyng' (working), 'philosofre' (philosopher), 'fals' (false), 'feendly' (fiendly), or 'shette the dore' (shut the door).
>
> (Ashton 1998: 5)

This approach, coupled with the use of a good glossary, make it possible to read the poetry in the original, which is recommended for A level study. However for KS3, and particularly Year 7, this approach will soon become tiresome and it is much better to introduce an easily accessible amount of text in the original Middle English but then to alternate with an easily accessible translation such as David Wright's verse translation, or the Harvard University interlinear translation readily found online.

I taught extracts from the General Prologue with a focus on how Chaucer had created the characters of the pilgrims to a Year 7 mixed-ability class of boys and girls over a series of lessons. They were a lively class who retained their primary school enthusiasm for all things new and I did not want to kill their enjoyment by having them write an extensive analysis of the poetry; instead the final assessment was to be a creative piece, where they described their own modern-day character by using some of the same techniques that Chaucer had used.

Prior to starting the poetry it was important to do some preparatory work on the Middle Ages (1066–1500). By questioning the class about life in the Middle Ages, I found they were most knowledgeable about the Black Death, which features in the KS2 curriculum, and we enjoyed watching an extract from *Monty Python's Holy Grail* where bodies are collected to the cry of 'Bring out your dead!' Teaching from the front, I led the discussion on the fact that medieval people were very superstitious and believed in both astrology and astronomy because there was a lack of scientific knowledge. Alongside this, people believed in a God who was more likely to punish than forgive, unlike our view of God today, and they often ascribed death and disease to God's punishment for misdemeanours. Finally we reviewed notions of class, propriety and the role of women by drawing a simple pyramid to show the social hierarchy of the times (see Figure 7.3).

Next I described the feudal system in simple terms, explaining that the land was owned by wealthy lords, and the peasants who worked the land were more or less owned by their master, to whom they were bound by duty and loyalty.

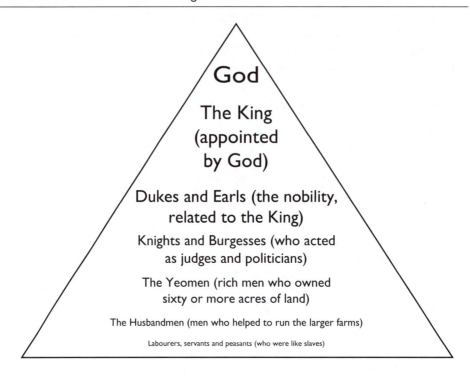

Figure 7.3 Pyramid for medieval social hierarchy

We finished our introductory lesson by watching a twenty-minute DVD of the *Horrible Histories Measly Middle Ages*, during which pupils made bullet points about life in the Middle Ages. Homework was set for pupils to do some research into the story of Thomas à Becket and why people went on pilgrimages to his shrine at Canterbury, using the website www.historylearningsite.co.uk/becket.htm.

The second lesson had language change as its focus. In the activities section of The Oxford Classic Playscripts of *The Canterbury Tales* adapted by Martin Riley, Jenny Roberts suggests three activities to complete which focus on how language changes, such as listing words from other languages which have come into common usage. The Year 7 class came up with mostly food-related words such as pizza, pasta and baguette, which show the preoccupation of the 11-year-old mind. The second activity is to list words for new inventions or discoveries, such as computer, television, email. Again, pupils were able to think of many new words, but

Table 7.1 Grid to demonstrate lexical change (Roberts 2003: 109)

Word	Old meaning	New meaning
wicked	evil	fun or interesting
cool	cold	

the activity they enjoyed most was to create a grid showing how the meaning of a word has changed over the years (see Table 7.1).

After completing these introductory activities, I told the class about *The Canterbury Tales*, where Chaucer had used the framing device of a Canterbury pilgrimage to bring together a wide variety of people, who would not normally mix, in order to create a collection of stories. Referring back to the hierarchy pyramid, I gave pupils a list of all the pilgrims, pointing out that Chaucer described them by their occupations. Pupils had a fairly clear idea of what most occupations were, but needed some explanation about the less well known, for example the Summoner and the Pardoner. We were therefore able to build on our previous discussion about the importance of religion in the Middle Ages. In groups, pupils tried to decide in what order the characters might travel, the highest-ranking going first.

Next we listened to a brief extract of the opening of the General Prologue spoken in Middle English on YouTube, which emphasises the rhyming couplets. Pupils were intrigued by this and commented that although it sounded like German, Scottish or Welsh they could not really understand it.

Focusing on character, I modelled annotating the description of the Miller on the IWB using the interlinear translation, again pointing out the rhyme of the original version. As a class we were able to highlight and discuss the details Chaucer had used, for example what a furnace is like (big, hot and dirty) and why Chaucer might have used this simile to describe the Miller's mouth, and what bagpipes sound like (loud and easily recognised) and what this tells us about the character of the Miller.

Pupils showed their understanding by writing down their first impressions of the Miller, one for example by a girl called Jane reproduced in Figure 7.4 as it was originally spelt and punctuated.

I next put pupils into pairs and gave each pair an interlinear version of the description of one of the following pilgrims: the Wife, the Yeoman, the Nun, the Monk, the Summoner, the Pardoner and the Squire, which allowed me to differentiate character by the ability of the pupils. Pupils read the description to each other, and on sugar paper they annotated the description in the same way that we had done previously with the Miller, underlining anything that described the character, such as details of physical appearance including adjectives and similes, details of clothing, occupation, habits or hobbies, the pilgrim's size and shape, likes and dislikes, whether they are associated with a particular colour and what that might repre-sent, and so on. This was a good way for pupils to focus on the language and detail of the description. The extracts are quite long so it is important to allow adequate time to complete the task. To extend the exploration of the more able pupils I asked them higher-order ques-tions, for example, to explain why they thought Chaucer had associated their character with particular possessions, similes and so on, and to say whether or not they thought Chaucer liked their character and what made them think this.

When they had completed this activity on sugar paper each pupil was given a grid to fill in using their own words, which would help them to synthesise what they had learned about the character and would be used in the second part of the activity, as in Figure 7.5.

Having completed their exploration of their character, I next asked the pairs to join in with another pair who had the same character, making a group of four. Crucial to the success of group work is that each group member knows what their role is and what they are responsible for: this is especially the case at Year 7 when pupils have often not yet developed the social skills to work successfully in a group.

In this case, I allocated the following tasks.

The Miller is a ugly, horrid, nasty, fat, drunken old bloke with no manners. He talks dirty and carries a sword and shield. He has a fox red beard and a wart with hair growing out of it. His head is big enough to brake through a door.

Figure 7.4 Jane's description of the Miller

Name ....   Number ....   Character ....

Body	
Face	
Hobbies and pastimes	
Similes	
Clothes	
Possessions	
Anything else	

Figure 7.5 Pupil grid for character exploration

- Director: to be the group leader and ensure all are on task.
- Artist: to draw a representation of your character and their possessions on A3 paper to show to the class.
- Scribe: to write a paragraph explaining who your character is and what they are like, to be read out to the class.
- Actor: to prepare a performance of how your character would walk and talk and the sort of things they would say.

As is to be expected, some argument ensued as to task allocation, which I allowed the groups to settle by negotiation.

First, the pairs compared their responses to their initial readings of the pilgrims' portraits, revising them where they felt the need. They next carried out their allotted tasks, guiding and advising each other as they attempted to represent their character through their agreed medium.

After the prearranged time, each group came to the front of the class and read out their synopsis of their character, one pupil holding up their picture and another representing him through actions, which the class found most amusing.

For the final lesson I wanted pupils to use their understanding of Chaucer's techniques to create their own characters who might go on a modern-day pilgrimage. As C. D. Benson points out, 'the General Prologue describes types rather than specific individuals' (1986: 96) so I encouraged the pupils to think in terms of stereotypes rather than individuals.

Before starting to write, as a class we agreed a list of rules for what should be included in creating their characters (see Figure 7.6.)

Using these rules, pupils advanced to describe a character. Unsurprisingly, many took the opportunity to describe teachers in a less than flattering light; for example the one in Figure 7.7 by a boy named Sam which starts off as a good approximation of Chaucer's style.

The most satisfying aspect for me as a teacher was when, on telling the class we had finished our work on Chaucer, they let out a loud groan and asked to continue with it. Even though it can seem a fairly daunting prospect to teach Chaucer to the lower years, their enthusiasm, love of word play and delight in the opportunity to be creative make them the perfect audience for Chaucer's imagery.

I	Different social classes – described by occupation.
2	How they looked – how they dressed/what colours, body shape or build, faces – small details.
3	What they did and had.
4	Described in similes.

Figure 7.6 Collaborative rules for creating characters

There once was a teacher who was wicked and cruel,
She liked to torture and torment the little kids at school.
She wore clothes so smart and cool,
She had white greasy hair which was as white as wool.
She was very skinny and lite, old and very hairy.
She had a pusy walt on her nose.
Her nose was as pointy as a pencil.

Figure 7.7 Sam's description

Chapter 8

Narrative in poetry

> He holds him with this glittering eye
> The Wedding-Guest stood still,
> And listens like a three years' child
> The Mariner hath his will.
>   (Coleridge, 'The Rime of the Ancient Mariner')

This chapter will consider the opportunities offered to pupils by the narrative form in poetry. We present a variety of aesthetic approaches in teaching Tennyson's 'The Lady of Shalott' at KS3, and follow this with Clarke's contemporary take on the lasting nature of poetry in 'Miracle on St David's Day' with KS4. We explore Rossetti's 'Goblin Market' for its teaching possibilities with KS5 and the case study, also with KS5, focuses on activities on Keats' 'The Eve of St Agnes'.

What does teaching narrative poetry offer?

Narrative poetry has a long and respectable history. By definition it is 'a poem ... that tells a story' (Preminger 1965: 452) and has two main forms, ballad and epic. Narrative poems were originally recited from memory or improvised. Like a priest or a magician, one who can channel the influence of the muses, a bard would retell a story. With its origins in religious ritual, an epic 'would be the joining of the narration with incantation' (Preminger 1965: 452). One branch of narrative poetry which developed in a secular manner is the heroic epic, in which the story itself becomes the focus rather than the religious element, and in which the hero is the focus of attention, such as *The Iliad*, *The Odyssey* and *Beowulf*. Popular as a form throughout the medieval period, in English the key work is, of course, Chaucer's *Canterbury Tales*, and later Milton's *Paradise Lost*, in which Milton returned to the origin of epic in its use of religious subject matter. The Romantics were interested in narrative poetry, with Wordsworth, Byron, Coleridge and Keats all turning their hands to the form. Yet today the form has fallen out of favour. What does the narrative poem offer contemporary students and how can we teach it? What are we looking for when we do teach it?

One place to start is a consideration of which genre narrative poetry draws on. Culler observes:

> Historically, many theorists of genre have followed the Greeks, who divided works among three broad classes according to who speaks: poetic or lyric, where the narrator

speaks in the first person, epic or narrative, where the narrator speaks in his own voice but allows characters to speak in theirs, and drama, where the characters do all the talking.

(Culler 1997: 74)

Narrative poetry operates somewhere in the midpoint between the genres of lyric and narrative. The form is definitely poetic, and lyrical in the use of stanza, rhythm and metaphor, whereas there are also characters present who 'speak' in their own voices. Whether we agree with Culler's definition above or not, what it does suggest is that in studying narrative poetry, we need to apply the principles of studying narrative, which at its most pared-down is character, plot and chronology and also those of studying poetry, such as language choice, metaphor and repetition.

That narrative poetry has a rich history cannot be denied. But what does it offer today's pupils? There is no doubt that as teachers we are inheritors of the legacy of the National Literacy Strategy (NLS), where the emphasis upon pace and focus 'tacitly encourages the promotion of a "snippet culture" in terms of engagement with literary texts' (Stevens and McGuinn 2004: 66). The legacy of NLS philosophy, which emphasises looking at aspects of texts, not necessarily at whole texts, leaves us in the situation summed up by McGuinn and Stevens in *The Art of Teaching Secondary English*:

> Cutting down on the time and space afforded to 'longer texts' allows less opportunity for that slow, often initially tentative and incremental sense of engagement which challenging works of literature can demand. There are fewer opportunities, too, for re-reading and re-negotiations of meanings, for exploring issues of context and intertextuality or for pursuing some exciting but unforeseen paths of enquiry inspired, perhaps, by a chance encounter with one word or line or ideas from the text.
>
> (Stevens and McGuinn 2004: 66)

When pupils are learning to engage quickly with a large variety of different texts in different forms, what place does narrative poetry have? Perhaps the biggest challenge is actually reading a narrative poem. How does one tackle this with a class? Do we read through quickly, all at once, and focus on the plot, or do we read it as a poem, pausing to meditate on the significance of specific words? In her Introduction to *The Oxford Book of Narrative Verse* Iona Opie writes, 'narrative verse needs a different reading technique from lyric and reflective poetry … A narrative poem is in the nature of a sea voyage … The reader must launch himself boldly…. the adventurer must hasten … He will find that the rewards are great'(Opie 1983: ix). The metaphor of a sea voyage is appropriate, as the reading is both strenuous and rewarding (for both 'he' and 'she'). The teacher must plan carefully the way that the reading is handled and think specifically about the outcome desired from it. With older pupils, such as those at Key Stage 5, an independent reading of the text first is a possible way in, but this will only provide a first impression of the text for most students, if indeed they read it at all. Further, more focused reading, aloud, in class, will support the students' meaning-making. One approach that ensures focused reading is suggested in the case study for this chapter, in reading Keats' 'The Eve of St Agnes'. The teacher needs to decide how to break down the narrative into manageable sections and set a reading task that requires students to be aware of certain qualities of the text as they read it. In the case study, for the opening of 'The Eve of St Agnes', the students were told to read stanzas 1–8 in groups, aloud, changing readers at a suitable punctuation point. In this first section the focus is the stillness and cold of the setting. This acts as an important frame for the later introduction of character and plot, and is therefore very important to structuring the plot element of the poem.

Berry and Madina in *Poems from the Past* suggest approaches to *The Rime of the Ancient Mariner* which are models of the approach to reading narrative poems with pupils at KS3 and 4. Before reading the text, the pupils put in order some pictures that depict incidents from the poem and 'Decide what story the pictures tell and perform it for the class' (Berry and Madina 1997: 104). The pupils will already have started to engage with aspects of the plot in this way and started to build up some imaginative engagement with elements of the pictures, such as the albatross and the sailors. The authors then suggest reading through the first section of the poem indicated in the text, giving the students a brief summary of the plot for that section. In groups of six, the instructions are, 'Read part 1 aloud. Change readers at each set of speech marks. After the reading, retell the story as dramatically and in as much detail as possible.' Reading aloud is crucial. Using the punctuation marks in the text, such as speech or semi-colons, and directing pupils to pay attention to them in this way, is a very significant contributor to the ways in which pupils pay attention to the text. Time must be allowed for the reading, and it is important, once the overall plot has been established by drama or other means, not to rush through detailed re-readings, or else the challenging nature of the subject matter can overwhelm the pupils.

In this chapter we have selected narrative poems that draw on the Romantic and Victorian fascination with medieval romance and epic themes. The level of intertextuality in these poems allows us to draw on a variety of different media to enable the pupils to experience the multiplicity of the texts. The use of references to art, music and other texts is a rich seam of influences to mine to stimulate pupils. One very flexible medium to use is film; it can be used as a tool to examine the techniques of narrative construction and framing in the text, as if preparing the text for filming. In this chapter's case study on 'The Eve of St Agnes', pupils chose to use filmic ideas to interpret the text. They chose to open with an establishing shot of the landscape, as Keats does in the poem. They then moved to the next significant setting in the poem, the chapel, and in order to move there they wanted the camera's viewpoint to swoop into the next shot on the back of the owl, into the chapel. In devising these sorts of activities we are addressing both the plot and stylistic elements of the narrative.

A very useful definition to work with when deciding which aspects to draw out of the poem in terms of the construction of the narrative is this:

> Narrative involves how the events and causes are shown, and the various methods used to do this showing. Exploring aspects of narrative involves looking at what the writer has chosen to include or not include, and how this choice leads the reader to certain conclusions.
>
> (Beard 2008: 4)

Looking at these elements from the study of prose will examine, for example, how a character is naturalised through speech and physical placement and explore the chronology of the text. Once the pupils have got a sense of the plot, we have to move into considering the aspects of the poem that make it different from prose. The elements of poetry that we may consider are the stanza form (see the case study on 'The Eve of St Agnes' for a discussion of Keats' use of the Spenserian stanza form in his narrative poem), and the use of detail, repetition, metaphor and simile. The final point for consideration, once these elements are in place, is reader positioning and the way in which the poet has presented the elements of the narrative to influence our reactions. If we manage to address even half of these issues in a narrative poem, we have been on a 'sea voyage' (Opie 1983: ix) with our pupils and certainly not only worked with snippets.

Narrative at KS3: 'The Lady of Shalott' by Alfred Lord Tennyson

Mark Pike, in *The Canon in the Classroom* (2002) argues convincingly for the opportunities offered by teaching pre-twentieth-century texts. One of their strengths is that they 'constitute a familiar world reproduced in an unfamiliar form' (Pike 2002: 258–9). These texts deal with emotions and human realities, such as joy or pain, which are familiar to us all. How texts from an earlier age appear to the ear and eye may be unfamiliar, but 'active and exploratory readings of the pre-20th century texts' provide 'opportunities for students to explore themselves as readers and to consider human experience in other times' (Pike 2002: 259). Alfred Lord Tennyson's 'The Lady of Shalott' is an accessible and popular narrative poem to use at any key stage. It deals with love, loss, isolation and entrapment, a whole gamut of human experience, which are the same now as at the time in which it was written, and also at the time in which it was set.

Pike continues in *The Canon in the Classroom* (2002) to discuss Jauss and his 'horizon of expectation' (Pike 2002: 360), in which 'all interpretations of past literature are created out of a dialogue between past and present' (Pike 2002: 360). The reader judges texts against what she has already read, so that reading a new work can expand the reader's 'horizon of expectation' (Pike 2002: 360). The greater the distance between reader and work read, or 'aesthetic distance', the more effect this reading will have on the reader's horizon. Similar to Iser's notion of gaps in texts (see Chapter 2), it is these gaps or 'indeterminacy' (Iser, in Pike 2002) that is to be regarded as challenging and fruitful for the reader, 'the indeterminate sections or gaps of literary texts are in no way to be regarded as a defect, on the contrary, they are a basic element for the aesthetic response' (Iser, in Pike 2002: 360). 'The Lady Of Shalott' is a text that is highly enjoyable for classes to work on in an aesthetic and creative way, and also offers many possibilities through the 'dialogue between past and present' (Pike 2002: 360) in a critical reading of the text. There are intriguing areas of indeterminacy in the text that can be explored in the classroom.

There is an abundance of material available on teaching 'The Lady of Shalott', and as teachers we will determine what we want our pupils to get out of the poem, and select resources that are useful. With a KS3 group, one starting point can be tackling the generic elements of the narrative, that is, the setting and characters. Pre-reading activities brings to the fore the intertexuality of these generic elements, as Tennyson has used aspects of the Arthurian legends. Engaging pupils with ideas they are already familiar with serves to arouse their curiosity and interest. Green and Davies have created materials on the text which provide background material and activities on King Arthur and Camelot (see http://www.collaborativelearning.org/ladyofshalott.pdf). Wood and Wood in *Cambridge Poetry Workshop 14+* also suggest working around the readers' previous knowledge of the connotations of Camelot. They provide an excellent plot summary of the poem, to use before coming to the text itself, and they suggest activities that ask pupils to speculate over the story, the possible landscape and the characters of Sir Lancelot and the lady. Having explored opening ideas and activities, reading the narrative aloud in groups or as a whole class is crucial and much can be made of the possibilities of group reading and performance. Again, Green and Davies suggest some lively ways into reading the text and paying attention to the rhythm of the language.

'The Lady of Shalott' lends itself to the use of art and music. There is a 'seductively illustrated version' (Goodwyn and Powell 2003: 51) by Charles Keeping (Oxford University

Press, 1986), in book form, and a very moving sung performance by Lorenna McKennit (see her website for details www.quinlanroad.com). Reading the poem with groups or a whole class, then listening to the sung version while following the text in the Charles Keeping illustrated text, has been known by the author to bring Year 10 boys to tears, most unexpectedly, in their English lesson. A Year 8 class found this so enticing that they asked again and again to repeat the activity in subsequent lessons, quite genuinely hoping to repeat the experience of encountering the poem in this moving and multi-modal way.

Andrew Stibbs, in his article 'For how long, where, and with whom: narrative time, place and company as generic distinguishers and ideological indicators' discusses ways of using place and time in narratives to study 'naturalised ideologies' (Stibbs 2001: 35) that are present in texts. He suggests activities for the classroom whereby narratives can be examined and discussed by pupils, referring particularly to concepts of Bahktin and Barthes. One of these concepts in narrative is the 'Barthesian nucleus' which Stibbs terms 'a "fork" because it presents two alternatives and prods on the plot' (Stibbs 2001: 36). The climactic structure of 'The Lady of Shalott' moves towards this crucial 'fork' in the narrative, and is characteristic of Tennyson's plotting in his narratives, whereby:

> the main character progresses through a series of discrete sections or panels that may take the form of landscapes, states of mind, arguments, or tests until he has a dream, vision, or other powerful revelation that effects a conversion to new ways of life and action.
>
> (Landow 1992)

That the lady leaves her web is a key moment in the narrative. She need not have done so and thereby would not have brought the curse upon herself. Michael and Peter Benton in their poetry textbook *Double Vision* are interested in the relationship between art and poetry, and have devised resources and activities around relating the two forms. In their section on 'The Lady of Shalott' they have group activities that are based around discussion of two artistic representations of the text. Holman Hunt's *The Lady of Shalott*, represents this 'fork' where she decides to leave her loom and the castle, and John William Waterhouse's painting of the lady floating to her death. Representing the plot of the poem using storyboards or sketches enables pupils to present their own visual conception of the poem, which is validated by the use of artists such as Charles Keeping or Holman Hunt and their interpretations of the poem. Activities around the plot, particularly why the lady has taken this decision, could take the form of debates or interviews.

Another of Stibbs's approaches that emerge in his article is the examination of time and place in a narrative. Physical space, he argues, has been 'gender-differentiated' (Stibbs 2001: 38) over time in narratives, and we see this in 'The Lady of Shalott'. The setting is highly significant – the river is beautiful, natural and people come and go along it. By contrast, the lady is 'embowered' in a grey, silent castle. Outside there is movement and life; inside the lady is condemned to experience life second-hand, through her mirror. Stibbs outlines methods of mapping the action of a narrative, using symbols for characters and identifying main settings for the action in the plot. Representing who is present where and when, in a narrative, soon demonstrates patterns such as 'confined and abandoned women' (Stibbs 2001: 37) and men in an active engagement in the world.

The language used in the poem is richly lyrical. The quality of the language changes dramatically at the entrance of Sir Lancelot into the scene. Green and Davies (1994) have devised a language activity that asks pupils to look for the way that he is described in terms of colour, fire, light, jewellery and astronomy. Yet the lady is not even given a name. Goodwyn and Powell examine the ways that using a text such as this in the classroom is a pleasure both in terms of the poetic experience, and also as a way of extending the critical literacy of the pupils. So a language activity such as the analysis of the language used to depict Sir Lancelot can lead into an unpicking of the Victorian cultural norms embedded in the narrative and the 'immense privileging of the male in the text' (Goodwyn and Powell 2003: 138).

If the reading of the 'The Lady of Shalott' is to fully engage pupils, the indeterminacy of the text, Iser's 'gaps', can be a good route to doing this. The text throws up a lot of questions. Why is the lady in the tower? Who put the curse on her? If she can leave the tower, has she chosen the imprisonment herself? What does she look like and what might she be called? All these areas can be exploited in a reading with a KS3 class; students could write a prequel or create a Facebook site for the lady. Equally mysterious is the ending. Sir Lancelot comments 'She has a lovely face' which Goodwyn and Powell call 'rather dismissive' (Goodwyn and Powell 2003: 13) but could equally be interpreted as very tragic: that had they met he would probably have loved the lady as much as she did him. Writing the newspaper coverage for the *Camelot Enquirer* investigating the mystery from the townspeople's perspective, including Sir Lancelot as a witness, is an activity with great potential. Here is another gap that can be filled with speculation and creative responses.

Narrative at KS4: 'Miracle on St David's Day' by Gillian Clarke

Miracle on St David's Day

"They flash upon that inward eye
Which is the bliss of solitude"
The Daffodils by W. Wordsworth

An afternoon yellow and open-mouthed
with daffodils. The sun treads the path
among cedars and enormous oaks.
It might be a country house, guests strolling,
the rumps of gardeners between nursery shrubs.

I am reading poetry to the insane.
An old woman, interrupting, offers
as many buckets of coal as I need.
A beautiful chestnut-haired boy listens
entirely absorbed. A schizophrenic

on a good day, they tell me later.
In a cage of first March sun a woman
sits not listening, not seeing, not feeling.
In her neat clothes the woman is absent.
A big, mild man is tenderly led

to his chair. He has never spoken.
His labourer's hands on his knees, he rocks
gently to the rhythms of the poems.
I read to their presences, absences,
to the big, dumb labouring man as he rocks.

He is suddenly standing silently,
huge and mild, but I feel afraid. Like slow
movement of spring water or the first bird
of the year in the breaking darkness,
the labourer's voice recites 'The Daffodils'.

The nurses are frozen, alert; the patients
seem to listen. He is hoarse but word-perfect.
Outside the daffodils are still as wax,
a thousand, ten thousand, their syllables
unspoken, their creams and yellows still.

Forty years ago, in a Valleys school,
the class recited poetry by rote.
Since the dumbness of misery fell
he has remembered there was a music
of speech and that once he had something to say.

When he's done, before the applause, we observe
the flowers' silence. A thrush sings
and the daffodils are flame.

(Clarke 1982: 9)

'Spots of time' are an important concept in Wordsworth's poetry, and refer to intense emotional experiences in life that can be recalled by the imagination many years later. In this poem, Clarke describes how a poetry recital has the effect of stimulating the memory of an emotional childhood event in the mind of the 'big, dumb labouring man', which causes him to break forty years of silence and recite the poetry he learned at that time: the miracle of the poem.

Because the poem is set in Wales, a useful starter activity prior to reading the poem would be to create a matching activity where pupils are asked to match up the national flags, flowers, saints and saints' days to the countries of the British Isles. This is an active way of reminding pupils that daffodils, St David and the first of March are all associated with Wales and is particularly important in a multicultural classroom where some pupils may never have known this. Also important is a mention of the Welsh mining industry; just enough comment is needed for pupils to understand the reference to 'buckets of coal' in the poem.

Following the matching activity, an exploration of the title including a brief dialogue about pupils' understanding of a miracle and whether they have ever experienced one will enable them to engage with the emotional territory of the poem. They will often tell you stories of accidents they have had where they have escaped unscathed, and some wag will usually quip that it is a miracle they have stayed awake so far into the lesson.

Gillian Clarke starts her poem with a quotation from Wordsworth's 'The Daffodils' so it is necessary to explain to pupils what that poem is about before reading 'Miracle on St David's Day'. Pupils are amused to learn that those of us who were at primary school some forty years ago did indeed learn 'The Daffodils' by rote. There is a nice reading by Jeremy Irons on YouTube which is probably enough for a KS4 class; it is possible to pause on the lines quoted at the beginning of the poem and to explain what they mean: that Wordsworth was so moved by the sight of the daffodils that he can still visualise them at times when he is alone and the memory of them fills his heart with pleasure all over again.

To capture pupils' interest, an exploration into a possible background to the story could be some teaching about the 1966 Aberfan disaster. One hundred and sixteen children and forty-eight adults were killed when a slag heap buried the mining village of Aberfan in South Wales. A PowerPoint or video from YouTube showing images of small children being pulled from the wrecked primary school and their mothers clawing at the wreckage with their bare hands will elicit a powerful emotional response from pupils, and serve to keep the memory of the disaster alive. Although Clarke does not herself make the link explicit, in the penultimate stanza she hints at the cause of the labourer's dumbness and it is possible that he was one of the few children who survived the destruction of the 'Valleys school' some forty years ago, and had not spoken since.

After this the poem itself can be introduced. The poem is read aloud by the teacher, and it does read like a narrative; the enjambment, lack of rhyme, use of present tense and first-person voice all reinforce the idea that Clarke is telling her own story.

Creating one of Tony Buzan's mind maps, using coloured pens and diagrams, will allow for a close investigation of the key features of the narrative, for example narrative voice, setting, time, character and how these are created using poetic techniques such as personi-fication, simile and repetition. They are an invaluable method of saving ideas and making connections between poems, which is a requirement of the examination syllabuses, and are very useful for gathering ideas prior to attempting an examination-style essay.

> Because Mind Maps fit so much on one page, they massively reduce the time needed to structure and prepare work, giving you a whole-picture view at all times. And because everything is so accessible – you're not dealing with pages and pages of notes – they eliminate the stress and unhappiness caused by disorganisation and feeling overwhelmed.
>
> (Buzan and Buzan 2010: 139)

Mind maps have the added attraction of appealing to visual learners: 'Their unique, colourful and creative designs bring to life something that, in linear note form, seemed so boring and "heavy"' (Buzan and Buzan 2010: 139). This visual appeal means they are also useful for revision as they can be displayed around the house in places frequented by teen-agers, such as by the refrigerator or microwave.

The principles of creating a mind map are very simple and are explained in Tony Buzan's books. The main guidelines are summarised in Figure 8.1.

If pupils are not familiar with creating mind maps, it would be useful to model a simple one (see Figure 8.2) on the board with them copying as you go along. This gives pupils a basis on which to add their own original thoughts and link ideas, enabling room for what the reader infers or brings to the poem from personal experience. By focusing on aspects of narrative in this way, pupils are given a framework for writing about narrative poetry when it comes to the inevitable examination.

Principles of creating a mind map
- You start by drawing a picture or symbol of the poem in the centre of the page, using at least three colours.
- Draw branches from the central image with key words and symbols printed on the branch; use one word per line.
- Draw smaller branches on from the main branches, adding facts and ideas.
- Link ideas and thoughts on different branches by using arrows, colours, underlining and boxes.

Figure 8.1 Principles of creating a mind map

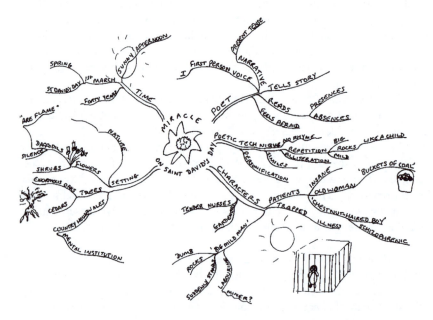

Figure 8.2 A mind map presenting aspects of narrative for study of Clarke's 'Miracle on St David's Day'

Narrative at KS5: 'Goblin Market' by Christina Rossetti

'Goblin Market' has been a popular and much praised narrative poem since its first publication in 1862. The poem is a cryptic fairytale which tells the story of two sisters, Lizzie and Laura, who are tempted to eat the fruit of the goblin men. Although Rossetti herself claimed there was no allegory in the poem, it is almost impossible for a modern reader to see the poem as a straightforward story about goblins and the disastrous consequences of eating the fruits they sell:

> Goblin Market is an enchanting and problematical poem. Its fantastic elements, its religious resonances, and its sexual undertones have led to a variety of critical interpretations, as has the relationship between the poem's two sisters, who have been depicted

variously as Freudian children, figural types, lesbians and, most recently, as 'sisters' in the feminist sense.

(Bentley 1987: 57)

The homoerotic undertones of the poem make possible the discussion of gay and lesbian issues. Kristin Comment describes a time when, as a new teacher, she missed an opportunity to open important dialogue about sexuality and problems of definition, and argues:

> it has become essential that we include this subject matter because gay, lesbian, bisexual, and transgender (GLBT) students both need and deserve to have their feelings and experiences validated. Moreover, most kids today are not just able to discuss these topics (as they were 16 years ago), they are also eager and excited to do so, and we need not look beyond our current curricula for opportunities to bring them up.
>
> (Comment 2009: 61)

We are not suggesting that you should bring up these themes intentionally, but it is highly likely that lines such as 'Hug me, kiss me, suck my juices' (l.468) will be commented on by the class and you should be prepared to respond. The *Teacher's Report* (2009) published by Stonewall, showed: '90 per cent of secondary school teachers say pupils in their schools are bullied, harassed or called names for being – or perceived to be – lesbian, gay or bisexual' (Stonewall 2011).

Teachers therefore have a responsibility to be open to discussions of this nature should they arise, as it is likely they will do in the course of exploring the imagery of this very sensuous poem.

In terms of teaching, the very length of the poem can be a problem, and it can be difficult to know where to begin. As a narrative it should be read in one sitting in order to appreciate the full impact of the storyline so it is probably best to set the initial reading as independent study, with instructions that students reflect upon their personal responses to the poem by making notes that they are prepared to share with the class. Benton *et al.* describe this activity as 'fundamental to the reader's early apprehension of a poem' and argue that the reader 'must have time to reflect on his own responses before participating in group discussion' (Benton *et al.* 1988: 206). As students have chosen to study English Literature at A level it is perfectly reasonable to expect them to read a poem in its entirety, but to help this process there is a very clear reading of the whole poem by Kate Reading available on YouTube to which students could listen as they read. It is important to hear the poem read aloud, particularly as the technical brilliance of the poem 'evinces an oral manner that converts even a reader into a listener, involving him or her in the gradual process of Laura's fall' (Bentley 1987: 69).

Jo Gill further develops the idea of the involvement of the reader right at the beginning of the poem by suggesting:

> the postponement in identification of precisely what fruits these are is supremely effective in placing us as readers in the same position as the 'Maids' .The reader, too, desires to know their true identity ... The poem thus solicits a reading process which re-enacts the very procedure it is describing. We are made to thirst for knowledge about Laura and Lizzie's thirst for knowledge.
>
> (Gill 2007: 120)

The narrative movement of the poem has three broad sections: the temptation of the two sisters by the goblins, the fall and decline of Laura and the happy ending enabled by the heroic and virtuous Lizzie. At A level students are expected to be able to write about how poets create characters, so a useful first activity would be to study the description of Laura, Lizzie and the goblins. Students can relate their understanding of what goblins are from prior knowledge of fairytales and then take some time to look at Arthur Rackham's lovely illustrations of 'Goblin Market' which are readily available online. Discussion on which of Rackham's creatures goes with each description will encourage students to focus on the language of the poem and help them to imagine what the goblins look like. Goblins are usually associated with evil and in this case the repetition of their words, 'Come buy, come buy' (l.4) shows them to be linked with an economic and materialistic view of the world, enticing both the sisters and readers with the attractiveness of their fruit. The goblins are described as having animalistic features and are said to be 'leering', 'queer' and 'sly' (ll. 93–6). The sensuous language and the structure of the verses should be explored alongside the descriptions of the goblins: 'Technically, the opening sections of "Goblin Market" are remarkable for their enactment, in sensual, incantatory, and cumulative (even hypnotic) rhythms, of the visual and aural appeal of the goblins and their fruit' (Bentley 1987: 69).

Following exploration of how Rossetti creates the goblins, another useful activity could be for half the class to investigate the character of Lizzie, and half to investigate Laura by creating mind maps. This will lead to a class discussion about the differences and similarities of the characters, the nature of their relationship and whether it seems to have altered by the end of the poem.

Laura is clearly enchanted by the goblins as she misunderstands their voices and addresses them as 'Good Folk' (l.116). She is described as being 'like a vessel at the launch/When its last restraint has gone' (ll.85–6) which shows the goblins had enticed her to the point she has lost all self-control; the word 'vessel' implying that she is ready to be filled, thus emphasising the sexual element of the poem. Bentley suggests:

> there is no reason to doubt that Rossetti intended her protagonist's frenetic guzzling of the merchants' fruits to be understood in a sexual sense. It was, after all, commonplace in the Victorian period to equate childhood with Eden, and the loss of innocence that occurred at the eating of the apple with a sexual awakening.
>
> (Bentley 1987: 70)

The second section of the poem deals with Laura's decline as she can no longer hear the cry of the goblin men and thus is not able to buy more fruit. Students could list the activities she no longer engages in and relate her physical description to how she declines. Her 'cankerous care' (l.300) bears deeper exploration; a canker is an ulcer so the implication is that the desire for the fruit is eating away at her. Students could do some research into cankers or ulcers and find out exactly what the symptoms are, and perhaps draw parallels between Laura's experience and the experience of drug addiction.

Unlike Laura, Lizzie is not deluded by the goblins and sees them for what they are. They become increasingly angry and attack her in an implicitly sexual manner. Eventually they give up and she runs home, 'The kind heart made her windy-paced' (l.461).

In studying narrative structure, students could be asked to focus on the ending of the poem and how the sisters' lives have changed. They are no longer 'Maids' but are adults with the responsibilities and fears that go with motherhood, which Bentley suggests is a 'confident affirmation that personal disaster can indeed be overcome and unblighted happiness achieved'

(Bentley 1987: 78). Gill, however, argues the ending is ambivalent and that perhaps Laura still desires the goblin fruit; 'one cannot help but see a twinge of nostalgia, a residue of longing, in [Laura's] recollection of the "quaint fruit-merchant men,/Their fruits like honey to the throat" (Gill 2007: 124). A very useful activity for examination preparation would be for students to discuss both viewpoints and find evidence in the text that supports both arguments, and to then articulate their own personal response.

Case study: 'The Eve of St Agnes' by John Keats at KS5

When reading 'The Eve of St Agnes', Keats is positioning us all the time to sympathise with his characters. He was influenced by his reading of *Romeo and Juliet* when writing this narrative and that play is a helpful starting place with KS5 students, as *Romeo and Juliet* is a text that most students are likely to be familiar with, in one way or another. I asked my students to summarise what they knew about the story of *Romeo and Juliet*, and their answers clustered around what they knew of the plot, that Romeo and Juliet are young people who 'fall in love', that Tybalt is killed and Romeo was banished. They recalled that the two characters are from rival families who 'have a long-running feud' and that their love is 'forbidden'.

The students were also very aware of the tragic genre of the play, that Romeo and Juliet die and that they are 'star-crossed lovers'. This is a helpful starting point for 'The Eve of St Agnes', as the narrative poem draws a great deal from *Romeo and Juliet*. The narrative poem is dramatic in its use of plot and dialogue and the time span of the narrative, taking place over one night, does seem to conform to the idea of Aristotelian dramatic unity with regard to time and action.

'The Eve of St Agnes' is concerned with love, and this is an area of the 'emotional territory' (Wood and Wood 1988: 2) that can be mapped out before actually coming to a reading of the poem. Building on the theme of *Romeo and Juliet*, I then asked the students to discuss what version of love the play offers. Some very pithy answers arose, such as 'cruel', 'so near and yet so far', 'bittersweet', 'eternal', 'true', 'doomed' and 'relentless'. These ideas were noted as a point of reference to return to once the version of love offered by 'The Eve of St Agnes' had been studied. I wanted now to move the discussion to the experiences that the students may have had of love, in order that some form of 'live circuit' (Rosenblatt 1970: 25) could be

---

Living somewhere in a medieval past, Porphyro and Madeline are young members of rival, warring families. Porphyro smuggles himself into Madeline's family castle, hoping to see her. It is St Agnes' Eve, in January, and on that night the old folks' tale is that virgins can follow certain customs, sleep and dream of their husbands. Porphyro finds this out from Madeline's old servant, Angela, and when he hears that Madeline is following the old customs, he plans to present himself to Madeline as she is dreaming of her future husband. He hides in her bedroom then wakes her, presenting her with a feast. She accepts his advances in a dream-like state, but when she realises that it is not a dream she is aghast. Porphyro says he has a home ready for her, and they escape the castle together, fleeing into the storm.

Figure 8.3 Plot summary for John Keats' 'The Eve of St Agnes'

prepared with the readers of the poem, before they came to the poem itself. Having worked in groups, I now asked the students to work individually, mindful that these are sensitive matters, and I asked them to reflect silently on what their idea was of a 'dream romance'. It is another area completely to analyse whether the student responses fell into gender stereotypes, but 'The Eve of St Agnes' does bring to the fore discussions about love and the gender depiction within the poem, so I will present the responses by gender. Responses from the males included 'instant spark', 'love at first sight', 'chase then both in love', 'put effort into pursuit' and some responses from the females were 'friendship', 'trust', 'happiness', 'are in love', 'physical attraction'. These responses are very interesting, especially in that the theme of 'pursuit' or 'chase' prefigures a key aspect of the plot in the poem, in that Porphyro pursues and then tricks Madeline. As the students study the poem further, monitoring their responses to the actions of the characters, a comparison to those which they suggested for 'dream romance' can give rise to discussion about how Keats is presenting the characters and positioning our responses.

Moving to the poem, I clustered the poem into particular sections and focused on various aspects of narrative in the separate activities. The first section, stanzas 1–8, focuses on the setting. Keats is very specific in his depiction of the atmosphere of the opening, the coldness of the landscape and the hostility of the rival families. There is much reference to death, age and stillness, which are key to the dramatic development of the poem. I asked one group to make preliminary designs for a theatre set for a dramatisation of the poem, and the other group to make preliminary notes for the opening shots of a film of the poem. The discussion of the text is really the focus here and the students are forced to focus on specific details and signifiers in the language. One very interesting piece of discussion for the design of the theatre set was regarding the character of the beadsman. He is a very old character, and significantly in the freezing night he is 'barefoot'. Why he is present and why he might be 'barefoot' is very much part of Keats's construction of the narrative and this activity forces a visual focus on him.

The discussion for the opening film shots brought into focus an aspect of Keats's construction of the narrative aspect of the poem. Watts comments, 'This the most cinematic of Keats's poems in its pictorial contrasts, colour-range, pace and tracking, and even – literally – in its "dissolves" (Watts 1985: 156). This cinematic quality was brought out in the students' work. They chose to open with an establishing shot of the landscape, noting: dusting of frost, moon, cold frost, trees, owl. The viewpoint then swoops into the next shot on the back of the owl, into the chapel, where the beadsman prays and where there are statues of the dead. It would be possible to see the beadsman's bare feet and the beadsman's breath. The students stressed the significance of the breath, which Keats portrays as being like 'pious incense' (Gilham 1988: 60), and the students wanted the breath to be conveyed in the film as having faces or spirits in it, so that it was as if the beadsman was in transition to heaven. Keats's telescoping of time came to the fore also in this section, as he moves quickly from the detailed, opening, cold deathly scene towards the interior of the castle and the focus for Porphyro, 'These let us wish away/And turn, sole-thoughted, to one Lady there' (Keats 1988: 60).

Reading the poetry aloud is crucial. For the first section, the students read aloud in groups, changing readers at a semi-colon, colon or full stop. The second section, stanzas 9–21, moves from setting to characterisation as its focus, so this time the groups were asked to read aloud in such a way that would dramatise the reading. They divided the narration between two readers and two others read the words of Angela and Porphyro. A very simple task on characterisation followed, whereby in groups they drew a large outline of Angela or Porphyro. With these instructions, they were asked to place labels around the outlines: What details are given to us about the characters? What signifiers? What indications of motive, internal and external? What is the effect of the direct speech? Is there any attributed speech, that is, speech not directly quoted but reported to us?

The groups had a great deal of fun with this task, but the analysis actually required is asking the students to look at the way in which the characters have been constructed through specific literary techniques, perhaps more familiar to the students from studying prose texts. In their pictures, Porphyro was depicted as having red lips, red brow, red heart and a 'heart on fire for Madeline'. The students found Porphyro's tears interesting when discussing the line, 'Believe me by these tears' (Keats 1988: 63) and as signifying a sort of obsession. They characterised him as infatuated: 'Now tell me where is Madeline' (Keats 1988: 60) and that he was perhaps a threat to Madeline, as Angela has her doubts about him: 'wicked men like thee' (Keats 1988: 64). They also felt Porphyro was creepy and sly: 'he stood hid from the torch's flame' (Keats 1988: 60) and manipulative: 'hide in closet' (Keats 1988: 60). I had not anticipated such a negative reaction to Porphyro from the students, as I tend to view him posi-tively, like Romeo, as a devoted lover. However, the students' perceptions mirror a number of critical reactions to the poem, especially more modern interpretations.

The students depicted Angela as witch-like, laughing 'St Agnes' Eve! Ha, ha, ha!' and being clearly associated with age and weakness: 'A poor, weak, palsy-stricken, churchyard thing' (Keats 1988: 64). The details of her 'palsied hand' (Keats 1988: 64) and her 'ivory headed wand' (Keats 1988: 64), along with her movement of shuffling along led them to conclude that Angela 'Plays on the fact she is old and weak, to try and change Porphyro's mind but ultimately she gives in.' The students felt that, generally, she was not a great guardian of Madeline's safety, and comparisons arose between her role in aiding and abetting Porphyro with that of the nurse in *Romeo and Juliet*, as both of these characters are morally ambiguous.

The next activity, which is based on stanzas 22–7, was undertaken before a reading of the specific section. Moving from the narrative elements of the poem, we were now starting to focus specifically on the poetic form and word choices of the stanzas. The students were all given a word cloud generated in the free program Wordle, easily accessed on Google, in which the text is arranged into random patterns, with words of greater frequency coming out in larger font. Individually, the students linked any words together in the word cloud that they felt were linked in any way, such as by sound quality, rhyming, meaning, or any kind of word association. The groupings that emerged were very interesting:

- Body parts: 'desire';
- Action: 'pressed knees';
- Sense of climax;
- Nature: 'seaweed', 'moonshine', 'sun';
- Death: 'darkness',' twilight', 'illness', 'age', 'frayed', 'wreathed', 'chilly', 'smoke';
- Lack of control: 'trembling', 'tongueless', 'heart-stripped', 'oppress'd', 'perplex'd';
- Contrast in emotions;
- Vulnerability and youth;
- Love: 'blushed', 'joy', 'light', 'heart', 'soul'.

The students commented that there did not seem to be much speech compared with the previous two sections, and that there were a lot of strong and effective adjectives, which were exactly the sort of language details that I wanted them to notice. We discussed what these words suggested about the content of the next five stanzas and predicted their content. Having read as a group stanzas 22–7, we labelled stanza 24 with the rhyme scheme and worked out rhythm. We then discussed why Keats' rhyme scheme for 'The Eve of St Agnes' has been described has having a 'sweet-slipping movement' (Sidney Colvin cited in Gilham 1988: 153).

The final activity undertaken for the first read-through of the poem was a written response from Keats to his publisher after Keats's revisions before publication were rejected as 'unfit for ladies' (see Gilham 1988: 154 for details). This was a popular activity, as both the stanza that was published, and Keats' revised one, are quite racy in their nature. See Figure 8.4 for a sample of a very able student's response.

Returning at the end to the students' own definitions of love and looking at the depiction of love in 'The Eve of St Agnes' is an interesting area for discussion. The way that the poem ends, as a fairytale, not as a tragedy, ensures that the poem is regarded by the reader in a completely different way to a tragedy such as *Romeo and Juliet*. It establishes a relationship with Keats' other poetic works, such as the great Odes, in that there is a central section of joy and connection, framed by opening and closing sections of bleakness and loss. 'Ode to a Nightingale' or 'Ode on a Grecian Urn' are good texts to compare this with, along with another of Keats' narrative poems, 'Lamia'.

Mr. Woodhouse,
Did you awake 'warm in the virgin morn'? Did you awake well rested and content after an all-encompassing and impenetrable sleep? Did you emerge from that 'dizzy stream' of fleeting, hyper-exaggerated emotion and accelerated vision satisfied with the world that slowly emerged around you, moving into focus as you opened your eyes?

I, Sir, did not.

How could I possibly awake 'warm in the virgin morn' when it is these very words which – amongst others – so offended your sensibilities, which attacked your moral worldview to the point of forcing you to demand their deletion? No: I did not enjoy the soothing embrace of sleep but instead spent a fitful night contemplating the notion that my poetic hand is no longer mine, that some invisible hand controls my own and crafts my verse.

Figure 8.4 Extract from a student's letter written as John Keats to his publisher

Chapter 9

The poetry of conflict

We few, we happy few, we band of brothers:
For he today that sheds his blood with me
Shall be my brother; be he ne'er so vile,
This day shall gentle his condition;
   (William Shakespeare, *Henry V*: Act 4, Scene 3, ll.60–3)

In this chapter we explore the changing nature of poetry in the face of war and how we might use this poetry with our pupils. 'The Sentry' by Wilfred Owen is used as a focus for approaches to a First World War poem with KS4. 'Vergissmeinnicht' by Keith Douglas is used with KS3 as a poem from the Second World War and the women's voice is considered through Vera Brittain's 'Perhaps' at KS5. The case study considers the experience of modern warfare, with an active approach to the study of poetry from the conflict in Afghanistan through 'The Last Patrol' by SSgt Colin Clark with KS4.

Introduction: teaching the poetry of conflict

Ever since ancient times poets have written about conflict; there is therefore much to choose from depending on what we as teachers want pupils to gain from the study. In the lower years, poetry lessons will often focus on the narrative form, the language of description and basic poetic techniques such as rhyme and rhythm. The Anglo-Saxon heroic epic *Beowulf*, dated between the eighth and the early eleventh century AD, is a lasting favourite, and can be made accessible by studying short extracts in translation alongside an illustrated prose publication, such as that by Michael Morpurgo, or Kevin Crossley-Holland's version illustrated by Charles Keeping. Younger pupils enjoy the story of battles and monsters, and particularly enjoy creating their own kennings.

The character of the knight came to the fore in poetry after William the Conqueror landed with his cavalry, and the early *chansons de geste*, narrative poems of heroic deeds composed in Old French, related real historical events such as experiences in the Crusades.

James Anderson Winn argues that primary sources from the Middle Ages reveal knights to be brutal, ruthless and violent, and that the values later associated with chivalry, such as courtesy, Christian piety, fairness to defeated enemies, chaste adoration of ladies and appreciation for poetry, owe very little to historic fact. He maintains they are a poetic construct derived from the poetry that followed the *chansons de geste*: the lyric songs of the troubadours, the chivalric romances recounting the legends connected with King Arthur and the elaborate chivalric epics of the Renaissance (Winn 2008: 109).

Whatever the historical truth, pupils very much enjoy learning about knights. Chaucer's description of the Squire from *The Canterbury Tales* is easily accessible to lower years and can be read with a focus on description and creation of character, whilst Tennyson's 'The Lady of Shalott' is a perennial favourite (see Chapter 8).

Poetic construct or not, Jon Stallworthy suggests that notions of chivalry which came with the knightly code of conduct pervade war poetry, and are a thread that can be followed right up until the Second World War in Keith Douglas' 'Aristocrats', which acknowledges 'both the stupidity and the chivalry, the folly and the glamour of cavalrymen on mechanical mounts duelling in the desert' (Stallworthy 1984: xxix).

Stallworthy describes how teaching at the first so-called 'public schools', which opened in the fourteenth century, and others later modelled on them, focused on a mixture of classical learning and 'chivalric training in honour, in sport, in military exercise, in social intercourse, in courtesy and generosity, in reverence and devotion, of the schools of Christian knighthood' (Hearnshaw 1928, cited in Stallworthy 1984: xxi). Notions of chivalry therefore became firmly embedded as part of the shared consciousness of the educated élite.

Stallworthy further suggests that Thomas Arnold's highly influential reforms to Rugby School in the 1830s, which were followed by other public schools, caused a revitalisation of the public school system resulting in many Anglican boarding schools admitting the sons of the middle classes in the 1850s to make 'Christian gentlemen' of them:

> The ethos of these schools was essentially chivalric … schoolboy fights were elevated into gentlemanly duels, and on the playing field the same school etiquette called for 'fair play' and 'team spirit' … and the curriculum was dominated by Latin, and to a lesser extent Greek.
>
> (Stallworthy 1984: xxiv)

Henry Newbolt's 'Vitaï Lampada' of 1892 neatly illustrates how a sporting code acquired on the playing fields of a public school came to be translated to the battlefields:

> The sand of the desert is sodden red –
> Red with the wreck of a square that broke
> The gatling's jammed and the colonel dead,
> And the regiment blind with dust and smoke.
> The river of death has brimmed its banks,
> And England's far, and Honour a name,
> But the voice of a schoolboy rallies the ranks –
> 'Play up! Play up! And play the game!'
>   (Henry Newbolt ll.9–16 in Stallworthy 1984: 146)

Notions of war as a game, which would somehow follow rules and be fair, can be seen in the early poetry of the First World War; Jessie Pope's patriotic 'Who's for the Game?' is a prime example. Prior to the First World War, battles had been localised affairs or fought on foreign soil, far removed from the everyday consciousness of the people of Britain. The sheer numbers involved in the First World War meant that almost everybody in Britain was touched in some way or other. The education of the working classes meant that for the first time in history Britain was sending to war a reasonably literate army. Working men sent letters home, and wrote poetry alongside the officer class who had been educated in the classical tradition of chivalry and saw war as a Hellenistic adventure. The poetry was full of moving and highly personal accounts of devastating experiences; it is this that makes the poetry of the First World War so compelling. For the first time the soldiers themselves described their lived experiences through the medium of poetry, rather than having a poet interpret and celebrate it for them.

Towards the end of KS3 and later, when we hope they have gained some emotional maturity, pupils are able to fully appreciate the moving impact of poetry from the First World War, which has long held a place in the English curriculum. The poetry goes through a series of transformations as the war progresses, exhibiting the influences of the natural imagery of Georgian poetry at the beginning of the war, as demonstrated by the optimistic patriotism of Rupert Brooke, through the bitter satire of Siegfried Sassoon and compassion for the troops expressed by Wilfred Owen.

The technological advances of modern warfare proved too much for the loyal steed as man and horse became tangled on the barbed wire of the battlefields, and the carnage of the Somme Offensive in 1916 meant it was no longer fitting to write poetry about the glories of fighting with your brother in arms. The nature of warfare had changed, and with it the nature of war poetry. Soldier-poets described warfare in new and uncompromising terms, and on the home front women were also using poetry as a means of expressing their grief.

Rosenberg's poem 'Dead Man's Dump' is now acknowledged as one of the undisputed masterpieces of First World War poetry. In the final stanza the poem changes viewpoint to that of the dying soldier who sees the mules and limber come crashing over him:

> Will they come? Will they ever come?
> Even as the mixed hooves of the mules,
> The quivering bellied mules,
> The rushing wheels all mixed
> With his tortured upturned sight.
> So we crashed around the bend,
> We heard his weak scream,
> We heard his very last sound,
> And our wheels grazed his dead face.
> (Isaac Rosenberg ll.78–86, in Stallworthy 1984: 185)

In the years following the First World War artists perceived a fragmentation of society which was reflected in the art and poetry of the time. Picasso and Braque had developed Cubism which enabled the breaking down of the subject so many facets could be seen at once; Dada, a European literary and artistic movement, was established as a reaction against the futility of the war. Had Rosenberg survived, it is possible his poetic style would have developed to convey numerous viewpoints, similar in style to the multiple voices of Eliot's 'The Waste Land'.

The poetry of the Second World War has received less attention than that of the First and is less often studied in schools; however, two poets worth noting are the British cavalryman Keith Douglas, who wrote of his experiences in the North Africa campaign, and the American airman Randall Jarrell. Lorrie Goldensohn suggests:

> In Great War poetry, the soldier is dominantly the victim, the hostage to the plans of others. But in World War II, Jarrell finally makes a significant alteration, asking the soldier to hold himself as agent as well as pawn of his society, although inexorably he also makes the responsibility for prosecuting and accepting war spread over all of us, combatant and non-combatant.
>
> (Goldensohn 2003: 180)

Goldensohn argues that Jarrell, who had doubts about the ethics of twentieth-century indus-trial war-making, 'stands stylistically, substantively, and historically between Wilfred Owen and Siegfried Sassoon, who came before him, and the American poets of the Vietnam War, who came after, in his accounts of soldier culpability within war's violence' (Goldensohn 2003: 178).

American poets of the Vietnam War are rarely studied in school, possibly because the sometimes graphic imagery can make them unsuitable for KS3 and KS4, and there is no room for them on the examination-driven curriculum at KS5. However, if space can be made, perhaps after Year 12 examinations and before starting Year 13 proper, these poems have much to offer as a means of gaining understanding of the individual voice of the soldier-poet and the pervasive damage war does to both individuals and families, as well as how form and structure support meaning. In these poems, the poets actively identify them-selves as 'agents of pain and war, as "agent-victims" of their own atrocities' (Goldensohn 2003: 237).

Students could fruitfully compare the subject matter of Bruce Weigl's 'Song of Napalm' (in which the image of a girl destroyed by napalm has burnt into his memory) with Wilfred Owen's nightmare visions of 'The Sentry', or Herbert Woodward Martin's 'A Negro Soldier's Viet Nam Diary' (in which a soldier discovers a dead mother and child in a river) with Robert Graves' graphic descriptions of 'A Dead Boche'. (Both American poems can be found in Mahony 1998.) Although methods of waging war have changed, the images of pain and suffering witnessed and written about by poets have not.

Much American poetry of the Vietnam War is written in *vers libre*, which Goldensohn suggests gives it 'an intense urgency and acts to restore narrative as a lyric force':

> In their late twentieth-century positioning, down go the walls of genre, and poets are free to plunder the richness of the novelist's range of detail. We see them draw, from a realism that stretched from Emile Zola to Tim O'Brien, the body and all the soldier body's acts: its sweats, its nightmares, as the body goes from the harrying of peasants to the shit-burning details of latrines and all the exigencies of its sexual needs.
>
> (Goldensohn 2003: 251)

Like poetry of conflict from earlier wars, American poetry of the Vietnam War expresses the most dramatic of human experiences and the most keenly felt emotions. The form may have changed but the emotions expressed and the poetry that results is some of the most moving and therefore most rewarding to teach.

Technological advances have meant that not only the methods of waging war have changed, but also the ways in which it is recorded. Servicemen and women now in Afghanistan and Iraq are able to keep in contact with their loved ones through social networking sites, and there are many poetry sites available for them to publish their poetry; the speed of publishing on the internet gives the poetry a sense of great immediacy. The public are able to read about real experiences and gain greater understanding of the emotional impact conflict has on service personnel. In teaching the poetry of conflict, we hope to enable pupils to reach a deeper understanding of the real sacrifices made by both those engaged in it, and their loved ones who are affected by it.

Conflict poetry at KS3: 'Vergissmeinnicht' by Keith Douglas

Vergissmeinnicht

Three weeks gone and the combatants gone
returning over the nightmare ground
we found the place again, and found
the soldier sprawling in the sun.

The frowning barrel of his gun
overshadowing. As we came on
that day, he hit my tank with one
like the entry of a demon.

Look. Here in the gunpit spoil
the dishonoured picture of his girl
who has put: *Steffi. Vergissmeinnicht*
in a copybook gothic script.

We see him almost with content,
abased, and seeming to have paid
and mocked at by his own equipment
that's hard and good when he's decayed.

But she would weep to see today
how on his skin the swart flies move;
the dust upon the paper eye
and the burst stomach like a cave.

For here the lover and killer are mingled
who had one body and one heart.
And death who had the soldier singled
has done the lover mortal hurt.
(Douglas 1978: 111)

Keith Douglas died on 9 June 1944 during the D-Day landings in Normandy, at the age of 24. Most of his war was spent in the desert conflicts of the Middle East and North Africa. He is now regarded as one of the foremost poets of the Second World War. His most commonly anthologised work is 'Vergissmeinnicht', in which he describes the experience of coming across the body of an enemy that the speaker had encountered three weeks previously. Should we tackle such a poem with pupils from KS3? Michael Morpurgo argues that we should. In an article by him that appeared in *The Times* in 2004, the strapline summarised his argument:

War IS sad. Don't hide it from your children. With Remembrance Day and Iraq our children are bombarded with images of war. What should we tell them? The Children's Laureate says that as the border between childhood and adulthood blurs, it's best to be honest.

Morpurgo argues that we cannot protect children from the images that bombard them through the media, and that books and poems have a role in helping them deal with what may be the consequence of this input. This is as true today as it was in 2004, with images of various conflicts and deaths ever-present on our screens.

Douglas wrote a prose account during his time in the desert, *Alamein to Zem Zem*, and it is worth taking this into account with the poem 'Vergissmeinnicht'. He writes of the way the men in the desert felt about what they were doing and the enemy they were fighting:

> Men ... at intervals moved by a feeling of comradeship with the men who kill them and whom they kill, because they are enduring and experiencing the same things. It is tremendously illogical – to read about it cannot convey the impression of having walked through the looking-glass which touches a man entering a battle.
>
> (*Alamein to Zem Zem*, Keith Douglas, cited in Piette 2008: 117)

In 'Vergissmeinnicht' the theme emerges of a 'looking-glass', where the enemy is essentially the double of the soldier himself, as the speaker muses on the humanity of his dead enemy. Another concern of Douglas' is the relationship between the machinery of a mass industrial war and the physical bodies and sacrifice of the soldiers. He sketched as well as writing poetry, and his sketches reflect the same concerns:

> The dead bodies littering the sands in Douglas's sketches are often draped over their jeeps and tanks, or juxtaposed against weapons, the line of scribble making animals of the machines, marionettes of the dead, and generating an indistinguishable man-machine.
>
> (Piette 2008: 119)

In 'Vergissmeinnicht', this theme occurs with the soldier 'sprawling' under the shadow of his own gun and his equipment being 'hard and good' whilst the soldier is 'decayed'.

'Vergissmeinnicht' opens with a style similar to reportage, with the speaker describing the area that they are in and hinting at what happened there previously, 'returning over the nightmare ground'. The voice is that of the professional soldier. He observes the area in which he fought with an enemy who 'hit my tank ... /like the entry of a demon.' Douglas wrote in a letter to another poet in 1943, 'reportage and extrospection (if the word exists) poetry ... seems to me the sort that has to be written just now' (Douglas cited in Piette 2009: 18). The use of this type of 'extrospective' reportage certainly characterises the observational quality of this poem. However, as the poem moves forward, through the observed detail, juxtaposition and visual imagery, the perception of the reader is changed, as the speaker's seems to. We come to see the dead enemy as a human, a lover, no longer a demon. It is this change in the perception of the reader that is the basis of the work suggested here for the pupils, as they investigate the way that the presentation of detail and use of imagery work to provoke a profound emotional response from the reader.

One place to start with a poem such as 'Vergissmeinnicht' is asking pupils to consider what might be needed from the individual in order to fight in a war. Pupils may well be familiar with *Private Peaceful*, a very popular text particularly for Year 8 pupils, or perhaps even younger than that. Morpurgo writes of where the idea for the text came from:

> Of all my books that touch on war *Private Peaceful* might seem the one that is too harsh, too painful for a young audience. ... I read of one young man of 18 who had fought through the Somme. In rest camp one day with the guns still firing he turned to his

friend and said that he 'couldn't stand the sound of the guns any more, that he was going home'. He was arrested, tried and condemned. Men from his own company were obliged to make up the firing squad. In protest they stood over his grave till sunset. I wanted to write that young soldier's story.

(Morpurgo 2004)

In order to fight effectively, individuals must have to believe that they are fighting for a just cause and to some degree dehumanise themselves and demonise the enemy. *Private Peaceful* explores the complexity of an individual soldier's experience, the pressures of war, in an introspective fashion, exploring the character's interior world. Building on what pupils are likely to know about this text, or using extracts from it, can open up the emotional territory of the poem. Working also on the use of propaganda in the Second World War to demonise the enemy, such as images of Hitler or of Nazis, can also prepare the ground.

One way of introducing the poem could be through presenting it as a word cloud generated in the free program Wordle, easily accessed on Google. The text can be cut and pasted into the program, which arranges it into various patterns, with words of greater frequency being presented in larger font. Word clouds can be produced in any colour and font combination and produce intriguing configurations of the words from the text. Pupils can use this to group words, speculate on word relationships and predict what the poem might be about, beside looking up unfamiliar words in the dictionary. Giving the pupils the meaning of *vergissmeinnicht*, forget-me-not, could entice the pupils to speculate further on the content of the text.

Another a very good introductory activity for the poem has been submitted to one of the Teachit discussion forums: 'cut out all individual lines of the poem, just give each group a sheet of sugar paper with the first line of each stanza and get them to place the rest of the lines' (Petra 2008). This activity requires that the pupils discuss in detail the progression of the poem, by addressing the changing movement of each stanza. The pupils will also be looking at the sentence structure and rhyme scheme to try to determine which sections go where. The rhyme scheme of the poem is unstable, which adds to the effect of a shifting perspective in the poem; the sentencing is variable, using fragments and enjambment to depict the cumulative and forward movement of the thoughts and reactions of the speaker.

Once the pupils have decided the final organisation of the poem, they will need to read it aloud, ideally in groups or pairs, at least twice. The authors recommend as standard practice that pupils read a poem first time line by line, and a second time from punctuation point to punctuation point, in groups, as this will always bring to the fore the poet's organisation of the language; without guidance pupils generally default to reading aloud line by line. There are two versions of the poem available on the internet; a reading by Ralph Fiennes (http://ralphfiennes-corner.net/poetry_corner/poetry_corner.php?id=25) and one on YouTube (http://wn.com/Vergissmeinnicht_by_Keith_Douglas_poetry_reading). The YouTube reading includes an image of Keith Douglas and a version of the postcard from the poem, which could be a useful resource.

Having read the poem, an activity which focuses on the progression through the poem from viewing the enemy as like a 'demon' to a 'lover' could be the use of a Twitter feed. Using the Twitter format, easily available on the internet, pupils devise, in groups or pairs, a Tweet for each stanza of the poem. This would engage them in text transformation, where they would have to elicit the essence of the stanza and transform that into a unit of 140 letters. The imagery of the poem is very visual, and another activity that pupils could engage in could be to plan, as a war photographer, a photo-journalism piece that includes six still images of the scene, that records the scene as the journalist travels with the combat group that includes Captain Douglas. This type of activity could also form the basis of drama work, creating freeze-frames for different moments in the poem or bringing in props that the pupils think relate to the poem.

Further creative approaches could be to consider what else the dead soldier might have in his pockets, to build up an idea of what he might have been like as a character. In R. C. Sheriff's *Journey's End* there is a moment in Act 3, Scene 1 where Osborne empties his pockets of significant objects, before he goes to his death. Using a clip from this (http://www.youtube.com/watch?v=x-x2_CExhJo&feature=related) and discussing the objects that a soldier might have, could lead to some very interesting suggestions about the construction of character and the use of detail that has wider signification. This could lead to drama work or creative writing either about the dead enemy soldier or improvisation and hot seating of the characters present at the scene with Captain Douglas. Creative writing outcomes might be text transformation pieces, such as a battlefield report by Captain Douglas or a letter home from him. If a literary critical analysis is required, the outcome of the Twitter feed or the photo-journalism exercise will have focused the pupils on the detail of the language, so that structuring an essay-style response will build on the active approaches taken towards the text.

Conflict poetry at KS4: 'The Sentry' by Wilfred Owen

When approaching a poem such as 'The Sentry' by Wilfred Owen, a variety of factors have to be considered. How much knowledge – lexical, contextual or historical – do the pupils need to make sense of the poem? In what ways do we want the pupils to interact with the poem? If we are committed to the notion of a 'live circuit' set up between reader and text, how can we put measures in place that enable this realisation of the text to occur? As Fleming (1996) comments, 'the balance is a delicate one because it is important not to convey a tacit message that the pupil's task is merely to uncover the poem's objective and correct meaning' (Fleming 1996: 39). We hope that we can facilitate some kind of 'dynamic happening' (Iser 1978: 22) between reader, or community of readers, and the text. As teachers, we need to start with pupils and their own experience, however far removed that seems at first glance at a poem. First World War poetry offers some particular difficulties here, as we are lucky enough to live in an age where most, although certainly not all, of our pupils will not have encountered being in a war zone or the realities of fighting. However, we need to find some way of accessing the experience in the poem that Owen is recounting if the pupils are to make meaning out of it for themselves. In that way, using the experience of being in a dug-out, somewhere underground, is one way into the territory of the poem. So, before reading the poem, the pupils can work on these questions and visualisation exercises, individually, to begin to 'map out the territory':

- Have you ever been underground – in a cave or a mine? Jot down some words or phrases to describe how it felt to be there.
- Close your eyes and imagine yourself underground, in a mine or a cave. How do you feel?
- How would you feel if there were a lot of people in there with you?
- How would you feel if there was no light? What might you smell or hear?

Working on the title, and exploring what our preconceptions of a sentry are, and what the poem might be about, again opens up the anticipation of the poem to come.

The importance of reading poetry out loud cannot be overestimated, and 'The Sentry' offers much dramatic potential. Reading the poem, aloud in groups, twice, is an excellent starting point. If groups read the poem first, line by line, which is often the way that groups will naturally incline, they are responding to the shape and rhyming on the page. If they are then required to read from punctuation point to punctuation point, each reader determining which punctuation point they read up to, immediately the poem starts to come alive. Doing a dramatic reading, in groups, in something that 'The Sentry' lends itself to, as there are elements of direct speech, recall and description that may determine how the groups choose to dramatise the text. An expert reading by the teacher, or one that is recorded, also allows the text to come alive. At this point, again moving back into individual work, pupils can record their initial reactions to the poem. In this way they can respond to any element of the poem, or the reading of it, without teacher intervention.

The 'delicate balance' that Fleming describes is one that always has to be borne in mind. There comes a point where the comprehension of a poem needs to be broadened further into the context of the poem. For WWI poetry there is a plethora of material easily accessed through the internet, and contemporary photographs and images are rich sources of inspiration. Using a selection of laminated images from the war, ask the pupils to look at the images and write, in a group, words and phrases that relate, in some way, to the images. For 'The Sentry', images of fighting on the First World War battlefields, dug-outs, gas masks and blinded and wounded soldiers have particular resonance. Responses to this exercise with pupils brought about comments on the relationship between the verb 'herded' (Owen 1981: 198) in the poem to an image of soldiers crowded in a trench. A very interesting discussion evolved around the similarity of the shape and appearance of a gas mask and Owen's image 'eyeballs, huge-bulged like squids' (Owen 1981: 199). A couple of images of the battleground and soldiers going over the top enabled the pupils to relate the noise and chaos apparent on the battlefield to evocation of the shells as 'frantic' (Owen 1981: 208) and to the proximity of the battlefield above and the dug-out below, where the shells 'hammered above' (Owen 1981: 208). Equally such an exercise with pupils combining images and text works using the IWB or PowerPoint. The key point is that the pupils are exploring the detail of the text, moving around it, making all the choices themselves.

Drama is a very powerful medium with which to further explore the poem. With 'The Sentry', it is possible to exploit the fact that Owen was invalided out of the army for a while and went to Craiglockhart hospital, suffering from shell shock, or as we might term it post-traumatic stress disorder (PTSD). The next activity that pupils can use to explore the poem can be a structured improvisation around a visit by Owen to his psychiatrist, who, for this purpose, was named Dr Frobisher. In using improvisation, the technique has to be carefully set up, so that pupils will take the exercise seriously. It is very useful to be able to tell some form of anecdote about Owen and his life, so the exercise springs from a real event.

The pupils then work in pairs, preparing for Owen's meeting with his doctor. One pupil is Owen and one is his psychiatrist, Dr Frobisher, who of course could be male or female. They will need, individually, to prepare for the improvisation. Dr Frobisher prepares questions for Owen, and the pupil playing Owen will need to reflect on the poem in detail, thinking about the impact of what he has experienced. If it is possible in terms of space, the pupils then need to set up a small space that will be the doctor's office, so that Owen can come into the space in order to discuss with his psychiatrist. The setting up of the space adds a further dimension of taking the activity seriously and preparing for it. The pupils are then told to improvise the discussion, along the lines of:

- Pupil 1: Dr Frobisher needs to explore what happened to Owen and how he is feeling now.
- Pupil 2: Owen has recurring nightmares and cannot sleep. He needs to go through the incident with the doctor, explain what happened and try and get it out of his system.

Feedback can be taken orally, or pupils can record the outcomes in the form of doctor's notes for Dr Frobisher and Owen's diary after the interview. Having undertaken this improvisation, it was clear that this activity really brought out for the pupils the impact that such an occurrence on the battlefield had for the speaker of the poem, from both the doctor's and the patient's perspective.

Having undertaken these activities, the pupils should be ready to consolidate and record their knowledge of the poem, as a basis for whatever assessment outcome might be required for the poem. They annotate the poem, but more or less without guidance from the teacher. They can be given a 'language hunt' sheet, and in pairs or groups annotate their own copy of the poem with the guidelines shown in Figure 9.1.

The pupils, having participated in a variety of readings, text selection and imaginative engagement, are very familiar with the poem by the time that they come to record their responses. They are confident in applying the technical terms and poetic analysis that they are, ultimately, required to do for assessment purposes.

Other written outcomes that are creative reinterpretations of the poem could be:

- Improvisation and/or script of the conversation of other men in the dug-out;
- Diary entry for the other soldiers in the dug-out;
- Letter home from another soldier in the dug-out to a relative, describing what happened to his friend;
- Letter home to the sentry's family from an army doctor or Owen himself as CO;
- Official report of Owen as officer to those in chain of command above him about the sentry's injury;
- Effect on Owen: his diary entry about this at Craiglockhart Hospital;
- Dr Frobisher's report on Owen.

Language Hunt! Highlight key words and annotate them with explanations for yourself

- Effective verbs, especially 'herded'
- Imagery: squid, smell of men as a curse
- Smells and animal associations
- The gaps between the verse paragraphs: what is the significance of these?
- Pronouns: move between 'we' and 'I'
- Use of direct speech
- Can you see a relationship between the rhythm and the rhyming and the meaning at any point here?

Figure 9.1 Language Hunt for use with 'The Sentry'

Pupils can compare 'The Sentry' very effectively with many other poems by Wilfred Owen, for example; 'Dulce et Decorum Est', 'Strange Meeting', 'Futility' and 'Exposure'.

The female voice in conflict poetry at KS5: 'Perhaps' by Vera Brittain

Perhaps

Perhaps some day the sun will shine again,
And I shall see that still the skies are blue,
And feel once more I do not live in vain,
Although bereft of You.

Perhaps the golden meadows at my feet
Will make the sunny hours of spring seem gay,
And I shall find the white May-blossoms sweet,
Though You have passed away.

Perhaps the summer woods will shimmer bright,
And crimson roses once again be fair,
And autumn harvest fields a rich delight,
Although You are not there.

Perhaps some day I shall not shrink in pain
To see the passing of the dying year,
And listen to Christmas songs again,
Although You cannot hear.

But though kind Time may many joys renew,
There is one greatest joy I shall not know
Again, because my heart for loss of You
Was broken, long ago.

(Brittain in Reilly 1981: 14)

Vera Brittain's moving poem was written in response to the death of her fiancé Roland Leighton, who was shot by a sniper in France in 1915. As a Voluntary Aid Detachment nurse, Brittain had first-hand knowledge of the horrors of trench warfare and recorded her experiences in her autobiography, *Testament of Youth* (1933).

Simon Featherstone suggests that while Owen's and Sassoon's early poetry had similar influences to that of Brittain, unlike the male poets whose poetry evolved in response to the extremity of their war experiences, the female poets published in Reilly's anthology *Scars Upon My Heart* (1981) suggest 'both formal limitations and uncertainty about the appropriate mode of writing to deal with the female experience of war' (Featherstone 1995: 96). Ultimately this is probably because the female experience was so vastly different; the deaths of millions of men meant there were millions of women whose lives were blighted by the loss not only of their men but also of their chance of motherhood. Yet despite the evident suffering of women, female writing about the First World War has been very much overshadowed by that of males.

Marcello Giovanelli suggests a pre-reading activity that is designed to encourage students to consider the possible causes of that misrepresentation which would be useful prior to the study of any First World War poetry written by women.

> 2225 British individuals wrote poetry during the First World War, of whom 532 were women.
>
> Why do you think that women's poetry during or about the First World War is so under-represented in anthologies and classrooms? What crucial differences might you imagine there to be between men and women's writing about the First World War? What different concerns might each have? Why?
>
> (Giovanelli 2010: 221)

Giovanelli suggests this question could lead to any number of responses, including those which focus on the position of women in Edwardian society and those that consider theme and content of the poetry (Giovanelli 2010: 226). It is certainly a very useful way of getting students to consider their own classroom experience, which may well have been dominated by the study of Sassoon, Owen, Brooke and Rosenberg, and whether or not their experience of studying literature written during or about the First World War had perpetuated the dominant ideology of patriarchy.

Brittain's poem expresses a grief not only for her loved one, but also for the many delights of nature that she can no longer experience as she is numbed by misery. The poem has a passive tone, which seems to indicate that she has been worn down by sorrow and has no fight left in her. The references to natural imagery mean that the poem can usefully be approached through giving students a 'crunched' version, where the words are rearranged into alphabetical order (see teachit.co.uk for an online tool that manipulates text). Students then have the task of sorting words into groups that they think go together, such as those that express sorrow and longing and those that describe the natural world. From this activity students should be able to comment on the juxtaposition of the two sets of imagery, and say how the beauty of one group of words makes the other seem all the more bleak as the speaker is no longer able to appreciate the splendour of the world around her.

Reading the poem aloud in its correct order will emphasise the simple rhyme scheme and long vowel sounds which accentuate the sad tone of the poem. Students should note that it was written in February following the December death of Brittain's fiancé, and appears to speculate on how she will get through the coming year, described season by season. Asking students to paraphrase the poem in their own words to express how the speaker expects to feel during each season may result in a paragraph that in effect says 'the sun will not shine again, the skies are not blue, my life is pointless' and so on. This activity effectively removes Brittain's poetic imagery, and an interesting discussion could ensue as to whether by doing this the voice becomes a more masculine expression of grief. Students will need to speculate on what the 'one greatest joy I shall not know /Again' might be, based on their understanding of sexual mores of the time and whether their understanding of the line is influenced by the fact it is a female voice.

The ambiguity of the capitalised 'You' also bears some exploration. Students may be familiar with the biblical tradition of capitalising God as 'You', and certainly Brittain would have been. This could therefore lead to another layer of interpretation and students should be encouraged to express their ideas on whether they think at this point Brittain may have lost faith in God and what might have caused this, or whether it is simply an expression of how important her fiancé was in her life.

Finally, the importance of the title needs to be assessed. By asking students to remove the word 'perhaps' from the poem and discussing the effect this has on the tone of the poem they may well reach the conclusion that the poem takes on an altogether more optimistic tone. The modal auxiliaries 'will' and 'shall' make the speaker seem certain that things will indeed improve for her, rather than experiencing the doubt that is associated with the word 'perhaps'. However, the final stanza does not conform to the anaphora of the first four and therefore serves to emphasise the 'one greatest joy' that Brittain does not expect to experience again; she does not imagine she will ever love again.

If the students were to place the poem in terms of when or where it is set, they will realise there is nothing in the poem that places it specifically as a First World War poem. This is another main difference between this poem and much male poetry of the period, and as such it becomes a timeless expression of grief pure and simple. It is just as poignant read at funerals today as it was when it was written 85 years ago.

Case study: poetry from the conflict in Afghanistan with KS3, 'The Last Patrol' by SSgt Colin N. Clark

The Last Patrol

White faced, we left the base,
time for one last look around.
But insurgents knew, as they do,
wasn't long 'til we are found.
Soon we take a frag grenade,
then RPG's were inward bound.
Men are falling, corporals calling.
Need to cross that open ground.
Legs pumping, hearts thumping,
have to reach the next compound.
Gunships flying, Taliban crying,
multi-rockets all hellhound.
Mortars popping; more men dropping,
bits of bodies all around.
Bodies flying, people dying,
screaming wounded; terrible sounds.
Then cross a ditch, where life's a bitch,
it's hand to hand; the victor crowned.
More men bleeding, wounded pleading,
thank God none make English sounds.
Then we see some escapees flee;
running, scampering, scared foxhounds.
But life's unfair because we call in air,
and bomb them where they've run to ground.
We count our men, a quick amen,
no time for speeches; too profound.
So it's sort our heads, count their dead,
and get our wounded safety bound.

But soon we hear, what squaddies fear,
artillery shells are inward-bound.
The leaders shout, 'Move on out,
this is no longer our playground'.
We dash out fast, before first blasts,
still no-one earns a Reaper shroud.
Then when we ask, for our next task,
Head-Quarters has us all spellbound.
For all you hear, was a great big cheer,
even now the echoes still resound.
'Get back to base, and pack your case,
Your job is done, you're homeward-bound!'
'Tour over!'

(Clark 2010)

Teaching a half-term course on literature from or about war to a mixed class of 34 high-ability Year 10 pupils as preparation for GCSE coursework, I felt it was important to include some study of contemporary war poetry written by serving soldiers, particularly as we had reached the sad position where most of now knew somebody who had been affected by the war in Afghanistan. The coursework assignment was to be a creative response to the poem, where pupils were to write an imaginative autobiography of the poem's speaker; one of the resources Long and Hopkins recommend for performers of poetry (Long and Hopkins 1982: 54).

While pupils are aware of the war from the wide news coverage, achieving a deeper level of empathy in response to poetry written from the battle zone requires careful preparation. In order to achieve this higher level of empathy, I based my lessons on Steven Athanasas' very interesting technique of studying poetry through performance, where pupils spend time looking deeply into a single poem and reflecting on what they have learnt through the process of rehearsal and performance. In his unit of work, Athanasas describes how he used the 'performers' resources' recommended by Long and Hopkins, adapted as in Figure 9.2.

Athanasas' pupils spent seven days working on one poem and he therefore recommends they should have a choice in the poem they select for such detailed study. Due to timetabling restrictions I had three ninety-minute lessons to spend on one poem and was not able to achieve the really deep exploration that Athanasas had; rather it was in this instance an introduction to the techniques he used in the hope of developing them in future lessons. I therefore chose one poem for the whole class to study, the main criterion being that it had what Athanasas calls 'the high definition speaker', that is, the 'I' or 'we' that invites role play of the speaker as a character' which Athanasas makes clear is the key to the success of this kind of study (Athanasas 2005: 89).

Because the poem was written by a soldier serving in Afghanistan, pupils were very receptive to it from the outset, which was a refreshing change to the usual groans that greet me when I say we are going to study some poetry. In order to attempt to understand the author's experiences, we first of all watched the trailer from *Restrepo* (2010) Tim Hetherington and Sebastian Junger's documentary which follows the lives of a US platoon deployed to Afghanistan's Korengal Valley. Pupils listened carefully to the soldiers' interviews and jotted down some of the emotions portrayed.

Following Athanasas' example, I planned lessons which would incorporate many of Long and Hopkins' 'performers' resources' in what I thought was a logical sequence. One boy volunteered to read the poem out to the class, after which pupils individually wrote down

- Read a text out loud as a means of exploring it.
- Get a sense of how it feels by hearing it read out.
- Carry on a 'mental discussion' with the text.
- Talk back to the author. Raise questions.
- Determine the 'plain sense' of the text.
- Find out the meanings of difficult references and vocabulary.
- Write a paraphrase.
- Clarify who is doing or saying what and when.
- Use physical, vocal, and psychological exercises to prepare for performance.
- Do warm ups to improve performance and try to create an inner monologue to help feel more like the speaker would.
- Find subtexts. Choose the appropriate subtext from among several possibilities.
- Find what lies behind the words and the reason they are said.
- Write an autobiography for the speaker.
- Imagine the wider life of the speaker.
- Dramatic analysis.
- State what is going on to whom at a literal level.
- Comparing responses.
- Compare your responses with a friend, critic or even the writer.
- Action of the lines.
- Name the verbs for what the speaker is doing as he speaks each line.
- Overall meaning.
- Say why you think the text is significant.

Figure 9.2 Performers' resources (adapted from Long and Hopkins 1982: 52–6)

their initial responses which included, 'quite sad, chaotic, fast, lots of death, pain'; 'real life, true, death, and blood' and 'full of pain and terror, loud and noisy'.

Working in pairs I asked the class to paraphrase any difficult passages, which did not take long as on the whole they found the language and surface ideas very accessible. Pupils then wrote down three questions they would like to ask the author, which was our first step in trying to construct an idea of the author's personality. Questions asked could be roughly divided into two types: those which focused on the specifics of life as a soldier, such as 'Did you see the RPG coming towards you?' and 'How long do you stay in Afghanistan at one time?' and those which sought deeper understanding of the emotions of the author, such as 'What did you feel when you found out your tour of duty was over?' and 'How does it feel to see your friends dying and knowing you could be next?' This type of questioning corresponds with the idea of having a 'mental discussion' with the text.

The next activity was for pupils to complete a 'dramatic analysis' of the poem, where they wrote down what they imagined the speaker to be doing on a literal level as the poem progressed. Pupils wrote down verbs such as 'running, shooting, shouting' which reflected their initial impressions of the poem as 'chaotic, fast, loud and noisy'.

Next I explained what finding the subtext means, using Athanasas' example of 'I wonder what time she'll get here' which in Athanasas' study communicated the subtexts:

1   She's always late.
2   I can't wait till she gets here.
3   She thinks she's all that!
4   We're going to miss the train.
            (Athanasas 2005: 90)

I allowed pupils to work in friendship groups of four, and instructed them to choose one or two lines per group, for which they would then generate the subtext. Every person in the group would speak the same lines, each attempting to communicate a different subtext by tone of voice, expression and body language, for example the line 'artillery shells are inward-bound' generated the subtext:

1   I don't want to die.
2   Will I be next?
3   Duck for cover, please stay safe.
4   Oh not again!

This activity enabled pupils to explore the emotions behind the lines, to gain a deeper understanding of how the author would be feeling and how he would express the lines were he to perform the poem. One boy commented that he found this a really useful activity because although he could usually understand the words on the page, this activity helped him to understand the meaning behind them, which of course was exactly what I was hoping for.

The second lesson began with a recap of the poem by getting pupils to explore the drama of the poem by writing down their answers to a series of questions as suggested by Athanasas, with the responses of a female pupil in italics, as seen in Figure 9.3.

The final exercise was to explore the poem through a physical enactment, in the same groups of four as the previous lesson. Pupils selected one person to perform the poem and the others in the group directed their enunciation and physical embodiment. Pupils were instructed to rehearse it aloud several times, practising until the words became familiar and comfortable. In Athanasas' words, to 'Make them your own so you speak meanings and subtext and not just someone else's words' (2005: 93).

When they were ready, the performer switched groups and performed to another group, who watched and listened and then provided specific feedback using the checklist recommended by Athanasas. The performers made notes of the feedback they were given, and then working individually pupils reflected on the activity by writing about any new discoveries they had made through the performance of the poem, again using Athanasas' prompt sheet, as in Figure 9.4.

Once the performances were completed pupils were asked to write down what new discoveries they had made through the performances. One of the performers read the lines 'Then we see some escapees flee; running, scampering, scared foxhounds' with a sense of heavy disdain, which prompted the response:

I discovered that underneath the tough exterior of the army, they are the same as everyone else, they're afraid of death. Underneath the sadness more feelings are there for example relief and even a bit of snideness and hierarchy over the Taliban.

1   WHO is the speaker in the poem (the character speaking the words of the text)? Tell anything you know about the speaker's gender, age, personality, attitude, tone.
    The speaker in the poem is the poet. I believe he is a male who is quite young. He has seen many terrible things he will remember for the rest of his life. I think he is very brave and determined and that is how he survived the war to tell his tale.

2   WHAT is the situation in the poem?
    In the poem the soldier had a last mission to complete and after that they get to go home.

3   WHERE and WHEN is the speaking of the poem happening?
    I think he wrote this after the war when he is back in his home country. It is not long after as the image must be clear in his head.

4   WHY is the drama of the poem being told? (For example, to explain, convince, delight in, and so forth)
    The poem is being told to explain about war and what it is actually like, how much pressure and stress you're under.

5   HOW is the drama of the poem told? (For example, any particular language devices, rhyme and meter special structure or style, and so forth).
    The poem is told with a rhyme scheme which is quite unusual but one that suits the poem. It flows very well.

Figure 9.3 Performance workshop – peer response groups: suggestions for listeners (Athanasas 2005: 94)

- Listen carefully to the performance; watch the performer, not the text.
- After the performance, consult the text. Praise the performer for any strengths you found in the performance of the poem. Be concrete. See sample responses below. Remember the risk of performing in front of others. Offer peer support, but be specific.
- Ask questions. Make suggestions. What would you like to see more of? What might be clearer, more fully conveyed in performance? Use the text to guide your suggestions. You are giving tips for a revision of this performance. Help the performer think about what specifically to do in rehearsals to strengthen this performance for the next time.
- Some sample questions and tips for support and revision
- I got a clear sense of your speaker's bitterness about bigotry among the townspeople, especially in lines three through five.
- Line two confused me in your performance. What subtext did you have for that line?
- I got a sense of mild anger in the lines about her husband's betrayal, but I wonder if intensifying that to rage might be more appropriate considering what she has experienced.
- The first eight or so lines seemed precise, but the rest seems to need more rehearsal.
- I didn't get a sense of how you meant the closing two lines to be delivered. What verbs did you have for the action?

Figure 9.4 Performance workshop – peer response groups: suggestions for listeners (Athanasas 2005: 94)

- Get serious. Treat the performance as a serious event. Give the poem and poet the respect they deserve.
- Take your time. Your poem performance may be brief. Let each moment of the poem live as you perform it fully.
- Embody the speaker. Look at listeners or focus your gaze in the distance, according to what the poem warrants. You may want to use a prop or two appropriate to your speaker and the poem's drama. Think about gestures your speaker might make to enhance the poem's full meanings and feelings. Assume the role of the poem's speaker.
- Make it a meaningful performance. Think of all the planning you have done (written responses, drama of the poem, subtext, action of the lines). Use all of these things in your performance: know your speaker's specific reasons for speaking each phrase and line of the poem, and try to convey these in your performance.
- Note feedback. During the feedback part, write notes on suggestions from your peers.
- Revise and rehearse carefully. Use feedback from your peers that seems reasonable to you as you rehearse for the final performance of your poem.

Figure 9.5 Performance workshop – peer response groups: performer preparation (Athanasas 2005: 94)

Performance of the poem meant that pupils had formed Rosenblatt's live circuit (see Chapter 2) and had been able to evoke the intellectual and emotional meanings required to create well thought out, plausible coursework assignments. As Athanasas observes,

> Performance … supports Rosenblatt's metaphor of a silent reader who 'performs the poem or the novel, as the violinist performs the sonata. But the instrument on which the reader plays, and from which he evokes the work, is—himself' (279) However more than just metaphorically 'performing' through silent reading, students turn a poem text into a notated script that guides an actual performance of particular embodied feelings and meanings.
>
> (Rosenblatt 1976: 279, cited by Athanasas 2005: 89)

Chapter 10

Multi-modality and new technologies

And therefore as a stranger give it welcome.
There are more things in heaven and earth, Horatio,
Than are dreamt of in your philosophy.
(*Hamlet*, Act 1, Scene 5, ll.165–167)

We consider in this chapter the use of information and communications technology (ICT) and multi-modal texts as a means of engaging pupils in the English classroom, with particular emphasis on the teaching of poetry. We stress the importance of using ICT as a way of encouraging higher-order thinking skills and promoting dialogic teaching, and present a number of examples where ICT has been used in this way with poetry. The complexity of issues surrounding multi-modality and the teaching of poetry are explored, and we emphasise the role of the teacher in setting up conditions for exploratory teaching.

With the updating of the National Curriculum in 2008, the use of multi-modality in English became fully embedded in the KS3 and KS4 curriculum. It was an acknowledgement that 'how young people relate to and understand media, and in particular moving image media, should be a central focus of our education system' (McCloskey 2005: 17). Sue Dymoke defines multi-modal texts as those which 'operate in two or more modes to create their meanings' (Dymoke 2009: 135). This can include a whole variety of options where text, images and sound can combine; moving images such as film, television, video, computer games; still images such as picture books, cartoon, comics, graphic novels, adverts, magazines, posters and web-based media platforms such as websites and social networking sites. Using the opportunities provided by multi-modality is a rich seam to be mined in the teaching of poetry. The use of multi-modal texts is inextricably linked with the use of ICT, although multi-modal texts are not exclusively technology based. In the classroom, the boundaries between print and electronic media are developing and shifting all the time. However, although the possibilities for using different media and ICT platforms are ever changing and developing with the affordances of the technology, the ultimate aim of using them with poetry remains the same: looking to create opportunities where, in the words of Ted Hughes, it is

occasionally possible, just for brief moments, to find the words that will unlock the doors of all those many mansions inside the head and express something ... of the deep complexity that makes us precisely the way we are ... when words can manage some of this ... we call it poetry.

(Hughes 1967a: 124)

ICT and the teacher

One of the most attractive ways of teaching multi-modal texts is through the use of ICT: whiteboards in classrooms, computer suites and bookable laptop facilities. The discussion of teaching methodologies about multi-modal texts comes under the wider umbrella of the use of ICT in English more generally. Schools have embraced technology wholeheartedly, as have all workplaces. We do not question the ubiquitous expectation to incorporate ICT into our lessons. However, Torgerson and Freeman describe the evidence base for the effectiveness of ICT and literacy learning as 'fragmented' (Torgerson and Freeman 2005: 218) and there is 'a challenge for government agencies and researchers to develop approaches which support evidence based informed practice by teacher' (Torgerson and Freeman 2005: 219). Andrews and Haythornthwaite discuss, in the introduction to the *Sage Handbook of E-learning Research* the example of the IWB:

> There is little substantial research on the topic … and yet many schools have installed them in place of blackboards or other forms of large-scale projection in the classroom. Reports are anecdotal, based on perceptions of pro-technology innovators and even of the technology vendors, with reviews of their use describing and justifying, post hoc, the use of whiteboards in the classroom.
>
> (Andrews and Haythornthwaite 2007: 25)

So, beyond anecdotal conversations and the publicity material of various technology companies, there is not a very extensive evidence base about the effectiveness of ICT on learning outcomes in the classroom.

Given that we are all using ICT in school, we need to ensure that we use it effectively to stimulate learning. The challenge in schools is that of moving beyond using ICT to 'write up assignments, Google or watch DVDs' (Burke 2008: 49) to a pedagogy of engagement and creativity. The use of ICT needs to promote active, not passive, learning. Lankshear and Knobel, in their chapter 'New technologies in the secondary English classroom' discuss the term 'digital busy work' operating in the English classroom, which they explain as being where:

> learners use new technologies to perform lower-order tasks – such as locating information within sources provided by the teacher, in order to answer pre-set questions, or to render text generated by pen and pencil as web pages, or as ornate 'slides' created with presentation software. Digital busy work contrasts with the kind of work where learners integrate the use of the technologies into higher-order challenges, such as conceptualising an issue or problem, designing strategies for addressing it, and evaluating the outcomes of implementing those strategies.
>
> (Lankshear and Knobel 2007: 101)

The references to Bloom's revised taxonomy are key here. Rather than giving pupils lower-order tasks, in which they do not go any further than describing and explaining, albeit using attractive visuals and whizzy features, ICT should rather encourage work at the higher-order end of the scale, generating new ideas and making judgements. ICT can help motivate pupils to become involved in creative activities, in which they synthesise ideas and recreate knowledge.

The most significant factor in the use of technology in the classroom is the teacher. One good definition of the role of the teacher is that of a 'mediating presence' (Andrews 2007: 131), who works to bridge the gap between 'the technology and the experience of language'

(Andrews 2007: 131) of the pupils in the classroom. Andrews argues that the teacher's 'values, disciplinary knowledge and pedagogical approach are critical to the student experience' (Andrews 2007: 131), that it is us and the way that we set up the classroom and the tasks that the pupils engage in which are crucial factors. It is not that students are using ICT that is creating a stimulating learning environment; rather it is how they are using it, how we are setting up their opportunities and how we structure the challenges for our learners.

Using multi-modality and poetry: a model of learning

Adrian Burke outlines one approach to the use of multi-modality and poetry using ICT, in which pupils interacted, enjoyed themselves and analysed in a creative and critical fashion in 'Filming poetry; an audiovisual approach to poetry appreciation' (2008). Burke wanted to explore the notion of 'mood' with KS3 pupils, support pupils in articulating their responses and exploit the potentiality of ICT to enhance their close reading. Burke's project took as its starting point the idea of mood and what that might be. Pupils were asked to respond to the mood of some visual images and musical clips. They were provided with a mood sheet, with a vocabulary list, which they could use to support their articulation of ways to describe mood. For the music, pupils in pairs worked on a variety of 20-second clips, listening to changes in mood in the music and how this was signified, such as through shifts of rhythm or volume. With images, pupils worked in close detail observing specific pictures. A viewing grid supported the pupils in the way that they observed the images, guiding them to pay attention to detail in the images (see Figure 10.1).

In encouraging the pupils to pay very careful attention to the signifiers of the mood shifts in art and music, the pupils were paying attention to important details. Burke wanted to promote the skill of close reading, as the aim of the project was ultimately to film one poem, 'Cold Tea' by Craig Bradley. In preparation for the filming, having worked on the idea of mood, the pupils then came to the poem and annotated it in two ways, for mood and for image. The annotated poem then formed the basis of the selection of still images, digital photos or pictures selected from other sources, that could be ordered and structured around the poem's changes in mood. In this way pupils were very much working collectively, creating and synthesising ideas, using the ICT as a tool and combining words, images and music. They were also working in minute detail with the language of the poem. As Burke suggests, 'In this project, the need for close reading skills arises because you need to unpack a poem's images and moods before you "shoot" the film' (Burke 2008: 50).

The introduction to the *Sage Handbook of E-learning Research* identifies four aspects that define learning, derived from the broad base of knowledge that exists on learning theory. In summary, these four elements are that learning produces new knowledge in a learner, that learning is based in community, that learning takes place in relation to other bodies of

Top left	Top middle	Top right
Centre left	Centre	Centre right
Bottom left	Bottom middle	Bottom right

Figure 10.1 Viewing grid (Burke 2008: 49)

knowledge and that knowledge is a 'transformative act' (Andrews 2007: 47) that charts new territory for the learner. Burke's project illustrates these principles. The first principle is that learning is a 'personal and social/political transformative act in which new knowledge is gained by the learner' (Andrews 2007: 47). In this, the individual learns something new by undergoing a transformation in her understanding of something. In Burke's project the pupils really came to grips with the notion of 'mood'. They took the idea and were able to apply it in different contexts and use it to create their own product.

The second principle is that although 'learning is experienced by the individual, it is essentially an effect of community: not only in knowledge generated and preserved by a community throughout history, it is also learnt as an effect of being part of a community' (Andrews 2007: 48). A community preserves knowledge, passes that on, and we learn, as with Vygotsky's argument, by talking together in a social environment. We have a body of knowledge that we, as a culture community, value and preserve, such as the poems we study. We construct knowledge with others, so that in the case of the project, the pupils worked together, constructing knowledge, working together on the features of 'mood' in images and music, then applying that to the poetry. They are using the technique of close reading, or in terms of Bloom's hierarchy, application and synthesis. The body of knowledge, in this instance, is what constitutes poetry, how it is written and how it creates its effects. The project deals with how, as readers, the pupils construct meaning in relation to the poem and its effects, and then how they communicate their interpretations of it, in another medium.

The third quality of learning, using Andrews' summary, is that learning is differentiated from simple experience, by taking place 'in relation to bodies of knowledge' (Andrews 2007: 48). Thus, the pupils have learnt about mood through their own experience, yet this work is defined by its relationship to a body of knowledge. Burke himself refers to T. S. Eliot's notion of the 'objective correlative' in poetry as a starting point for defining 'mood' for the pupils, referring to Eliot's use of the location in 'The Love Song of J. Alfred Prufrock' as an objective correlative for 'the loneliness and desolation of modern life' (Burke 2008: 49). Burke rendered this relationship with a body of knowledge more simply for the context of the pupils that he was working with, but nevertheless they were working with this in mind. He also made reference to the fact that 'close reading is an ability which teachers at A Level and beyond often say their students lack' (Burke 2008: 50).

The final quality, outlined by Andrews, is that 'the transformative act creates new knowledge that is the product of a learner's (or learners') research and exploration in territory previously unrecognised or uncharted' (Andrews 2007: 49). That the pupils can create a new form for the poem, using images and sound, moves to a new level their understanding of the poem and the way that its effects are created. This is definitely a project that exemplifies the way in which using multi-modality with poetry can promote 'higher-order challenges' (Lankshear and Knobel 2007: 101) and exploit the possibilities of working collaboratively.

Multi-modality and dialogic teaching

Kennewell and Beauchamp studied and continue to study the impact of the use of ICT on the interactivity of teaching. One of their findings has been that ICT is at its most effective when it is used to promote dialogic teaching. In their article 'The influence of ICT on the interactivity of teaching' (2008), they conclude that when ICT is used as a tool for interaction, setting up discussion and collaboration, it is at its most effective. When it is used, lecture-style, as a part of a didactic, authoritative style of teaching, its impact on achievement is much less than when it is part of a rich, interactive classroom environment. One of their conclusions is that:

It is the depth of interactivity which is more important in stimulating learning (Kennewell *et al.* 2007). Most teachers adopting ICT use it for relatively authoritative teaching approaches, and our results suggest that they should try to identify how it can help them achieve a more dialogic approach to whole-class teaching.

(Beauchamp and Kennewell 2008: 312–3)

They conclude that it is not using ICT that stimulates learning, it is how it is used. If ICT is used for a more 'authoritative' lecture, PowerPoint style learning, then it is less effective than when a dialogic approach is taken to the pedagogy in the classroom. They discuss whether stimulating learning and interactivity is linked to the 'scale of learner influence over the course of activity' (Kennewell and Beauchamp 2007: 306), but conclude that 'more research and development is needed concerning how ICT can be used to support deeper interactivity in groupwork … and more dialogic interactivity when used with individual students' (Kennewell and Beauchamp 2007: 313).

The features of good teaching, those of promoting dialogue, independence and interactivity, are present when teachers use ICT effectively. Kennewell and Beauchamp relate these to the notion of 'dialogic teaching' (Alexander 2008), which is an approach that has its roots in a great deal of research into the effectiveness of talk in the classroom since the 1970s. Drawing on Vygotsky's principles of the interrelatedness between thought and language, the idea of a dialogic pedagogy is defined as being characterised with dialogue in the classroom, explained here as:

> being collective (teachers and students address the learning task together), reciprocal (teachers and students listen to each other to share ideas and consider alternative viewpoints), supportive (students articulate their ideas freely without fear of embarrassment over 'wrong' answers and support each other to reach common understandings), cumulative (teachers and students build on their own and each other's ideas to chain them into coherent lines of thinking and enquiry), and purposeful (teachers plan and facilitate dialogic teaching with educational goals in mind). Most importantly, it can take place in whole class, group-based and individual interactions between teacher and students.
>
> (Hardman 2011: 36)

It is crucial, then, that talk is at the heart of what we do in the classroom, and that we build that into our use of ICT, as we would any other approach to English. Exploratory talk is a crucial means of building learning together, or what Neil Mercer terms 'thinking together' (Mercer 2000). Mercer defines this type of talk, which is a collaborative venture and a joint construction of knowledge, thus:

> Exploratory talk is that in which partners engage critically but constructively with each other's ideas. Relevant information is offered for joint consideration. Proposals may be challenged and counter-challenged, but if so reasons are given and alternatives are offered. Agreement is sought as a basis for joint progress. Knowledge is made publicly accountable and reasoning is visible in the talk.
>
> (Mercer 2000: 98)

In the next section we present a number of examples of where ICT has been used in an interactive way with poetry and multi-modality, where individual teachers have modelled the principles of dialogic teaching and the use of talk within their planning and teaching of poetry.

Using multi-modality with poetry: promoting dialogic teaching

So what are the ways in which we can pursue these higher-order skills and provide for dialogic teaching using ICT? The English classroom has become a 'home for a complex range of pursuits' (Lankshear and Knobel 2007: 99) but what it is, above all, is a community. Community is crucial to learning. Vygotsky argued that learning is a social process; we learn by talking to each other and 'human learning presupposes a specific social nature and a process by which children grow into the intellectual life of those around them' (Vygotsky 1978: 88). ICT can exploit this aspect of community and provide ways of accessing activities and processes that require higher-order thinking.

One example of work with poetry in the classroom and ICT that promoted a dialogic pedagogy through the use of ICT is the work with 'The Lady of Shalott' described by David Gibbons in his project 'Talking with Tennyson: interpreting The Lady of Shalott in the internet age' (2007). Even the title of the project foregrounds the significance of talk to the project. Working with Year 6 students to produce a film for a real audience, the members of the Tennyson Society, the teachers and students worked collectively towards the outcome, and worked reciprocally. As Gibbons notes, 'we all learned from and challenged each other' (Gibbons 2007: 2). The pupils undertook activities such as selecting and photographing images in the local neighbourhood to capture the visual imagery of the poem, and as Gibbon comments, 'the quality of debate about what to photograph and why, constantly referencing the text, was very high' (Gibbons 2007: 2). Here the students are genuinely in control of the decisions that were made and the collaborative discussion about the process.

The photographic work was then built upon by drama work, using the visual imagery of the poem and the lady's dilemma: whether or not she should look out of the window at Sir Lancelot. The pupils were involved with empathising with the lady, debating over a 'conscience alley' piece of drama, and using their imagination to work through her situation (for information on this technique see http://www.dramaresource.com/strategies/conscience-alley). Next the pupils explored the artwork and visual imagery that has derived from 'The Lady of Shalott' and is available on the internet, researching in a self-determined way. Thus the activities built in a supportive, cumulative and purposeful way towards an outcome. Finally, using Photo Story 3 software, the 'pupils worked collaboratively to produce just one film' (Gibbons 2007: 2), which combined images with lines from the original texts, along with music selected by the pupils. Pupils also recorded the drama piece they devised earlier using Audacity software, for the end of the film.

Bearne and Wolstencroft, in *Visual Approaches to Teaching Writing*, look in great detail at multi-modality and ways to draw on what pupils know and how to use this in creating texts, both written and multi-modal. The approaches are drawn from research into writing at primary level, but are equally applicable to secondary level. They have formulated a model for planning and teaching a sequence of lessons with either multi-modal or written outcomes. There are three main phases that have in total seven constituent parts:

* Becoming familiar with the text type, capturing ideas and planning
* Drafting, revising and proof reading
* Presenting.

(Bearne and Wolstencroft 2007: 34)

The planning sequence is flexible, in that the amount of time spent on each of the seven sections will vary; however, all seven need to be addressed in order to scaffold the pupils' understanding and ability to address the task. Bearne and Wolstencroft are clear that at each stage teachers must model 'responses, choices, attitudes and behaviours' (Bearne and Wolstencroft, 2007: 36), and that equally pupils must have the chance, at all seven stages, of being able to 'investigate, use and apply' (Bearne and Wolstencroft, 2007: 36) what they have learnt. An account is then provided by a classroom teacher of his approach to using the planning sequence in a special school, to writing a whole-class narrative poem. Being familiar with the genre of narrative poetry and elements of rhyme, in order to prompt ideas for the narrative poem, Peter Fifield created his own digital images to use on the IWB, that were the character of a dragon in a variety of different poses (Bearne and Wolstencroft 2007: 118–19). The pupils' contributions were then captured on a class grid in the IWB, and Fifield then modelled telling the story of the character, using the pupils' ideas. In order to structure these initial plans, one key word per picture was selected and all the pupils suggested rhyming words.

The sequence moved into the second main stage, that of drafting, with a revision of the planning grids on the IWB and the allocation of one picture per pupil, for them to write lines to go with that picture. Again, Fifield modelled writing for the pupils, this time a rhyming couplet. The pupils composed their lines, and if necessary worked on drafting them. For the final element of the sequence, the work was presented, typed up and presented on the IWB for the class and then in school assembly.

In both of these teacher accounts of poetry work the emphasis has been on the interactive quality of the learning. The students have worked collectively towards a collaborative endpoint, that culminates in a presentation for a real audience. As Bearne and Wolstencroft comment, 'poetry is probably the perfect multi-modal text, combing all the dimensions of representation' (Bearne and Wolstencroft 2007: 114). The accounts from the teachers here demonstrate how, through a process that utilises the features of dialogic teaching (pedagogy which is collective, reciprocal, supportive, sustained, cumulative and purposeful), the teachers have moved the pupils' learning into the higher-order domains of creativity, synthesis and production of new knowledge.

Textual instability

We are living in a period of very fast technological change. As the role of the teacher adapts to becoming a mediator in the classroom, we are always developers with technology, rather than users of a finished product that is stable. Andrews states 'The rapid development of computing technology, at first the personal computer revolution and now the mobile technology revolution, have pushed change ahead of planned fit' (Andrews 2007: 55). Our planning for the use and capabilities of ICT, 'planned fit', cannot be fixed or stable. Anticipating where systems will fit in to an organised existing system and preparing for that has to be flexible as the pace of change is so fast and the affordances change too quickly. This puts us as teachers into the role of 'developers' rather than just 'users' (Andrews 2007: 55), such that we have to roll with the changes, adapting them to our purposes, as they come, rather than really being able to anticipate them. As with those changes discussed in Chapter 1 of the Early Modern period, where the development in printing practices and the relationship between manuscript and print was being both blurred and explored, so with writing practices today. Poetic culture was influenced by the fact that printing was developing, and the distinctions blurred between manuscript and print, so today there is instability of form and much mixed-mode writing. The use of text, email, social networking and other ICT media have led to a very fluid world of writing, where speech features are far more prevalent and used by young people on a consistent basis. Working with ICT we can exploit this instability of form and seek to utilise forms of language that are familiar to our pupils but rarely validated in the classroom.

Sue Dymoke, in *Drafting and Assessing Poetry* (2003), outlines a way that text message poetry can be used in the classroom. Text messaging inhabits a world that is somewhere between speech and writing and is mostly a spontaneous form. Pupils' voracious appetite for texts can be used by the teacher, by incorporating this potential into developing writing. Dymoke suggests some guidelines for text poetry that are derived from the work of Andrew Wilson, the text message poet. She suggests:

> Students can only have a maximum of 160 characters in the poems. Therefore stress the importance of economic use of words.
>
> - They should avoid trying to tell a complicated story.
> - Text poems can be jokey but they do not have to be.
> - Mobile phones all have different layouts so it is difficult to predict how someone will receive/read the poem. This means the students should focus on how their word and punctuation choices can drive the rhythm and pace of their poems.
> - Experiment with internal rhymes.
> - Make use of abbreviations where appropriate but be aware of their impact on the reader and tone of poem.
> - Ask students to experiment with writing straight onto screen and drafting on paper, and talk about the differences. How is the process of texting a poem different from writing one with pen and paper or a word processor?
>
> (Dymoke 2010: 123–4)

Pupils can benefit from their familiarity with technology to focus carefully on the process of writing. Dymoke compares this process to Rosenblatt's definition of poetry: 'the poem itself is a space between what the writer provides and what the reader brings with them to the poem' (Dymoke 2009: 14). Using technology in this way to compose poetry enables a 'blurring of the boundaries between reader and writer' (Dymoke 2009: 14) which can occur 'naturally and instantly' (Dymoke 2009: 14). An extension of this idea is to write text message poetry in the form of poem and answer, building on this tradition of writing poetry from the Early Modern period.

We have looked in this chapter at the complexity of issues around multi-modality and poetry teaching. Teaching poetry has to be seen within the larger umbrella of teaching English with ICT, and the interconnectedness of ICT with learning. The role of the teacher as a 'mediating presence' (Andrews 2007: 131) is crucial here, in setting up the conditions for learning that is dialogic and exploratory. However, the last word is appropriately expressed by Seamus Heaney, one of our most respected contemporary poets:

> What matters most in the end is the value that attaches to a few poems intimately experienced and well remembered. If at the end of each year spent in school, students have been marked by even one poem that is going to stay with them, that will be a considerable achievement.
>
> (Heaney 2003)

The Haward Version of 'To His Coy Mistress'

Had I but world enough, & tyme,
This Coynesse, Madam, were noe Crime.
I could sitte downs and thinke, which way
To walke, & pass our long-loue's day.
     e

You by y Indian Ganges side
Should Rubyes seek, I by the Tide
Of Humber would complaine, I woud
     e

Love you ten years before y Floud,
And you should, if you please, refuse,
     e

Till y Conuersion of the Jewes.
My vegetable Loue should grow
Vaster, then Empires, and more slow.
One hundred yeares should goe, to prayse
Your brow, and on your forehead gaze;
Two hundred to adore your eyes,
But thirty thousand to your Thighes.

An age att least to euery part,
And the last Age to shew your heart.
For, Madam, you deserue this state,
Nor can I loue att lower Rate.
But hark, behind meethinks I heare
Tyme's winged Charriot hurrying neare.
And yonder all before vs lyes
Desarts of vast Eternityes.
Your beauty will stand need of Salt,
For, in the hollow Marble Vault
Will my Songs Eccho, Wormes must try
Your long preseru'd Virginity.
     e

Now then, while y youthfull Glue
Stickes on your Cheeke, like Morning Dew,
Or like amorous Bird of prey,
Scorning to admitt delay,
Lett vs att once our Selves deuoure,
Not linger in Tyme's slow-Chop't power,
And since we cannot make the Sun
Goe back, nor Stand, wee'l make him run.

(Kelliher, J. H. 1970)

References

Alexander, R. (2008) *Towards Dialogic Teaching*, 4th edn, Thirsk: Dialogos.

Allott, K. (ed.) (1965) *The Poems of Matthew Arnold*, London: Longman.

Andrews, R. (2001) *Teaching and Learning English*, London: Continuum.

Andrews, R. (2007) 'Research on teaching secondary English with ICT' in A. Adams and S. Brindley (eds) *Teaching Secondary English with ICT*, Maidenhead: Open University Press.

Andrews, R. and Haythornthwaite, C. (2007) *The Sage Handbook of E-learning Research*, London: Sage.

Angelou, M. (1978) *And Still I Rise*, New York: Random House.

Applebee, A. (1974) *Tradition and Reform in the Teaching of English: A History*, Urbana, IL: NCTE.

Arnold, M. (1910) *Reports on Elementary Schools 1852–1887*, London: HMSO/Eyre and Spottiswoode.

Arnold, M. (1932) *Culture and Anarchy* (ed. Dover Wilson), Cambridge: Cambridge University Press.

Arnold, M. (2000) 'The superior adequacy of poetry' in V. Cunningham (ed.) *The Victorians: An Anthology of Poetry and Poetics*, Oxford: Blackwell.

Ashton, G. (1998) *Chaucer: The Canterbury Tales*, Basingstoke: Macmillan.

Athanasas, S. Z. (2005) 'Performing the drama of the poem: workshop, rehearsal, and reflection', *English Journal* 95(1): 88–96.

Barrell, J. and Bull, J. (1974) *The Penguin Book of Pastoral Verse*, London: Penguin.

Bayn, N. (ed.) (1998) *The Norton Anthology of American Literature, Volume 2*, 5th edn, New York: Norton.

Beard, A. and Bunton, P. (2008) *AQA English Literature B*, Cheltenham: Nelson Thornes.

Beard, R. (1987) *Developing Reading 3–13*, Oxford: Hodder & Stoughton.

Bearne, E. and Wolstencroft, H. (2007) *Visual Approaches to Teaching Writing*, London: Sage.

Beauchamp, G. and Kennewell, S. (2008) 'The influence of ICT on the interactivity of teaching', *Education and Information Technologies*, Special Issue, 13(4): 305–15.

Benson, C. D. (1986) 'The Canterbury Tales: personal drama or experiments in poetic variety?' in P. Boitani and J. Mann (eds) *The Cambridge Chaucer Companion*, Cambridge: Cambridge University Press.

Bentley, D. M. R. (1987) 'The meretricious and the meritorious in Goblin Market: a conjecture and analysis', in D. Kent (ed.) *The Achievement of Christina Rossetti*, New York: Cornell University Press.

Benton, M. and Benton, P. (1990) *Double Vision*, London: Hodder & Stoughton.

Benton, M., Teasey, J., Bell, R. and Hurst, K. (1988) *Young Readers Responding to Poems*, [poetry in Ch 2] London: Routledge.

Berry, M. and Madina, A. (1997) *Poems from the Past*, Cambridge: Cambridge University Press.

Blake, W. (1992) *Songs of Innocence and of Experience*, London: The Folio Society.

Blake, W. (1995) Stevens (ed.) *Selected Works*, Cambridge: Cambridge University Press.

Bleiman, B. (1995) *The Poetry Pack; Exploring Poems at GCSE and A Level*, London: English and Media Centre.

Bleiman, B. and Webster, L. (2007) *Studying The World's Wife*, English and Media Centre Advanced Literature Series, London: English and Media Centre.

Blunden, E. (ed.) (1963) *The Collected Poems of Wilfred Owen*, London: Chatto & Windus.

Boagey, E. (1978) *Poetry Workbook*, Slough: University Tutorial Press Ltd.

Boden, M. (2001) 'Creativity and knowledge', in A. Craft, B. Jeffrey and M. Leibling (eds) *Creativity in Education*, London: Continuum.

Brown, D. (2000) 'Victorian poetry and science', in J. Bristow (ed.) *Cambridge Guide to Victorian Poetry*, Cambridge: Cambridge University Press.

Brownjohn, S. (1980) *Does It Have to Rhyme?*, London: Hodder & Stoughton.

Burke, A. (2008) 'Filming poetry: an audiovisual approach to poetry appreciation', *NATE Classroom*, 4: 49–51.

Buzan, A. and Buzan, B. (2010) *The Mind Map Book*, Harlow: Pearson.

Campbell, K. (2008) *Matthew Arnold*, Tavistock: Northcote House.

Cardinal, R. (1997) 'Romantic travel', in R. Porter (ed.) *Rewriting the Self: Histories from the Renaissance to the Present*, London: Routledge.

Causley, C. (1992) *Collected Poems 1951–1997*, London: Macmillan.

Clark, SSgt Colin N. (2010) 'The Last Patrol' in *The Sapper*, June 2010.

Clarke, G. (1982) *Letter from a Far Country*, Manchester: Carcenet.

Coleridge, S. (2000) 'Biographia Literaria', in M. H. Abrams (ed.) *The Norton Anthology of English Literature*, New York: Norton.

Comment, K. M. (2009)'"Wasn't she a lesbian?" Teaching homoerotic themes in Dickinson and Whitman', *English Journal*, 98(4): 61–6.

Cox, B. (1995) *Cox on the Battle for the English Curriculum*, London: Hodder & Stoughton.

Cressy, D. (1980) *Literacy and the Social Order: Reading and Writing in Tudor and Stuart England*, Cambridge: Cambridge University Press.

Culler, J. (1994) 'Structuralism and Literature' in D. Keesey (ed.), *Contexts for Criticism* (pp.280–9), Mountain View, CA: Mayfield Publishing Co.

Culler, J. (1997) *Literary Theory: A Very Short Introduction*, Oxford: Oxford University Press.

Davison, J. and Dowson, J. (2009) *Learning to Teach English in the Secondary School*, Oxford: Routledge.

de Bono, E. (1985) *Six Thinking Hats*, London: Penguin.

DES (1989) *Report of the English from 5 to 16 Working Party* (The Cox Report), London: HMSO.

Dias, P. and Hayhoe, M. (1988) *Developing Response to Poetry*, Oxford: Oxford University Press.

di Cesare, M. (ed.) (1978) *George Herbert and the Seventeenth Century Religious Poets*, London: Norton.

Dickens, C. (1837) *Oliver Twist*, London: The Folio Society.

Dixon, J. (2009) 'English renewed: visions of English among teachers of 1966', *English in Education*, (43)3: 241–50.

Douglas, K. [n.d.] 'Vergissmeinnicht', http://wn.com/Vergissmeinnicht_by_Keith_Douglas_poetry_reading (accessed 28 March 2011).

Douglas, K. (1978) *The Complete Poems of Keith Douglas*, Oxford: Oxford University Press.

Drabble, M. (ed.) (2000) *The Oxford Companion to English Literature*, 6th edn, Oxford: Oxford University Press.

Duffy, C.A. (1999) *The World's Wife*, London: Picador.

Duffy, C. A. 'Mrs Midas', available at http://peoplereadingpoems.org/2010/05/07/mrs-midas/ (accessed 28 January 2011).

Duffy, C. A. interview, available at http://www.sheerpoetry.co.uk/advanced/interviews/carol-ann-duffy-the-world-s-wife (accessed 28 January 2011).

Duffy, C.A. (2004) *New Selected Poems*, London: Picador.

Dymoke, S. (2003*) Drafting and Assessing Poetry: A Guide for Teacher*, London: Sage.

Dymoke, S. (2009) *Teaching English Texts 11–18*, London: Continuum.

Eagleton, T. (1996) *Literary Theory: An Introduction*, Oxford: Blackwell.

Eliot, T. S. (1933) *The Use of Poetry and the Use of Criticism: Studies in the Relation of Criticism to Poetry in England*, Cambridge Mass: Harvard University Press.

Eliot, T. S. (1957) 'The three voices of poetry' in *On Poetry and Poets*, London: Faber & Faber.

Eliot, T. S. (1963) *Collected Poems 1909–1962*, London: Faber & Faber.

Eliot, T. S. (1964) *The Use of Poetry and the Use of Criticism*, London: Faber & Faber.

Eliot, T. S (1975) 'Andrew Marvell', in F. Kermode (ed.) *Selected Prose of T. S. Eliot*, London: Faber & Faber.

Evans, B. (ed.) (1996)) *The Sonnets*, Cambridge: Cambridge University Press.

Featherstone, S. (1995) *War Poetry: An Introductory Reader*, London: Routledge.

Ferguson,W., Salter, M. and Stallworthy, J. (eds) (1996) *The Norton Anthology of Poetry*, 5th edn, New York: W. W. Norton.

Fernie, E. *et al.* (2005) *Reconceiving the Renaissance: A Critical Reader*, Oxford: Oxford University Press.

Fiennes, R. reading, available at http://ralphfiennes-corner.net/poetry_corner/poetry_corner.php?id=15 (accessed 23 March 2011).

Fish, S. (1980) *Is there a text in this class? The authority of interpretive communities*, London: Harvard University Press.

Fleming, M. (1996) 'Poetry teaching in the secondary school: the concept of "difficulty"', in L. Thompson (ed.) *The Teaching of Poetry: European Perspectives*, London: Cassell.

Fleming, M. and Steven, D. (1998) *English Teaching in the Secondary School*, London: David Fulton.

Fraser, G. S. (1970) *Metre, Rhythm and Free Verse*, London: Methuen.

Gascoigne, G. (1998) 'The Adventures of Master F.J.' in P. Salzman (ed.) *An Anthology of Elizabethan Prose Fiction*, Oxford: Oxford University Press.

Gee, J. P. (1994) 'First language acquisition as a guide for theories of learning and pedagogy', *Linguistics and Education* 6, 331–53.

Gibbons, D. (2007) 'Talking with Tennyson: interpreting The Lady of Shalott in the internet age' *NATE Classroom* (online) 3: 1–3. Available at http://findarticles.com/p/articles/mi_6950/is_3/ai_n28481673/ (accessed 24 March 2011).

Giddings, R. (1998) *The War Poets: The Lives and Writings of the 1914–18 War Poets*, London: Bloomsbury.

Gifford, T. (1999) *Pastoral*, London: Routledge.

Gilham, D. J (ed.) (1988) *John Keats: Poems of 1820*, 2nd edn, Plymouth: Northcote House.

Gill, J. (2007) *Women's Poetry*, Edinburgh: Edinburgh University Press.

Giovanelli, M. (2010) 'Pedagogical stylistics: a text world theory approach to the teaching of poetry', *English in Education*, 44(3), Autumn.

Goldensohn, L. (2003) *Dismantling Glory*, New York: Columbia University Press.

Goodwyn, A. and Powell, M. (2003) 'Canonical texts, critical literacy and the classroom: the case of the Lady of Shalott', *English in Australia*, 138: 51–5.

Graham, D. (ed.) (1978) *The Complete Poems of Keith Douglas*, Oxford: Oxford University Press.

Green, P. and Davies, S. (1994) 'The Lady of Shalott', available at http://www.collaborativelearning.org /ladyofshalott.pdf (accessed 4 February 2011).

Greenblatt, S. (1980) *Renaissance Self-Fashioning: From More to Shakespeare*, London: University of Chicago Press.

Gunn, T. (1976) *Jack Straw's Castle*, London: Faber & Faber.

Hall, L. (1989) *Poetry for Life: A Practical Guide to Teaching Poetry in the Primary School*, London: Cassell.

Hardman, F. (2011) 'Promoting a dialogic pedagogy in English teaching', in Davison, J., Daly, C. and Moss, J. *Debates in English Teaching*, London: Routledge.

Hawlin, S. (2002) *Robert Browning*, Abingdon: Routledge.

Hayhoe, J., Taylor, R. and Hayhoe, M. (1990) *Between the Lines*, Oxford, Heinemann.

Hayhoe, M. and Parker, S. (1989) *Words Large as Apples*, Cambridge: Cambridge University Press.

Heaney, S. (1980) *Selected Poems 1965–1975*. London: Faber & Faber.

Heaney, S. (2003) 'Bags of enlightenment', *Guardian*, Saturday 25 October, available at http://www.guardian.co.uk/books/2003/oct/25/poetry.highereducation (accessed 29 March 2011).

Hearnshaw, F. J. C. (1928) 'Chivalry and its place in history' in E. Prestage (ed.) *Chivalry*, London: Kegan Paul, Trench, Trübner & Co.

Hebron, M. (2008) *Key Concepts in Renaissance Literature*, Basingstoke: Palgrave Macmillan.

Herbert, G. (1991) *The Complete English Poems*, (P. Tobin, ed.), London: Penguin.

Hollander, J. and Kermode, F. (1973) *The Literature of Renaissance England*, Oxford: Oxford University Press.

Homer (1996) *The Odyssey*, tr. Robert Fitzgerald, London: The Harvill Press.

Hobsbaum, P. (1996) *Metre, Rhythm and Verse Form*, London: Routledge.

Hughes, M. (1999) *Closing the Learning Gap*, Stafford: Network Educational Press.

Hughes, T. (1967a) *Poetry in the Making*, London: Faber & Faber.

Hughes, T. (1967b) *Wodwo*, London: Faber & Faber.

Hughes, T. (1995) *What is the Truth?* London: Faber & Faber.

Iser, W. (1978) *The Act of Reading: A Theory of Aesthetic Response*, London: Routledge.

Iser, W. (1988) 'The reading process; a phenomenological approach' in D. Lodge and N. Wood (eds) *Modern Criticism and Theory*, Edinburgh: Pearson.

Jespersen, O. (1967) 'Notes on metre' in S. Chatman and S. Levin (eds) *Essays on the Language of Literature*, Boston: Houghton Mifflin.

Kelliher, J. H. (1970) 'A new text of Marvell's "To his Coy Mistress"', *Notes and Queries* 7: 254–6.

Kennewell, S. and Beauchamp, G. (2007) 'The features of interactive whiteboards and their influence on learning', *Learning, Media and Technology*, 32(3): 227–41.

Kermode, F. (ed.) (1975) *The Selected Prose of T.S. Eliot*, London: Faber & Faber.

Kingsley, C. (1863) *The Water Babies*, London: The Heirloom Library.

Landow, G. P. (1992) Tennyson's Poetic Project. Online, available at http://www.victorianweb.org/authors/tennyson/im/improject.html (accessed 4 February 2011).

Lankshear, C. and Knobel, M. (2007) 'New technologies in the secondary English classroom' in A. Adams and S. Brindley (eds) *Teaching Secondary English with ICT*, Maidenhead: Open University Press.

Learning Site [n.d.] Available at www.historylearningsite.co.uk/becket.htm (accessed 28 March 2011).

Leavis, F. R. (1952) *The Common Pursuit*, London: Chatto & Windus.

Leishman, J. B. (1966) *The Art of Marvell's Poetry*, London: Hutchinson.

Long, B. W. and Hopkins, M. F. (1982) *Performing Literature: An Introduction to Oral Interpretation*, Englewood Cliffs: Prentice-Hall.

Love, H. (1986) *The Culture and Commerce of Texts: Scribal Publication in Seventeenth Century England*, Amherst: University of Wisconsin Press.

Low, A. and Pival, P. (1969) 'Rhetorical pattern in Marvell's "To His Coy Mistress"', *Journal of English and Germanic Philology* 68: 414–21.

Mahony, P. (ed.) (1998) *From Both Sides Now*, New York: Scribner Poetry.

Marlowe, C. (1995) *Doctor Faustus* (J. Butcher, ed.), London: Longman.

Marotti, A. F. (1995) *Manuscript, Print and the English Renaissance Lyric*, Ithaca: Cornell University Press.

Marsh, N. (2001) *William Blake, The Poems*, Basingstoke: Palgrave.

McCloskey (2005) 'A wider literacy: media education and the moving image in Northern Ireland', in *English Media Drama* 3: 17–20.

McGuinn, N. (1986) *Seamus Heaney: A Student's Guide to the Selected Poems 1965–75*, Leeds: Arnold-Wheaton.

McLeod, I. R. (1916) *Songs to Save a Soul*, London: Chatto & Windus.

McManus, C. (2005) 'Identities' in E. Fernie, R. Wray, M. Thornton Burnett and C. McManus (eds) *Reconceiving the Renaissance: A Critical Reader*, Oxford: Oxford University Press.

Mercer, N. (2000) *Words and Minds: How We Use Language to Think Together*, London: Routledge.

Merrick, B. and Fox, G. (1987) 'Thirty-six things to do with a poem', in *The English Curriculum: Poetry*, London: English and Media Centre/NATE.

Millay, E. St Vincent (1992) *Selected Poems* (Falck, ed.), Manchester: Carcanet Press.

Michelis, A. and Rowland, A. (2003) *The Poetry of Carol Ann Duffy: 'Choosing Tough Words'*, Manchester: Manchester University Press.

Morpurgo, M. (2004) 'War IS sad; don't hide it from your children', available at http://www.timesonline.co.uk/tol/life_and_style/article389173.ece 10 Nov 2004 (accessed 27 March 2011).

Motion, A. (1980) *The Poetry of Edward Thomas*, London: The Hogarth Press.

Novak, B. (2002) 'Humanizing democracy: Matthew Arnold's nineteenth-century call for a common, higher, educative pursuit of happiness and its relevance to twenty-first-century democratic life', *American Educational Research Journal*, 39(3): 593–637, Autumn.

O'Brien, V. (1985) *Teaching Poetry in the Secondary School*, London: Edward Arnold.

Okara, G. (1978) *The Fisherman's Invocation*, London: Heinemann.

Onions, C. T. (ed.) (1973) *The Shorter Oxford English Dictionary*, 3rd edn, Oxford: Oxford University Press.

Opie, I. and Opie, P. (eds) (1983) *The Oxford Book of Narrative Verse*, Oxford: Oxford University Press.

Owen, W. (1981) 'The Sentry' in J. Silkin (ed.) *The Penguin Book of First World War Poetry*, Harmondsworth: Penguin.

Owen, W. (1984) *The Oxford Book of War Poetry*, (J. Stallworthy, ed.), Oxford: Oxford University Press.

Palmer, D. J. (1965) *The Rise of English Studies*, Oxford: Oxford University Press.

Peskin, J. (2007) 'The genre of poetry: secondary school students' conventional expectations and interpretive operations', *English in Education*, 41(3), Autumn.

Petra (2008) Available at http://www.poetryshuffle.com/poetry.asp?forum_action=show_message& (accessed 23 March 2011).

Pettigrew, J. (1981) *Robert Browning: The Poems*, Aylesbury: Penguin Books.

Piette, A. (2008) 'Keith Douglas and the poetry of the Second World War', in *The Cambridge Guide to the Poetry of the Second World War*, Cambridge: Cambridge University Press.

Piette, A. (2009) 'War poetry in Britain' in *The Cambridge Companion to the Literature of World War Two*, Cambridge: Cambridge University Press.

Pike, M. (2003) 'The canon in the classroom', *Journal of Curriculum Studies*, 35(3): 355–70

Pinder, B. (1990) *Shakespeare: An Active Approach*, London: Collins Educational.

Pope, R. (2002) *The English Studies Book: An Introduction to Language, Literature and Culture*, London: Routledge.

Porter, R. (ed.) (1997) *Rewriting the Self: Histories from the Renaissance to the Present*, London: Routledge.

Preminger, A. (ed.) (1965) *Princeton Encyclopedia of Poetry and Poetics*, Princeton: Princeton University Press.

Puttenham, G. (1970) *The Arte of English Poesie*, (G. Wilcock and A. Walker, eds), Cambridge: Cambridge University Press.

Puttenham, G. (2004) 'The Art of English Poesy' in G. Alexander (ed.) *Sidney's 'The Defence of Poesy' and Selected Renaissance Literary Criticism*, London: Penguin.

QCA (n.d.) National Curriculum Programme of Study Key Stage Three. Available at http://curriculum. qcda.gov.uk / key-stages-3-and-4/ subjects/key-stage-3/english/programme-of-study/index.aspx (accessed 1 February 2011).

Quiller-Couch, A. (1927) *The Oxford Book of English Verse 1250–1900*, Oxford: Clarendon Press.

Reading, K. 'Goblin Market', available at http://www.youtube.com/watch?v=raQETd3pJVU&feature =related (accessed 21 Feb 2011).

Reilly, C. (ed.) (1981) *Scars Upon My Heart*, London: Virago.

Roberts, D. (ed.) (1999) *Out in the Dark: Poetry of the First World War*, Burgess Hill: Saxon Books.

Rosen, M. (2009) What is children's poetry for? Towards a new, child-specific "Apologie for Poetrie" (Philip Sidney, 1579) available at http:www.michaelrosen.co.uk/apologie.html (accessed 29 March 2011).

Rosenblatt, L. (1970) *Literature as Exploration*, London: Heinemann.

Rosenblatt, L. (1976) *Literature as Exploration*, 3rd edn, New York: Noble.

Rosenblatt, L. (1978) *The Reader, the Text and the Poem*, Carbondale and Edwardsville: Southern Illinois University Press.

Russell, S. (2001) *Grammar, Structure and Style*, Oxford: Oxford University Press.

Saunders, J. W. (1951) 'The stigma of print: a note on the social basis of Tudor poetry', *Essays in Criticism* 1: 139–64.

Scafe, S. (2004) 'Out of the ghetto: teaching black literature', in S. Brindley (ed.) *Teaching English*, London: Routledge.

Schillinger, T., Meyer, T. and Vinz, R. (2010) 'Poetry immersion: reading, writing and performing with secondary students', *English in Education*, 44(2), Summer.

Selby, N. (1999) *T. S. Eliot, The Waste Land*, Cambridge: Icon Books.

Shakespeare, W. (1992) *Othello* (J. Coles, ed.), Cambridge: Cambridge University Press.

Shakespeare, W. (1996) *The Sonnets* (B. Evans, ed.), Cambridge: Cambridge University Press.

Shaw, F. (2008) 'A Game of Chess' [online video] available at http://www.youtube.com/watch?v=k8QKvCflFWU (accessed 27 May 1010).

Shaw, R. B. (2007) *Blank Verse: A Guide to Its History and Use*, Athens: Ohio University Press.

Silcox, M. V. (1999) 'Ornament of civil life; the device in Puttenham's Arte of English Poetry' in Peter M. Daly and J. Manning (eds), *Aspects of Renaissance and Baroque Symbol Theory 1500–1700*, New York: AMS Press.

Silkin, J. (ed.) (1979) *The Penguin Book of First World War Poetry*, London; Penguin

Smith, R. (1997) 'Self reflection and the self', in R. Porter (ed.) *Rewriting the Self: Histories from the Renaissance to the Present*, London: Routledge.

Smith, W. 'On a Stupendous Leg of Granite, Discovered Standing by Itself in the Deserts of Egypt, with the Inscription Inserted Below', available at http://www.rc.umd.edu /rchs /reader/smith.html (accessed 30 January 2011).

Stallworthy, J. (1984) *The Oxford Book of War Poetry*, Oxford: Oxford University Press.

Steiner, G. (1978) *On Difficulty and Other Essays*, Oxford: Oxford University Press.

Stephen, M. (ed.) (1993) *Poems of the First World War: 'Never Such Innocence'*, London: Everyman.

Stevens, D. and McGuinn, N. (2004) *The Art of Teaching Secondary English*, London: Routledge Falmer.

Stibbs, A. (2001) 'For how long, where, and with whom: narrative time, place and company as generic distinguishers and ideological indicators', *Changing English*, 8(1): 35–42.

Stonewall (2011) Teachers' Report, *Times Educational Supplement* 11 February.

Taylor, J. (2004) 'Teaching poetry in the secondary school' in S. Brindley (ed.) *Teaching English*, London: Routledge.

Tennyson, A., Lord (1986) *The Lady Of Shalott*, Oxford: Oxford University Press.

Theroux, L. (2003) online video, available at http://documentarystorm.com/lifestyle/ louis-and-the-nazis/ (accessed 31 January 2011).

Thomas, G. R. (ed.) (1978) *The Collected Poems of Edward Thomas*, Oxford: Oxford University Press.

Torgerson, C. and Freeman, A. (2005) 'The evidence base for effective ICT practice in literacy learning', in M. Leask and N. Pachler, *Learning to Teach Using ICT in the Secondary School*, 2nd edn, London: Sage.

Vygotsky, L. (1978) *Mind in Society*, Cambridge, MA: Harvard University Press.

Wainwright, J. (2004) *Poetry: The Basics*, Oxford: Routledge.

War Poetry Website [n.d.] Online. Available at www.warpoetry.co.uk (accessed 28 March 2011).

Wardle, D. (1970) *English Popular Education 1780–1970*, Cambridge: Cambridge University Press.

Watts, C. (1985) *A Preface to Keats*, Longman: London.

Webb, T. (1977) *Poems and Prose: Percy Bysshe Shelley*, London: J. M. Dent.

Williams, R. (1996) *Keywords*, London: Fontana.

Williamson, J., Fleming, M., Harman, F. and Stevens, D. (2001) *Meeting the Standards in Secondary English: A Guide to the ITT NC*, London: Routledge Falmer.

Willinsky, J. (1990) 'Matthew Arnold's legacy: the powers of literature', *Research in the Teaching of English*, 24(4): 343–61, December.

Winn, J. A. (2008) *The Poetry of War*, Cambridge: Cambridge University Press.

Wood, J. and Wood, L. (1988) *Cambridge Poetry Workshop: GCSE*, Cambridge: Cambridge University Press.

Wood, L. and Wood, J. (1989) *Cambridge Poetry Workshop 14+*, Cambridge: Cambridge University Press.

Wordsworth, W. (1998) 'Poems in Two Volumes', in D. Wu (ed.) *Romanticism: An Anthology*, 2nd edn, Oxford: Blackwell.

Wright, D. (1985) *Geoffrey Chaucer: The Canterbury Tales*, Oxford: Oxford University Press.

Wright, S. (2005) *How to be a Brilliant English Teacher*, London: Routledge.

Yates, C. (1999) *Jumpstart: Poetry in the Secondary School*, London: The Poetry Society.

Young, R.V. (1985) '"To His Mistress" as Characterisation', *Postscript* 2: 39–48. Available at http://www2.unca.edu/postscript/postscript2/ps2.5.pdf (accessed 7 September 2010).

Zephaniah, B. (1997) *School's Out: Poems Not for School*, Edinburgh: AK Press.

Index

accessibility 2, 105
aesthetic tradition 95–6, 105
alliteration 31, 56
analysis 13, 38, 50, 90, 96, 131–2
Angelou, M. 56–60
annotation 49, 89, 99
Arnold, Matthew 1–5; *Culture and Anarchy* 4
Art of English Poesy, The 7, 23
associations 40, 55

Baby Song 45–8
Ballad of Charlotte Dymond, The 26–8
ballads 26, 27, 102
barn line drawing 71f6.1
Barn, The 69–71
Beard, R. 38f4.1, 68, 104; *Developing Reading 3-13* 37
Bearne, E.: *Visual Approaches to Teaching Writing* 140–1
Bentley, D.M.R. 110–11, 112
Benton, P.: *Double Vision* 106; frames of discussion 21f2.3; Goblin Market 111; methodology 22f2.4; poetry teaching 62; pre-reading tasks 44; stories 52; *Young Readers Responding to Poems* 20
Berry, M.: *Poems from the Past* 25, 55, 104
Blake, W.: Chimney Sweeper, The 85, 94–7; London 78–82; *Songs of Innocence, The* 85, 94; student responses 80f6.3
Bono, Edward de 59, 82t6.1
Brittain, V.: Perhaps 127–9; *Testament of Youth* 127
Browning, R.: My Last Duchess 61–4

Canterbury Tales, The 97–9, 100f7.4, 100f7.5, 101, 118
case studies: First World War Poetry 48–50; form 33–5; KS3 97–101, 129–34; KS4 78–82; KS5 61–4, 113–16
Causley, C.: *Ballad of Charlotte Dymond, The* 26–8
challenges 76, 103, 105
characters: *Canterbury Tales, The* 97, 99, 100f7.4; children 94, 97; chivalry 117–18; construction 83–5; creation 101f7.6; Eve of St Agnes 113, 114–15; exploration 100f7.5; Marsh, N. 96; Mrs Midas 85, 90
Chaucer, G. 118; *Canterbury Tales, The* 84, 97–101
children 23, 94–7, 121–2
Chimney Sweeper, The 85, 94–7

City Blues 71–4
Clark, C.: Last Patrol, The 129–34
Clarke, G.: Miracle on St David's Day 107–10
class 83–4, 97, 118
Coleridge, S. 17, 23; Rime of the Ancient Mariner, The 102
communication 38, 138, 139
conflict poetry 117, 121–9
construction of characters 83–5
context 77, 95
Cox, B. 12, 13
creative activity 17, 101f7.6, 136
creative learning 58f5.1
culture 4, 12, 15, 87, 141

Daffodils 67–8
Davies, S. 105, 106–7
Dead Man's Dump 119
deconstruction 88f7.1
descriptions 101f7.7
dialogic teaching 138–9, 140–1
discussion 59, 62–3, 76, 80–1, 131
Donne, J.: *Flea, The* 33–5; *Good Morrow, The* 23
Douglas, K. 119; *Alamein to Zem Zem* 122; Aristocrats 118; Vergissmeinnicht 121–4
Dr Faustus 31–2
drama 33, 34, 125–6
dramatic reading 26, 92, 93, 125, 132
Duffy, C.A.: Medusa 53; Mrs Midas 85, 86–90; *World's Wife, The* 87
Dulce et Decorum Est 48–9

Early Modern Period 5, 76, 84
education 3–4, 5, 79, 85, 118
Eliot, T.S. 26, 51, 58, 92; *Love Songs of J. Alfred Prufrock, The* 29; Three Voices of Poetry, The 52; Waste Land, The 60–1
emotional territory: Eve of St Agnes 113; To His Coy Mistress 92; Last Patrol, The 132, 134; poetry 34–5; pre-reading tasks 43; reading aloud 108; tranquility 68; Vergissmeinnicht 123
English 11t2.1, 12–15
English literature 1, 12, 19–20
Eve of St Agnes 113–16
experience: aesthetic tradition 95; learning 138; poetry 69; *Private Peaceful* 123; students 72–3, 113; texts 43
exploration 60, 100f7.5

fairytales 88f7.1
female voice 86–90, 97, 127–9
first person voice 56–60
First World War Poetry 48–50, 119, 125, 127
Flea, The 33–5
Fleming, M. 77, 124, 125; Poetry teaching in the
    secondary school: the concept of 'difficulty' 76
follow-up activities 88, 93
form: heroic epic 102; KS3 26–8; KS4 28–31;
    KS5 31–5; narrative poetry 103; poetry 23–6
fragments 89f7.2
frames of discussion 21f2.3
free verse 28–31, 53

Garden, The 74–8
gender 83, 88, 106
Goblin Market 110–13
Green, P. 105, 106–7
group work 82t6.1
Gunn, T.: Baby Song 45–8

Hall, L. 28, 29–30; *Poetry for Life: A Practical
    Guide to Teaching Poetry in the Primary School*
    26
Hamlet 36, 83, 135
Hardman, F. 13–14, 139
Hardy, T.: I Look Into My Glass 72f6.2
Hayhoe, M. 72f6.2; City Blues 71–4; *Developing
    Response to Poetry* 13; *Words Large as Apples*
    39
Heaney, S.: Barn, The 69–71; *Death of a Naturalist*
    71; poetry 142; *Rattle Bag, The* 9; *School Bag,
    The* 9
Hughes, T.: poetry 135; *Poetry in the Making*
    10; *Rattle Bag, The* 9; Roger the Dog 38–42;
    School Bag, The 9; Thistles 42–5
Hurst, K. 52, 62

I Look Into My Glass 72f6.2
ICT: communities 140; instability 141; interactive
    whiteboards (IWB) 141; Lady of Shalott, The
    140; students 142; teachers 136–7; teaching
    methods 77, 135; viewing grid 137f10.1
identity 83, 84, 97
imagery: Dulce et Decorum Est 49; First World
    War Poetry 125; Garden, The 77; To His Coy
    Mistress 92–3; KS4 42–5; poetry 36–8; pre-
    reading tasks 88; sexuality 111; storyboards 78;
    Vergissmeinnicht 123–4
interpretation 15, 46, 74, 81, 105
Iser, W. 11, 18f2.2, 19, 60, 105; *Act of Reading,
    The* 17
It's Work 45–8

Keats, J. 116f8.4; Eve of St Agnes 113–16
KS3: case studies 97–101, 129–34; conflict poetry
    121–4; female voice 86–90; First World War
    Poetry 48–50; form 26–8; lexis 38–42; narra-
    tive poetry 105–7; Ozymandias 54–6; pastoral
    setting 69–71
KS4: case studies 78–82; conflict poetry 124–7;
    first person voice 56–60; form 28–31; imagery
    42–5; male voice 90–3; narrative poetry
    107–10

KS5: case studies 61–4, 113–16; child's voice
    94–7; form 31–3; narrative poetry 110–13;
    pastoral poetry 74–8; rhythm 45–8; Waste
    Land, The 60–1

Lady of Shalott, The 105–7
language: awareness 72; *Canterbury Tales, The*
    99; dialogic teaching 139; Eve of St Agnes
    115; examination 59; form 35; intensity 34;
    Lady of Shalott, The 106; Perhaps 128–9;
    poetry 1, 10; processing 37; Sentry, The
    126f9.1
Last Patrol, The 129–34
learning 1, 37, 59, 70–1, 137–8
Leavis, F.R. 12–13
lexis 36, 38–42, 98t7.1
literary work 18f2.2, 105
Literature as Exploration 16
live circuit 16f2.1, 41, 113, 134
London 78–82
Lone Dog 39–42
Love Songs of J. Alfred Prufrock, The 29

Madina, A.: *Poems from the Past* 25, 55, 104
male voice 90–3
Marlowe, C.: *Dr Faustus* 31–2; Passionate
    Shepherd to His Love, The 65–6
Marvell, A.: Garden, The 74–8; To His Coy
    Mistress 84, 90–3
McGuinn, N. 58, 71
meanings: context 77; narrative poetry 103; poetry
    30, 46; rhythm 36, 47–8; texts 16
medieval society 98f7.3
Middle Ages 97, 99, 117
Midsummer Night's Dream, A 1, 51
Miller: *Canterbury Tales, The* 100f7.4
mind maps 109, 110f8.1, 110f8.2
Miracle on St David's Day 107–9, 110f8.2
models 70–1, 137–8, 140–1
Moon on the Tides 83
Morpurgo, M. 121–2; *Private Peaceful* 122–3
Mrs Midas 85, 86–8, 89f7.2, 90
multi-modality 135, 137–9, 140–1
My Last Duchess 61–4

narrative poetry 102, 105–16
narratives 26, 52
National Curriculum 8, 14, 48, 135

O'Brien, V. 27, 44, 92
On Difficulty and Other Essays 43, 45
oral tradition 26, 51
organisation 82t6.1, 123
Owen, W.: Dulce et Decorum Est 48–9; Sentry, The
    124–7
Ozymandias 54–6

Passionate Shepherd to His Love, The 65–6
pastoral poetry 65–6, 74–8
pastoral setting 69–71
patterns 37, 39, 46
perceptions 58, 115, 122, 124
performance: conflict poetry 130; Lady of Shalott,
    The 105–6; Last Patrol, The 132–4; poetry 46,

59; reading 20; resources 131f9.2; workshop 133f9.3, 133f9.4, 134f9.5
Perhaps 127–9
perspective 11, 24, 83–4, 85, 93
Poems from the Past 25, 55, 104
PowerPoint 73, 79, 109
pre-reading tasks: Barn, The 69–70; *Canterbury Tales, The* 97; Charlotte Dymond 26; emotional territory 34–5, 43; Eve of St Agnes 115; First World War Poetry 128; Lady of Shalott, The 105; Miracle on St David's Day 108–9; mythology 88; Ozymandias 55; *Poems from the Past* 104; poetry 72; research 95; Sentry, The 124; Still I Rise 58; Vergissmeinnicht 122, 123; visualisation 76; Waste Land, The 60
Puttenham, G.: *Art of English Poesy, The* 7, 23

QCA 14–15, 36
qualities 41f4.2, 141

racism 58–9, 83
Reader, the Text and the Poem, The 15–16, 17
readers 15–21
reading: *Canterbury Tales, The* 100; communication 38; creative activity 17, 137; dramatic reading 26; Goblin Market 111; patterns 37; performance 20; poetry 44, 92; taxonomy of reading 38f4.1
reading aloud: emotional territory 108; Eve of St Agnes 114; narrative poetry 103, 104; Perhaps 128; poetry 59; Sentry, The 125; Vergissmeinnicht 123
religion 1–5, 84, 99
research 77, 79, 95, 98
resources 131f9.2
responses 80
rhyme 1, 23, 27, 31, 115–16, 128
rhythm: *Ballad of Charlotte Dymond, The* 27; children 23; Duffy, C.A. 89; Eve of St Agnes 116; KS5 45–8; language 1; meanings 36; This is Just to Say 53
Richards, I.A. 12–13, 17
Roger the Dog 38–42
Rosenberg, I.: Dead Man's Dump 119
Rosenblatt, L.: compenetration 46; *Literature as Exploration* 16; live circuit 41; performance 134; poetry 11, 24; *Reader, the Text and the Poem, The* 15–16, 17
Rossetti, C.: Goblin Market 110–13
rural landscapes 66, 69, 76

Second World War Poetry 119
self 25, 83, 84, 85
Sentry, The 124–5, 126f9.1, 127
settings 65–74, 106, 114
sexuality 25, 35, 83, 111, 112
Shakespeare, W.: *Hamlet* 36, 83, 135; *Henry V* 117; *Midsummer Night's Dream, A* 1, 51; pastoral poetry 66; *Romeo and Juliet* 113; sonnets 25; *Tempest, The* 11, 65; *Twelfth Night* 36
Shelley, P.B.: Ozymandias 54–6
social hierarchy 98f7.3, 128

Socratic seminars 61–2, 63f5.2, 64
Songs of Innocence, The 85, 94
sonnets 23, 24, 55, 56
Steiner, G. 77, 85; *On Difficulty and Other Essays* 43, 45
stereotyping 88, 100
Stevens, D. 58, 77
Still I Rise 56–60
structures 37, 47, 58f5.1
students: Blake, W. 80f6.3; discussion 62–3; ICT 142; interaction 32; knowledge 124; learning 141; research 77, 79; rhythm 45–6; war poetry 120
Studying the World's Wife 88

taxonomy of reading 38f4.1, 136
teachers 136–7, 141
teaching methods: aesthetic tradition 95–6; English literature 19–20; Eve of St Agnes 115, 116f8.4; Garden, The 77; ICT 135; moral tradition 96–7; *Poems from the Past* 104; poetic exchange 67; poetry of conflict 117; PowerPoint 73, 79, 109; reading 37; settings 65; Socratic seminars 61–4
Tennyson, Alfred Lord: Lady of Shalott, The 105–7
texts: analysis 96; attention 13; constructed subjects 83; cultural knowledge 18; details 125; discussion 131; experience 43; gaps in texts 105; imagery 78; instability 141–2; multi-modal texts 135; National Literacy Strategy 103; readers 15–21; transformation 123
themes 92, 94, 122
third person 54–6
This is Just to Say 52–3
Thistles 42–5
time 83–5, 108, 114
To His Coy Mistress 84, 90–3
traditional teaching 12–15

Vergissmeinnicht 121–4
vers libre 29, 120
viewing grid 137f10.1
visualisation 76, 109, 124
voice 51–4, 55, 60–1, 83, 86–90, 127

war poetry 119–20, 130
War Poets: The Lives and Writings of the 1914-18 War Poets, The 48
Waste Land, The 60–1
Webster, L.: *Studying the World's Wife* 88
Williams, W.C.: This is Just to Say 52–3
Wood, J. 34, 43, 92; *Cambridge Poetry Workshop 14+* 55, 105
Wood, L. 34, 43, 92; *Cambridge Poetry Workshop 14+* 55, 105
words 36–8, 40, 44, 50, 72
Words Large as Apples 39
Wordsworth, W.: Daffodils 67–8, 108–9
workshop 133f9.3, 133f9.4, 134f9.5
writing 1, 15, 54–6, 76

Zephaniah, B.: It's Work 45–8